# SHIP PERFORMANCE

Technical, Safety, Environmental and
Commercial Aspects

## SECOND EDITION

# OTHER TITLES IN THIS SERIES

*Ship Finance*
by Peter Stokes
(1992)

*Ship Management*
SECOND EDITION
by John Spruyt
(1994)

*Ship Registration*
SECOND EDITION
by Nigel Ready
(1994)

*Bunkers*
SECOND EDITION
by Christopher Fisher and Jonathon Lux
(1994)

*Shipbroking and Chartering Practice*
FOURTH EDITION
by Gorton, Ihre, Sandevarn
(1995)

*Shipping Pools*
SECOND EDITION
by William Packard
(1995)

# SHIP PERFORMANCE

## Technical, Safety, Environmental and Commercial Aspects

BY

### CYRIL HUGHES
*C. Eng., M.I.Mar.E.*

## SECOND EDITION

## BUSINESS OF SHIPPING SERIES

**|L|L|P|**

LONDON   NEW YORK   HONG KONG
1996

LLP Limited
Legal & Business Publishing Division
27 Swinton Street
London WC1X 9NW

USA AND CANADA
LLP Inc.
Suite 308, 611 Broadway
New York, NY 10012 USA

SOUTH-EAST ASIA
LLP Asia Limited
Room 1101, Hollywood Centre
233 Hollywood Road
Hong Kong

© C. N. Hughes

First published 1987
Second edition 1996

*British Library Cataloguing in Publication Data*
A catalogue record for this
book is available from
the British Library

ISBN 1-85978-069-5

Text set in 10 on 12 pt Times Roman by
Mendip Communications, Frome, Somerset
Printed in Great Britain by
WBC Limited,
Bridgend, Mid-Glamorgan

# PREFACE

Since this book was first published in 1987 the shipping industry has experienced many changes, the most important probably being a softening in fuel prices scarcely thought possible when the book was first written, although these could easily start rising again.

The emphasis has now shifted from technical to commercial performance as owners strive to retain a competitive edge and this is covered more extensively in this edition.

Technical considerations are of course still included but have been updated to reflect current developments.

New chapters have been added on the currently fashionable subjects of safety and the environment, and passenger ship performance has also been included.

*May 1996*                                                    C. N. HUGHES

# TABLE OF CONTENTS

*Preface*                                          v
*List of Tables*                                   xiii
*List of Figures*                                  xv

CHAPTER ONE    TECHNICAL CONSIDERATIONS            *Page*

1.  Main propulsion system                          1
2.  Underwater hull                                 2
3.  "Bolt-on" improvers                             5
    A. Slow steaming                                5
    B. Power take-offs                              6
    C. Exhaust gas recovery                         6
    D. Use of blended or residual fuel in diesel generators   7
    E. Upgrading existing Main Engines              9
    F. Ducted and other propellers                  9
4.  Energy conservation                            14
    A. Minimum ballast—optimal trim                14
    B. Adaptive steering modules                   15
    C. Self-polishing underwater paint             15
    D. Underwater air lubrication                  16
    E. Propeller polishing                         16
    F. Underwater scrubbing                        16
    G. Reduction of electrical load                17
    H. Increase in deadweight                      17
    I. Other action                                18
5.  Other performance improvers                    19
    A. Fuel oil storage tanks                      19
    B. Combined incinerator/boilers                19
    C. Accommodation heating                       19
    D. Two-speed pumps                             19
6.  Summary of Chapter One                         20

CHAPTER TWO    MAIN PROPULSION PERFORMANCE

1.  Introduction                                   23
2.  Steam turbine                                  23

3. Diesel engines                                     25
4. Oil tanker propulsion                              27
5. Container ship propulsion                          29
6. Passenger ship propulsion                          30
7. Bulk carrier propulsion                            32
8. Other propulsion systems                           34
9. Summary of Chapter Two                             35


CHAPTER THREE    FUELS

1. Crude oil                                          37
2. Refinery process                                   38
3. Residual fuel oil (heavy oil)                      40
4. Distillate fuel (diesel and gas oil)               41
5. Viscosity                                          41
6. Density                                            44
7. Compatibility                                      44
8. Calorific value                                    45
9. Quality testing                                    46
10. Documentation                                     48
11. Combustibility                                    50
12. Fuel additives                                    50
13. Quantity audit                                    52
14. Cost control                                      52
15. Summary of Chapter Three                          53


CHAPTER FOUR    PERFORMANCE MONITORING

1. Measuring methods used                             55
2. Ship's speed                                       56
3. Horsepower                                         57
4. Revolutions/slip                                   57
5. Fuel consumption                                   58
6. Weather                                            60
7. Pressures—temperatures                             62
8. Monitoring systems                                 65
9. Speed versus consumption                           67
10. Summary of Chapter Four                           68

CHAPTER FIVE    COMMERCIAL PERFORMANCE

| | | |
|---|---|---|
| 1. | Introduction | 71 |
| 2. | Bulk carriers | 71 |
| 3. | Tankers | 77 |
| 4. | Container ships | 79 |
| 5. | Passenger ships | 81 |
| 6. | Summary of Chapter Five | 83 |

CHAPTER SIX    FACTORS AFFECTING CHOICE OF A VESSEL, ITS MACHINERY AND EQUIPMENT

| | | |
|---|---|---|
| 1. | Basic philosophy | 85 |
| 2. | Long-term time charter | 85 |
| 3. | Speculative charters and spot voyages | 87 |
| 4. | Charter of affreightment | 89 |
| 5. | Bareboat charter | 90 |
| 6. | Cargo related operations | 90 |
| 7. | Labour saving devices | 92 |
| 8. | Registry and manning considerations | 95 |
| 9. | Secondhand tonnage | 96 |
| 10. | Commercial aspects | 97 |
| 11. | Summary of Chapter Six | 97 |

CHAPTER SEVEN    SAFETY PERFORMANCE

| | | |
|---|---|---|
| 1. | Introduction | 99 |
| 2. | International Maritime Organisation | 99 |
| 3. | Classification Societies | 102 |
| 4. | Shipowners | 107 |
| 5. | Ship's staff | 109 |
| 6. | Summary of Chapter Seven | 111 |

CHAPTER EIGHT    ENVIRONMENTAL PERFORMANCE

| | | |
|---|---|---|
| 1. | Introduction | 113 |
| 2. | Oil pollution | 113 |
| 3. | Chemical pollution | 117 |
| 4. | Harmful substances | 117 |
| 5. | Sewage | 118 |
| 6. | Garbage | 118 |

7.  Gaseous emissions                                    119
8.  Anti-fouling paint                                   119
9.  Summary of Chapter Eight                             120


CHAPTER NINE    CHARTERPARTY PERFORMANCE CLAIMS

1.  Bulk carriers                                        123
2.  Galley fuel                                          130
3.  Hold cleaning                                        132
4.  Tankers                                              132
5.  Summary of Chapter Nine                              134


CHAPTER TEN    COMPUTER APPLICATION

1.  Introduction                                         135
2.  Computer required                                    135
3.  Data input                                           136
4.  Passage summary                                      139
5.  Database                                             141
6.  Graphic illustration of trend analysis              141
7.  Charterparty calculations                           145
8.  Main Engine performance                             153
9.  Cargo heating performance                           156
10. Voyage strategy                                      156
11. Communications                                       157
12. Diagnostic and predictive programs                   158
13. Summary of Chapter Ten                               159


CHAPTER ELEVEN    REMAINING COMPETITIVE BY OPTIMISING
PERFORMANCE

1.  Introduction                                         161
2.  Dry docking                                          161
3.  Voyage repairs/maintenance                          164
4.  Condition monitoring                                 166
5.  Planned maintenance                                  167
6.  Unplanned maintenance                                168
7.  Spares and supplies                                  168
8.  Lubricating oil                                      169
9.  Insurance and P & I                                  172

10.  Miscellaneous charges                                    175
11.  Summary of Chapter Eleven                                175


CHAPTER TWELVE    PAST, PRESENT AND FUTURE

1.  Introduction                                              177
2.  The past                                                  177
3.  The present                                               180
4.  The future                                                181
5.  Summary of Chapter Twelve                                 182


CONCLUSION                                                    185


GLOSSARY                                                      187


Index                                                         205

# LIST OF TABLES

*Table*     *Page*

1. Fuel coefficients and Admiralty Constants     3
2. Performance improvers—sensitivity     13
3. VLCC fuel costs     28
4. VLCC Main Engines     28
5. Panamax Main Engines     34
6. Energy performance of various fuels     45
7. Beaufort Scale     60
8. Swell represented in order of magnitude     60
9. Log abstract or passage summary     61
10. Simple digital system for daily recording     62
11. Charter of affreightment calculations     90
12. Passage summary—all weather     125
13. Passage summary—fairweather     126
14. Summary of charterparty clauses     127
15. Galley fuel cost table     132
16. Expected performance—computer input     140
17. Lubricating oil performance     171

# LIST OF FIGURES

| *Figure* | | *Page* |
|---|---|---|
| 1. | MAN–B&W Power take-off with turbine | 8 |
| 2. | Flow straightening nozzle or wake improvement duct | 10 |
| 3. | Integrated duct | 11 |
| 4. | Vane wheel | 12 |
| 5. | B&W Panamax aft end | 20 |
| 6. | High speed ship (HSS) and water jet | 33 |
| 7. | Refinery flow diagram | 38 |
| 8. | Refinery complex | 39 |
| 9. | Distillate fuel classification | 42 |
| 10. | Residual fuel classification | 43 |
| 11. | Fuel oil test kit | 47 |
| 12. | Bunker delivery note | 48 |
| 13. | Nomograph for determining CCAI | 51 |
| 14. | Simple sector system | 61 |
| 15. | Manual ship performance monitoring system | 66 |
| 16. | Speed and fuel consumption graph—Panamax | 68 |
| 17. | Speed and fuel consumption graph—various vessels | 69 |
| 18. | Typical bulk carrier | 72 |
| 19. | Fully open bulk carrier | 75 |
| 20. | On deck cell guides | 80 |
| 21. | Speed and consumption graph showing sea margin | 88 |
| 22. | Tank arrangement—modern product carrier | 93 |
| 23. | Bulk carrier structural problems | 105 |
| 24. | Bulk carrier loss rate | 106 |
| 25. | Corrosion in a double bottom tank | 107 |
| 26. | Selective catalytic reduction plant (SCR) | 120 |
| 27. | Passage summary—computer printout | 137 |
| 28. | Speed summary—computer printout | 139 |
| 29. | Performance summary—computer printout | 140 |
| 30. | Database—computer printout | 141 |
| 31. | Unsmoothed trend graphs | 142 |
| 32. | Smoothed trend graphs | 143 |

| 33. | Regression analysis graphs | 144 |
| 34. | Main Engine absorbed load | 146 |
| 35. | Charterparty claim all weather: New Orleans–Rotterdam | 148 |
| 36. | Charterparty claim fairweather: New Orleans–Rotterdam | 149 |
| 37. | Charterparty claim all weather: NSW–Rotterdam | 150 |
| 38. | Charterparty claim fairweather: NSW–Rotterdam | 151 |
| 39. | Database printout | 151 |
| 40. | Database weather screening | 152 |
| 41. | Main Engine cylinder data—computer printout | 153 |
| 42. | Main Engine general data—computer printout | 154 |
| 43. | Main Engine compression/scavenge pressure ratio | 155 |
| 44. | Cylinder liner wear graph | 173 |
| 45. | World oil supply and demand (million barrels daily) | 183 |

CHAPTER ONE

# TECHNICAL CONSIDERATIONS

## 1. MAIN PROPULSION SYSTEM

The performance of the main propulsion unit *per se* will be more fully discussed in Chapter Two but other items associated with the propulsion system as a whole will be discussed here.

Generally, the choice of Main Engine will be between slow speed and medium speed diesel. Both types have their supporters but the trend in recent years comes out in favour of slow speed diesels for so-called conventional vessels. Assuming a slow speed diesel has been selected, we currently have two European and one Far Eastern design to choose from. All three designs have closely similar performances from a fuel consumption, in relation to horse-power, point of view. We will in future refer to this particular parameter as specific fuel consumption (SFC).

There are, however, various measures available to shipowners to enable them to improve performance of the propulsion system at the design stage. The most important of these options is probably to choose a derated engine having the highest possible stroke/bore ratio. It should, perhaps, be mentioned that derating is sometimes referred to as economy rating depending on the engine builder.

The principle behind derating concerns choosing a more powerful engine than that necessary for the selected ship's speed, and then operating it at a lower output but still using the maximum design combustion pressure. There is a twofold benefit operating in the derating mode in that the thermodynamic performance is improved by around 3% and propeller performance is similarly enhanced by operating at lower revolutions; this a well known principle in optimising propeller efficiency.

It should be mentioned that after choosing the derated option it is not possible to operate the engine at its full output without changing the propeller and fitting larger pumps, coolers, etc. One disadvantage of the derated engine is its high initial cost as the unused horsepower must, of course, be paid for by the shipowner, it being general practice that engines are sold on a horsepower basis, at their full rating.

This brings us to another important point which will be briefly mentioned

1

here. Irrespective of whether a derated engine has been chosen, it is vitally important to determine what ship's speed is likely to be over the vessel's life-cycle. Ship's speed determines the output of the engine, and the advent of slow steaming in the early 1970s made most conventional vessels greatly overpowered. Many billions of dollars are locked up in unused horsepower, some of which has never been used on these early vessels although many have subsequently been broken up.

A brief mention of the medium speed option will be made even though it is outside the scope of the subject-matter of this chapter. Medium speed diesel engines generally operate better at their rather high design revolutions and they are generally used in conjunction with gearboxes and clutches, and sometimes with controllable pitch propellers. Therefore, a possibility of reducing propeller revolutions is instantly available, perhaps more so than with a derated long stroke slow speed engine, depending on the limitations of the propeller diameter, itself a function of many other considerations.

We can say that gearbox transmission losses could negate the possibility of any improvement due to reduced propeller revolutions, leaving us with a straight thermodynamic efficiency contest in which the slow speed diesel appears to have a slight edge. Very many other considerations can be brought into the contest of slow speed versus medium speed diesels, but as we are only concerned with performance these will be left for others to discuss.

## 2. UNDERWATER HULL

The design of the underwater hull plays an important part in the overall performance of a vessel. There are many establishments around the world which tank test various designs submitted to them, usually by a shipbuilder.

For bulk carriers and tankers a compromise is generally reached between maximising cargo cubic capacity without having too fine underwater lines. Fine lines are normally associated with high speed passenger ships and a different approach is necessary for these specialised vessels. Some very good designs have been produced in recent years. One of the most successful known to the author was the Burmister & Wain Panamax Bulker and it is rather sad to learn that this long established shipyard has recently ceased trading, yet another casualty in the war of survival.

So how is the performance of a vessel measured? There is an international test tank association which standardises the methods used in towing tank calculations, but this does not really help anybody but the most technically trained observer. In any case, the performance of a hull in a test tank and under seagoing conditions can be somewhat different, as many readers will know.

A well-known method of measuring overall vessel performance in service is the non-dimensional fuel coefficient, which is suitable for comparing vessels having similar particulars. The simple formula used calculating the coefficient is:

$$\frac{D^{2/3} \, V^3}{C}$$

where D = displacement tonnage, V = ship's speed, C = fuel consumption (propulsion only or total consumption).

By introducing fuel consumption into the formula the machinery perform-ance is also taken into consideration and a 3% less fuel consumption would increase the numerical value of the fuel coefficient by approximately the same amount.

It will also be seen that speed cubed is used to tie up with the well-known propeller law which uses this cube relationship as a basis for many calculations on hydrodynamic performance. This cube relationship illustrates the penal effect of speed on fuel consumption, and it can be shown that a 10% increase in speed requires a 30% increase in fuel consumption.

Some ship operators use the Admiralty Constant, which uses horsepower instead of fuel consumption in the fuel coefficient formula. However, not many vessels are fitted with accurate meters for measuring horsepower, so a more practical approach using fuel consumption is preferred by the author. Strictly speaking, the Admiralty Constant is a more accurate measurement of the ship's hull. If we substitute horsepower instead of fuel consumption the performance of the engine, whether it be a fuel-thirsty turbine or a modern diesel, is not taken into account. What sort of fuel coefficient or Admiralty Constant values can we expect in service? A lot depends on the type of vessel, and expected figures for fully laden conditions using 9,600/K.cal/kg fuel are given in Table 1. For ballast conditions, the numerical values of both the Admiralty Constant and fuel coefficient are somewhat lower.

*Table 1. Fuel coefficients and Admiralty Constants*

| VESSEL TYPE | FUEL COEFFICIENT | | ADMIRALTY CONSTANT | |
|---|---|---|---|---|
| | *Sea trials* | *In service fairweather* | *Sea trials* | *In service fairweather* |
| VLCC/VLBC | 185,000 | 165,000 | 580 | 520 |
| Cape sized bulker | 185,000 | 165,000 | 570 | 510 |
| Panamax bulker/tanker | 175,000 | 147,000 | 550 | 470 |
| 30,000 TDW bulker/tanker | 140,000 | 125,000 | 385 | 335 |
| 26-year-old VLCC | 137,000 | | 535 | |

The vessels in the table are assumed to have the latest propulsion systems with specific fuel consumptions of around 130 gms/b.h.p./hr basis heavy fuel of net calorific value 9,600 K.cals/kg or 40.20 megajoules/kg, to use this recently introduced unit. Corrections can be made for older and newer vessels by making allowance for changes in specific fuel consumption and propeller revolutions.

By way of example, we could take a 1970-built diesel VLCC which had a sea trial fuel coefficient of around 137,000, an Admiralty Constant of around 535 and a specific fuel consumption of 167 gms/b.h.p./hr at 9,600 K.cals with Main Engine revolutions of 100.

The increase in fuel coefficient over the modern vessel shown in the table is nearly 35%, but the improvement in the Admiralty Constant is only around 8%. Most of the 35% improvement in fuel coefficient is explained by a 28% improvement in specific fuel consumption and the remainder by the reduced RPM of the propeller coupled with improved aft-end geometry. The increase in Admiralty Constant is due to reduced RPM and aft-end geometry only. As a rough rule of thumb it is generally accepted that a 10% reduction in propeller revolutions equates to a 1% increase in speed for the same power or a 3% reduction in power for the same speed.

Using this approach, we can compare the 100 RPM of the older vessel and the 80 RPM of the modern vessel, which gives a 25% reduction in RPM equal to a 7.5% reduction in power, closely that of the improvement in Admiralty Constant.

Differences between sea trials and in-service results are occasioned first by the so-called Sea Margin normally added to sea trials results to take account of weather, and secondly by the expected deterioration in hull and propeller roughness after entering service. Sea trials on bulkers are invariably carried out in the ballast condition and corrections are made for loaded displacement conditions, whereas tankers generally carry out their sea trials in loaded displacement condition and no displacement corrections are necessary.

Contractual conditions for carrying out sea trials usually specify calm weather, and additionally various corrections are made for wind speed, water depth, tide, water density and temperature. All these add up to, perhaps, 15–20% increased power being necessary to maintain sea trials speed in service. A lot depends on the expected trading pattern of the vessel with its effect regarding sea state and weather conditions, and also hull fouling organisms. Only the shipowner can determine what figure to use, based on his experience.

Modern underwater paint systems have been especially formulated to cope with the current practice of extending dry dock intervals to combat high operating costs in a critical expense area, although the use of TBT, which is present in the more efficient paints, is subject to some constraints as mentioned in a later chapter. The use of the fuel coefficient and Admiralty Constant can detect a trend in performance fall-off and help shipowners decide if a dry docking, or underwater scrubbing operation, is necessary.

They are also useful for determining if a shipyard's design is a good performer or not. The main drawback to their unqualified use is that the cube relationship between speed and horsepower has, in some instances, been measured as high as the fifth power, which can make direct comparisons a little dangerous.

## 3. "BOLT-ON" IMPROVERS

With the advent of the progressive fuel cost hikes experienced starting from the autumn of 1973 until the spring of 1986, many innovative ideas to improve the performance of vessels were introduced, although the recent softening in fuel costs have made many of these uneconomical.

### A. Slow steaming

Not strictly in this category was the widely practised slow steaming mode of operation. However, when carried out properly, slow steaming requires specific fuel nozzles to be fitted which basically increase fuel injection pressures to sustain acceptable combustion conditions below that originally thought necessary in the original design.

Various operational measures of a protective nature were also introduced simply to counter the possible deleterious effect of continuous operation at ultra-low powers which have been allowed to drop to around 25% in suitable cases. In this category are included diesel VLCCs returning to the Arabian Gulf for an indefinite stay when worldscale levels of under 20 prevailed.

Other measures to obtain more dramatic improvements in slow steaming performance involve fitting new propellers and in the case of steam turbine vessels altering the gear ratio or turbine layout. This course of action enables much lower propeller revolutions to be used more economically, but still maintaining the turbine efficiency at almost full power output.

Modern diesel engines have fairly constant specific fuel consumptions throughout their operating range; steam turbines decidedly do not have this attractive feature, hence the need for major surgery to enhance the steam turbine's relatively poor performance—especially at low power output.

To improve the specific fuel consumption of older diesel engines at lower outputs or if slow steaming, the economy fuel pump was developed. This loosely follows the derating principle mentioned earlier, and the economy fuel pump increases maximum combustion pressure at lower powers with a corresponding increase in thermodynamic performance of around 2–3% depending on the chosen power. The economy fuel pump loses its effect above 85% and below 40% output.

The practice of slow steaming, with or without the bolt-on benefits, was arguably the most cost-effective method of improving performance as measured by a miles per tonne of fuel basis.

## B. Power take-offs

The generation of auxiliary power, normally in the form of electrical energy, has scope for improvement in the overall performance of the machinery within the vessel. Normally, electrical energy is provided by independent diesel generators using a distillate fuel, originally diesel oil, but more latterly blended or even heavy fuel.

A development gaining recent popularity is to use a power take-off from the Main Engine in the form of a shaft generator mounted directly on the intermediate shaft or free end of the crankshaft. Variations on this theme include hydraulic or geared drives taken from the crankshaft. Some versions have a novel revolution regulating system which permits less expensive voltage regulation control. This is an important consideration when a Main Engine of variable output is used to perform a duty normally requiring fairly constant revolutions.

The main benefit in using a power take-off is that the fuel used in the Main Engine, which—if of slow speed design—can tolerate fuel of quite low quality, is used to generate electrical energy whilst at sea. It should be remembered that the amount of electrical energy used must be deducted from the developed propulsion energy with a resultant loss of the ship's speed. Another benefit of using power take-offs is that maintenance costs of the diesel generator engines are reduced because they are only used in port or whilst manoeuvring.

The main disadvantage in power take-offs is the rather large capital cost, which probably can be justified when fuel costs are high but not when they are low. Each shipowner will have his own ideas on the cost-effectiveness of power take-offs.

It should perhaps be mentioned in closing that in a depressed shipbuilding market it is possible to obtain extras such as this at cost price. We must not forget that the universal trend to use lower cost crews makes achievement of the technical aspect necessary for highly technical innovations that much more difficult in service.

## C. Exhaust gas recovery

As mentioned in the previous section, power take-offs do not make a positive contribution to performance improvement, in that the power used is redirected rather than conserved. This was not the case in exhaust gas recovery schemes, which provided energy without detracting from the Main Engine output.

Most vessels have simple exhaust gas recovery schemes, generally in the form of economisers or boilers, which supply steam for all heating purposes by utilising the waste heat in the Main Engine exhaust gases. Such were the benefits of this scheme that in recent years it was extended to recovering heat from the exhaust gases of diesel generators, albeit at a rather lower value than that from Main Engines.

In sophisticated exhaust gas recovery schemes, much larger economisers were provided and all the available heat in the gases was converted to steam. Sufficient steam was generated to drive a steam turbine coupled to an alternator which could supply all seagoing electrical demands. On vessels fitted with rather large powered Main Engines, alternators having outputs of around 1,000kW were not unknown.

Recent improvements in Main Engine thermal efficiencies, which now exceed 50%, have dealt a severe blow to these steam driven alternator schemes. This improved efficiency has manifested itself in lower Main Engine exhaust gas exit temperatures so the amount of heat capable of being recovered has dropped dramatically. The situation was partially retrieved by the adoption of air-cooled turbochargers, which have higher gas outlet temperatures and, therefore, have a higher heat input into the economiser, allowing more steam to be generated.

Another innovation was the hot gas bypass, which allowed a certain amount of high temperature exhaust gas from the exhaust manifold to flow direct into the economiser. Unlike the air-cooled turbocharger, which has no effect on Main Engine performance, the hot gas bypass does represent a slight loss of Main Engine efficiency, albeit very small.

Exhaust gas turbochargers have also had their efficiency improved and any excess power available can be returned to the propeller shaft by introducing an additional power turbine, utilising a novel system of gears similar to that used in some of the power take-off schemes described earlier. The contribution from this turbocharger scheme is around 3–4% in suitably powered vessels.

It is even possible to have a combined system whereby the output from the power turbine can be directed to the Main Engine crankshaft or to an electrical alternator supplying the ship's electrical needs, as shown in Fig. 1.

Sophisticated exhaust gas recovery systems are rather expensive but when fuel costs are pitched at what might be called their normal level an economic case can be put forward, providing a large enough Main Engine is available to generate sufficient waste heat from the exhaust gases or surplus power from the turbochargers. Retrofitting sophisticated exhaust gas systems is not an attractive proposition and their use is generally confined to new buildings, but it must be said that they are rarely used these days.

### D.  Use of blended or residual fuel in diesel generators

As mentioned in a previous section, the generation of electrical power was normally by diesel generators using distillate fuel. In recent years the cost of distillate fuel has fallen sharply and the use of blended or heavy fuel oil, which became very popular when distillate fuel costs were high, is not so commercially attractive any more, but even so many generators still use either of these fuels.

Distillate fuel, normally diesel oil, has rather low viscosity and does not require heating. Residual heavy fuel, by having a high viscosity, requires substantial heating and when these fuels are mixed or blended a degree of

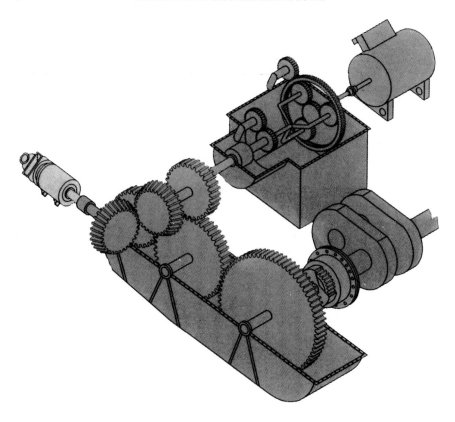

**Fig. 1. *MAN-B & W power take-off with turbine*** (courtesy of Man-B & W
Diesel A/S)

heating is required. This is the main modification required when blended fuel is
used and a fuel heating system, as well as a static or dynamic blender, must be
provided to ensure the blend is adequately mixed and heated.

Because the resultant blend will contain some of the naturally occurring
contaminants normally associated with residual heavy fuel, it may be necessary
to upgrade some of the components in the diesel generator engines. These
contaminants are not normally present in distillate fuel, and engines designed
to run on this good quality fuel could run into operational problems—unless
fitted with high grade exhaust valves and other modified components.

A logical progression is to use straight residual heavy fuel in the generator
engines after experience gained running on blended fuel. Most manufacturers
now market diesel generator engines for use on residual fuel and many "one
fuel ships", as they are called, are in service.

Retrofitting existing plants to run on blended or residual fuel is sensitive to
ruling fuel costs, and pay-back periods are now quite lengthy due to the

aforementioned fall in distillate fuel costs. Another disadvantage is the increased cost of maintenance and possibly increased lubricating oil costs which should be included in any calculations.

### E. Upgrading existing Main Engines

Some of the earlier Main Diesel Engines in service today have rather low thermal efficiencies when compared to the engines currently available. However, it does appear that we are reaching the practical limit, and it is doubtful if any significant increase in thermal efficiency above the 53% or so presently attainable will be made. This 53% should be compared with the 40% of the older engines and, although it would be possible to re-engine many vessels, this expensive exercise has rarely been undertaken in recent years. Compared with the 30% efficiency of the steam turbine, even the older diesels look good, and many steam-to-diesel conversions have taken place. There exists a possibility of upgrading certain diesel engines and some of the options available are outlined.

One of these options is to convert from impulse turbocharging to constant pressure turbocharging, which increases thermal efficiency by around 10%. It is quite a major operation to convert to constant pressure turbocharging—new turbochargers and a new exhaust manifold are necessary.

It is also possible to increase the stroke/bore ratio of some earlier engines by fitting cylinders of a smaller bore diameter. One disadvantage of this option is that the output of the engine is considerably reduced, which may not suit all shipowners' requirements.

Generally, both these operations are carried out in conjunction so the combined effect in improved performance almost approaches that of the latest engines, but it must be said that they would only become popular if fuel costs rose dramatically.

### F. Ducted and other propellers

The performance of conventional fixed pitch propellers has probably reached its limit and the only possibility left is to increase diameter with a corresponding reduction in revolutions and a corresponding increase in efficiency. There is a practical limit to the size to which a propeller diameter can go, mainly because of draught restrictions. Propeller efficiency can also be improved by using various means which are described below.

*Flow straightening nozzle or wake improvement duct (Fig. 2)*

This is fitted in front of the propeller and its purpose, as its name suggests, is to even out the flow of water into the propeller. It consists of a nozzle which is made in two halves and welded to the stern frame. Propeller efficiency can increase upwards of 6%, especially if high speed vessels are under consideration. The nozzles are not so effective when fitted to slow speed vessels.

*Fig. 2  Flow straightening nozzle or wake improvement duct*

*Integrated duct (Fig. 3)*

This is mounted in front of the propeller and requires to be a quite massive structure compared to the flow straightening nozzle and is, therefore, rather expensive. The theory involved is to recapture some of the energy lost in turbulent forces and redirect it to the forward propulsive force. In suitable cases, gains of up to 8% increased efficiency can arise.

***Fig. 3 Integrated duct***

*Reaction fins*

These are fitted in front of the propeller and are sometimes fitted with a shroud to combat dynamic forces in this critical area. Their purpose is to improve the propulsive performance by inducing a swirl to the propeller inflow which will counter slipstream rotation, a source of efficiency loss. Gains of 4% to 8% are claimed by fitting these reaction fins. Retrofitting costs are rather high if a shroud is necessary but, if the reaction fins are designed for a new vessel, the shroud could probably be eliminated and the cost would, therefore, be much less.

*Vane wheel (Fig. 4)*

The vane wheel consists of what might be termed a free running propeller mounted directly behind the existing propeller. The vane wheel is larger in diameter than the main propeller and has a larger number of blades. The purpose of the vane wheel is to convert tangential forces in the propeller slipstream into additional thrust. Gains in propulsive efficiency of around 10% have been quoted and payback times of 12 months indicated. One problem is that not all existing single screw ships have aft-end arrangements capable of accommodating this rather large appendage without major restructuring, and serious technical problems have apparently been experienced in service.

***Fig. 4 Vane wheel***

*High skew*

This type of propeller is becoming increasingly popular, but it has never been claimed to be a performance improver. It could be said that it permits the same blade area to be developed over a smaller diameter, which allows vessels with a draught restriction to be fitted with more effective propellers.

*Contra rotating propeller*

The use of contra rotating propellers was first promulgated many years ago but as far as is known only one was actually fitted. Quite recently a VLCC was provided with such a propeller and the improvement in propulsive performance claimed to be around 15%.

*Tip vortex free*

In its original form the tip vortex free propeller was used in conjunction with a duct and trial results indicated satisfactory savings—especially on VLCCs.

More recently, it has been developed without a duct and renamed CLT (Contracted and Loaded Tip). The tips of the CLT propeller are provided with end plates which permit a finite load to be developed in this part of the propeller, so having an advantage over a conventional propeller.

*Asymmetrical stern*

The aft-end lines of the vessel are offset to improve the water flow into the propeller and compensate for the side thrust generated by the direction of turning. It is not strictly a bolt-on performance improver, as it would be difficult and cost prohibitive to modify an existing vessel. Improvements in perform-ance of around 8% are claimed and, if the asymmetrical stern is negotiated during contractual discussions, only negligible cost would be involved.

*Controllable pitch*

Controllable pitch propellers are generally used in cross-channel ferries and other vessels having a high manoeuvrability requirement coupled with multi-engine configurations. They have only rarely been used in our so-called conventional vessels, which, of course, do not have such high manoeuvrability requirements.

Because of the large difference in the loaded and ballast draughts of conventional vessels, controllable pitch propellers do have a part to play as they can be adjusted to optimise the displacement condition. They are also useful when used in conjunction with a shaft generator as revolution control is made much easier. It would be difficult to calculate what improvement in perform-ance would arise, as controllable pitch propellers are not specifically marketed for this reason. They are rather costly and are not particularly efficient, mainly due to their increased weight and reduced blade area, compared with a fixed pitch propeller.

**Table 2. *Performance improvers—sensitivity***

| Performance improver | Capital cost | Percentage improvement | Recovery period in months with various fuel costs | | | |
|---|---|---|---|---|---|---|
| | $ | Full steam | $50 | $100 | $150 | $200 |
| Increased stroke/ bore—constant pressure | 800,000 | 17 | 75 | 38 | 25 | 19 |
| Constant pressure only | 400,000 | 12 | 53 | 27 | 18 | 13 |
| Vane wheel | 200,000 | 10 | 32 | 16 | 11 | 8 |
| Flow straightening nozzles | 50,000 | 8 | 10 | 5 | 3 | 2 |
| Economy fuel pumps | 20,000 | 1 | 32 | 16 | 11 | 8 |

Faced with this array of bolt-on performance improvers it is difficult for any shipowner to make a choice—especially as the drop in fuel costs, starting in spring 1986, made most alternatives financially unattractive. As will be discussed later on in the book, a lot depends on whether the vessel is time chartered or not. However, as a rough guide to measure the financial attractiveness of some of the performance improvers mentioned, Table 2 will give some idea in order of magnitude for a typical Panamax bulker.

Capital costs are given in good faith at 1996 levels, but US$ cross-rates and geographical location of the work done could cause these to be somewhat different. The power of the Main Engine also plays an important part in the decision-making process. The vessel chosen in the example has a rather high powered engine, and lower powered vessels would give less savings. A word of caution about the percentage improvements shown. These, generally, cannot be guaranteed by the manufacturers and it is for the shipowner to decide if the claims made are achievable in service.

## 4. ENERGY CONSERVATION

This subject is closely allied to that of performance improvers mentioned in the previous paragraph. For ease of reference, the items included in this paragraph will be those not of a large capital outlay.

### A. Minimum ballast—optimal trim

Our conventional vessel will probably spend 50% of sea time loaded, and the other 50% in the ballast condition. There is a lot of scope for improving performance in the ballast condition, particularly on the larger vessels. If we take as an example a Panamax bulker, the difference between the light and heavy ballast condition is something in the order of 10,000 tonnes. This represents a speed increase of around 0.2 knots if the vessel were operated wholly in the light ballast condition on ballast voyages. On larger vessels, the speed difference can be greater on account of the greater reduction in ballast capacity.

Of course safety considerations must prevail, especially when severe weather is forecast. Most shipmasters frown upon filling the deep tank (cargo hold) at sea, but a close study of the problem has shown that on many vessels it is possible to achieve a light ballast condition with the deep tank full—thus allaying fears of having to fill this tank in inclement weather. In the case of tankers, MARPOL regulations relating to minimum draught must be considered and, in the case of large bulkers registered in the UK, similar DOT recommendations should be observed.

Most vessels have the possibility of choosing an optimum trim by adjustment of loading or ballasting operations within certain limits. The only problem is knowing what this optimum trim actually is. Although there are various microprocessors on the market which allegedly calculate the answer for you, the technical aspects are not sound. Each vessel type will have its own characteristics, which could change in different sea states, and a series of extensive—and expensive—tank tests would appear necessary before making any firm recommendations. The type of bulbous bow fitted would appear to have an influence on both aspects considered in this section. Only detailed analysis of service results can give an indication of what improvements are likely.

## B. Adaptive steering modules

There are also microprocessors available which allegedly improve steering capabilities and, therefore, set a course that minimises the distance between ports. The theory is sound but, in the author's experience, the service results did not live up to the claims made. This is not to say that all steering modules would fall into the same bracket, but the subject is very difficult and measuring the results perhaps requires an approach beyond present measurement techniques.

## C. Self-polishing underwater paint

The use of self-polishing copolymer underwater paint has spread in recent years; its main purpose is to allow extended periods between dry dockings. Frictional resistance probably accounts for 70% of the total ship resistance, the balance being made up of wave, eddy and air resistance. Conventional underwater paint was originally based on the almost universally adopted annual dry docking. As dry dock intervals were extended as a cost-cutting exercise, paints having more aggressive anti-fouling properties were developed.

The high fuel cost era, starting in 1973, highlighted the need to reduce frictional resistance, which eventually led to self-polishing copolymer paint being marketed which has the duel function of combating marine growth and reducing frictional resistance. This latter property is achieved by using the action of the vessel proceeding through the water to slowly abrade the paint surface, making it progressively smoother. Obviously, paint film thicknesses must be that much greater when using self-polishing paint and this, coupled with a higher product cost, makes the operation that much more expensive than conventional paint systems. As will be discussed in Chapter Eight, the use of underwater paints containing TBT (tributyltin) are subject to certain restrictions.

A very important factor is the roughness of the hull, which must be maintained as smooth as possible. Latest thinking is to take regular hull roughness readings at each dry docking to monitor the situation. Shot blasting is really the only answer, starting from when the ship is built and then maintaining damaged areas by blasting as necessary at subsequent dry dockings. A sophisticated sacrificial cathodic protection system is a good idea or, if trading in areas where underwater damage is expected, ice for example, an impressed current cathodic system will greatly help control corrosion.

### D. Underwater air lubrication

Towing tests carried out at the Feltham Tank in 1979 gave encouraging results when using, first, a simple plate and, latterly, a model. However, when the system was fitted on a vessel no significant reduction in hull resistance could be measured. It would appear that the theoretical reasoning is sound but the practical difficulties in obtaining an air film under seagoing conditions are insurmountable.

### E. Propeller polishing

Propeller surfaces are as much likely to be affected by fouling as is the underwater hull, although corrosion is not normally a threat because of the non-ferrous metals used in propeller manufacture. It is important that the propeller blade surfaces are maintained as smooth as possible and this is normally carried out by discing at the dry dock.

Specialist firms for carrying out this operation afloat have recently been formed and they claim that, by doing the work underwater, a better finish is obtained—a claim which has some substance. No significant increase in performance was measured after several underwater polishing operations were carried out by the author's company.

It is difficult to say if the propeller polishings carried out at dry docking are effective, as the maintenance work carried out on the underwater hull would tend to overshadow that carried out on the propeller.

### F. Underwater scrubbing

This operation has been in practice many years and gained popularity in the early 1970s when it looked likely that the availability of large dry docks would be unable to meet the rising number of vessels of ever-increasing size entering service. This situation did not last for very long, but extended dry dock intervals became the norm for economic rather than logistic reasons.

Many stations for carrying out underwater scrubbing operations are now available worldwide and can do the work quickly and efficiently. Video tapes showing before and after conditions are normally available. Performance improvement is usually dramatic in the days after the operation, but it generally falls off after a period, which varies for reasons which are at present unknown.

There is a possibility that the scrubbing brushes remove the anti-fouling ingredient in the paint, which leaves the remaining surface more vulnerable to attack by marine growth. A further possibility is that the brushes scatter the spores of the organisms, thus promoting further growth.

## G. Reduction of electrical load

Electricity costs money, especially when diesel oil costs were as high as they were in the early 1980s. To leave a 100 watt light burning would then cost around $50 per year if conventional diesel generators using diesel oil were in use. This gives some scope for conserving energy aboard ship by reducing the electrical load. An approach which has met with some success is to introduce an energy audit, whereby every item consuming electricity is examined with a view to either stopping it completely, limiting its output or using an alternative means of performing its function.

A prime example is a typical sea-water cooling system, which normally comprises a main circulating pump and possibly two auxiliary pumps. It was found possible to stop one of the auxiliary pumps as the main pump could adequately supply the auxiliary system, mainly because the Main Engine was being operated in a slow steaming mode. In other cases, a simple cross-connection between main and auxiliary systems made it possible to stop an auxiliary pump.

Another idea with possibilities is to reduce the electrical frequency by slowing down the generators—this in turn slows down all the electric motors and reduces the output of whatever is being driven by the motors. When slow steaming this is quite acceptable: reducing the frequency causes no problems as long as it is increased to normal when full steaming is restored. During the power supply problems of the 1950s the Central Electricity Generating Board reduced the frequency of the entire grid system to conserve energy during peak demand periods.

Apart from switching off many lights, the audit was able to find various examples whereby other electrical consumers could be switched off. Hold ventilation fans, even radars, came into this category. It was not uncommon to find that reductions of 30kW in electrical load were possible at an annual cost saving of around $15,000 without any adverse effect. A cautionary note regarding reduction of frequency must point out that unless this is accomplished with a corresponding reduction in voltage overheating of electrical motors could occur.

## H. Increase in deadweight

It is possible to increase the deadweight and hence earning capacity of many vessels, particularly larger-sized older bulkers by adopting the B-60 freeboard. As a typical example, a 1974-built CAPE sized bulker—constructed under the then existing freeboard regulations—had a summer deadweight of 123,132 tons. By carrying out certain work to the classification society's specification, it was possible to increase the summer deadweight to 129,193 tons, a very useful contribution to the vessel's earning capacity, particularly in times of reasonable freight rates. There is a penalty to pay in increased wetted area leading to higher frictional losses with a corresponding loss in speed or increase in fuel consumption. But this is only in the fully laden condition. We also have to consider the capital cost of the conversion, but generally it would appear the benefits outweigh these penalties.

## I. Other action

This section could also be called good housekeeping, as the subject-matter is mainly just that. Many apparently similar vessels perform quite differently, and the reasons for this will be examined.

One of the most common faults concerns the number of diesel generators in use at sea. Some vessels use two machines as a misguided security operation whereas one machine could adequately cope with the anticipated additional load. Using two machines costs many thousands of dollars per year in additional fuel consumption.

Correct maintenance of Main Engine temperatures is very important if thermal efficiency is to be kept at the design figures. Again, some vessels—as a misguided security measure—keep certain critical temperatures below the recommended value with resultant loss of efficiency.

The same applies to combustion pressures, especially as fuel quality variations are now frequently met with. The net effect of not maintaining these critical temperatures and pressures represents a loss of performance, manifesting itself in increased fuel consumption.

It has been found that some vessels still use diesel oil whilst manoeuvring, even though the fuel system has been designed for operation on heavy oil when entering and leaving port.

Probably the most important aspect is maintenance of the underwater hull. We have learnt that frictional resistance accounts for 70% of the total propulsive resistance. If this resistance is allowed to increase by not keeping the hull surfaces in reasonably good condition, then fuel consumption will rise dramatically. Choice of paint system, regularity of dry docking, geographical area of operation and weather conditions when applying underwater paint, all contribute to the overall equation.

Not all these factors are controllable; for example, vessels still dry dock in unsatisfactory weather conditions, they are still anchored awaiting discharge in high temperature sea water areas and are always subject to possible mechanical damage to the underwater paint surfaces. It is possible nowadays to measure the hull roughness by means of a fairly cheap instrument. The proper use of this piece of equipment can help maintain hull roughness at acceptable levels when used during scheduled dry dockings.

## 5. OTHER PERFORMANCE IMPROVERS

There are other items which can be incorporated into a vessel when it is at the building stage, but these are not suitable candidates for retrofitting mainly because of the high cost.

### A. Fuel oil storage tanks

Quite a large amount of heat is lost when storage tanks are mounted in direct contact with the sea. If double bottom tanks are involved, little can be done, but if deep tanks are provided it is a comparatively simple matter to provide a cofferdam between side shell and the tank's outboard bulkhead. This works on a similar principle to that used for double glazing in that air is a poor conductor of heat.

### B. Combined incinerator/boilers

We will read in a later chapter about the deterioration of fuel quality. One side effect is the generation of appreciable amounts of sludge recovered from the fuel, either in the settling tanks or from the purifier. This sludge does have a reasonable heat content and when suitably treated can be burnt in a combined incinerator/boiler, thus producing useful steam at a rather low cost. When burnt in a conventional incinerator, the sludge has no useful contribution to the performance of the auxiliary plant. The sludge can be quite expensive to get rid of in certain parts of the world, and burning it in an incinerator/boiler can produce substantial savings.

### C. Accommodation heating

It is possible to provide a link from the main cooling system to the accommodation heating system, thus allowing the heat in the cooling system to heat the accommodation. This saves valuable steam which can be redirected to the steam alternator, if fitted, which in turn will produce more kW.

### D. Two-speed pumps

When operating in cold sea water temperatures, only small quantities of sea water are necessary for cooling the various systems. The provision of two-speed motors on the sea-water cooling pumps represents a considerable energy saving when operating in the colder climates.


## 6. SUMMARY OF CHAPTER ONE

Some of the various technical possibilities for improving performance have been reviewed. There are many others which have not been mentioned and the author apologises to those who may feel slighted by these omissions.

Shipowners must decide which of the possibilities are the most suitable for

*Fig. 5.  B & W Panamax aft end*

their needs, bearing in mind that vessels on existing long-term charters already performing within the warranted performance need do nothing unless it is paid for by the charterer.

A sobering thought is that one of the most successful Panamax designs known to the author does not employ any of the sophisticated means for improving flow into the propeller, but relies simply on a good underwater hull geometry coupled with a simple barge type after body with Skeg (as shown in Fig. 5). Many shipbuilders now adopt this approach to improving hydro-dynamic efficiency by paying special attention to the design of the after body to the detriment of providing more expensive alternatives.

# CHAPTER TWO

# MAIN PROPULSION PERFORMANCE

## 1. INTRODUCTION

In this chapter the performance of the main propulsion system for the various types of vessel currently in service will be discussed. The thermodynamic performance of an engine is usually expressed by either its thermal efficiency or specific fuel consumption (SFC). The former is a measure of the useful work delivered by the engine compared with the heat available in the fuel, and the latter is the output of the engine expressed in grams of fuel consumed per brake horsepower per hour (Gms/BHP/Hr). The SFC is usually measured on the test bed using distillate fuel at the engine manufacturer's works before the engine is installed in the vessel. Many owners ask for a check on the SFC on the sea trials when using heavy viscosity fuel oil. Whilst the thermodynamic performance of an engine is arguably the most important issue in the eyes of many, other performance criteria should be considered, as will be discussed.

## 2. STEAM TURBINE

The demise of the steam turbine coincided with the introduction of the large diesel engine; when the power output of the diesel engine could match that of the steam turbine, coupled with the huge increase in fuel costs starting in the autumn of 1973, the latter's days were numbered.

The SFC of the steam turbine at that time was in the region of 210 Gms/SHP/Hr (expressed as shaft horsepower SHP) and an equivalent sized diesel engine about 167 Gms/BHP/Hr. This 26% or so advantage the diesel engine had over the steam turbine was to become very important as heavy fuel oil costs appeared then to be on an ever-rising trend until they peaked at around $180 per tonne towards the end of the 1980s.

Steam turbines are nowadays only used for those gas carriers (LNG) who use cargo boil off as fuel for the boilers supplying steam to the turbines and for nuclear propelled warships as used by certain of the world's navies. In the case of LNG carriers the major diesel licensors have designed engines to burn boil off gas but at the moment (1996) no firm contracts have been signed for these engines for shipboard application, although several land-based diesel plants use LNG.

One probable reason for diesels not being popular on LNG carriers is the lack of boil off gas on the lengthy ballast voyage and the lack of operational experience with dual fuel engines.

Mainly due to the high fuel costs prevailing in the 1980s, many vessels originally built with steam turbine propulsion were converted to diesel engine propulsion. The most notable example of this was the QE II passenger ship, but many container ships were also converted from steam to diesel propulsion at this time.

Fuel oil costs as of late have stabilised around the $100 per tonne mark for a typical 380 cst heavy fuel over a mix of bunkering ports and if we take into account historical inflationary increases in other sectors of industry then today's fuel costs are probably at pre-1973 levels.

Recent forecasts have in fact predicted that worldwide oil consumption will be comfortably below available capacity and, coupled with a glut in the gas production sector, it is possible that oil prices could fall in the short to medium term. It would appear unlikely that many of these rather expensive steam to diesel conversions would have taken place if this unexpected softening of oil prices could have been predicted.

There has been no recent improvement in the thermodynamic performance of marine steam turbines; neither does there appear to be any likelihood of any significant improvement in the future. It is an accepted fact that steam turbines can burn fuel of inferior quality to that currently used by diesel engines, but this would not appear to be a factor in their unlikely resurrection as the cost difference is only in the region of $1 per tonne.

Coal, of course, can be used as fuel in steam turbine plants and indeed coal was the original fuel when turbines were first introduced at the end of the last century. When fuel oil costs peaked in the 1980s the coal burning steam turbine 75510 TDW bulk carrier "River Boyne" was built in Japan. This vessel was unique in that it was the first coal-fired ship to employ automatic coal handling and combustion control equipment. However, it did not set a trend and as far as is known no further coal burning steam turbine vessels were built, although an existing large gas carrier with serious hull defects was converted to a coal burning bulker in Korea around this time.

It could be said that the poor thermodynamic performance of the steam turbine led to its demise at a time when fuel costs took off. Its future will be restricted to the relatively small number of LNG gas carriers and even that market could be compromised if diesel propulsion is introduced. By using boil off gas as a fuel in these vessels the provision of an expensive re-liquefaction plant is avoided. If the provision of such plants is contemplated for future LNG vessels then the choice of propulsion plant would appear to lie with the diesel.

## 3. DIESEL ENGINES

Probably over 99% of the world's merchant fleet is now propelled by a diesel engine and its long-term future appears unassailable due to the lack of any serious contenders to its present dominant position. Unlike the steam turbine, the thermodynamic performance of the diesel engine has experienced a remarkable improvement in recent years. This improvement was as a direct result of the fuel cost hikes starting in the autumn of 1973, which forced the designers to improve performance of their engines in order to minimise the effect the fuel costs had on shipowners.

In the case of slow speed 2-stroke diesel engines, the SFC can today be as low as 120 Gms/BHP/Hr depending on the price the customer is prepared to pay for achieving this low figure by adopting various measures. It should be added that unless otherwise mentioned the SFC figures given are based on using fuel normally used in service, typically 380 cst with a calorific value of 9,600 K Cals/Kg.

Specific fuel consumption figures given by enginebuilders are usually based on distillate fuels with calorific values in the region of 10,200 K Cals/Kg as generally used on the test bed. This 6% or so difference between the heat values of the fuels must of course be taken into account when converting SFC design figures into actual daily fuel consumptions when the vessel enters service.

We have learnt that the SFC of diesel engines prior to the 1973 fuel crisis was in the region of 167 Gms/BHP/Hr and that nowadays (1996) an SFC of 120 Gms/BHP/Hr can be obtained. This remarkable improvement in performance of around 39% was achieved in several stages as outlined below.

As a first step, the cyclical combustion pressures were increased, which has the effect of increasing combustion temperatures and this is the determining factor in increasing thermodynamic efficiency. It can be shown that the higher the combustion temperature and the lower the gas outlet temperature from the engine, so the more efficient the engine is from a thermodynamic point of view.

In order to increase the combustion pressure it was necessary to provide more air into the combustion chamber and this was achieved by increasing both the output and efficiency of the exhaust gas turbochargers supplying this combustion air. In some instances this meant converting the turbochargers from impulse into constant pressure turbocharging.

Early on in the quest for improved performance, the derating concept was introduced by the slow speed 2-stroke engine designers. The principle behind derating concerns operating an engine at below its full power capability whilst maintaining the maximum combustion pressure (P Max) for which it was designed.

Derating increases the ratio of P Max to Brake Mean Effective Pressure (BMEP) and this also has the effect of increasing the thermodynamic performance of an engine. Many modern 2-stroke diesel engines are now offered with a selection of design points relating to the degree of derating chosen. The RPM, P Max and SFC can all be designated to meet the requirement of the shipowner and in general terms the higher the degree of derating the lower the SFC. The cost of the engine in terms of $ per BHP utilised would of course be higher for a derated engine as the enginebuilder still has to build an engine with similar dimensions whatever level of derating is chosen.

It must be said that derating was first introduced when fuel costs were at their peak and the quest for improved thermodynamic performance arguably the engine designer's first priority. It was then more or less taken for granted that most shipowners would specify an engine with some level of derating, depending on what they perceived was the likely cost of fuel oil over the vessel's life cycle. Sophisticated computer programs were introduced by the enginebuilders which could make the shipowner aware of all the various parameters needed to make the most cost-effective choice of engine from a fuel performance point of view.

Not usually included in the computer program was the capital cost of the engine as this is usually the shipbuilder's responsibility, in that all the ancillary equipment and associated services have to be taken into account when assessing the true cost of an engine.

The actual dimensions of the chosen engine, particularly its length, have a profound effect on the cost of the ship and this must also be taken into account. The RPM of the chosen engine is also a factor which has an effect on the cost of a ship in that the diameter of the line shafting and propeller, as well as the aft-end geometry, has to be taken into account. If an engine with the lowest available RPM is chosen, then the hydrodynamic performance of the ship is improved in that the largest possible propeller diameter is then a possibility, a prerequisite to maximising performance.

It would appear that due to the fairly recent stabilisation of fuel costs the choice of a Main Engine is nowadays of much less importance from a fuel performance point of view than it was in the relatively high fuel cost era and the emphasis on derating not so significant, and many shipowners now specify a fully rated engine as they only see the capital (or credit) cost of a ship as the determining factor when placing an order and are not really interested in its fuel economy performance.

For example, the shipowner may have a long-term charterparty in mind whereby the charterer pays for the fuel, and of course the shipowner would not be interested in paying extra for a more fuel-efficient engine unless a higher freight rate could be negotiated with the charterer. Long-term charters are, however, not so easily obtained nowadays and the more prudent shipowner will endeavour to obtain the most fuel-efficient engine providing he can justify any additional cost. This assumes he will be operating his vessel on the spot market and he himself would therefore be paying for the fuel consumed.

Another category of shipowner could be identified as one who has his own captive market, for example an oil major, container consortia member or perhaps a cruise line operator. These shipowners control their own destiny with respect to choice of vessel, its service speed and this in turn allows them free choice of engine. By and large it could be said that a large number of shipowners are therefore only interested in choosing the most fuel-efficient engine if any additional cost can be justified from a return on investment point of view.

Some of the factors involved in making this choice will now be reviewed for various ship types.

## 4. OIL TANKER PROPULSION

One of the major successes of the diesel engine protagonists was when they wrested away the former dominance of the steam turbine as the chosen form of propulsion for large tankers in the early 1970s. Steam turbine propulsion for these vessels was then very convenient in that a large steam plant was needed for the steam driven cargo pumps and also, in some instances, cargo heating coils. It therefore made sense to utilise some of the steam needed for the Main Engine for these other consumers.

Diesel engines chosen to propel large tankers have a distinct advantage over many other types of vessel in that because of their deep draught there is virtually no practical limit to the propeller diameter and a Main Engine with very low RPM can be chosen. This, incidentally, was one of the attractions of the steam turbine, which could be geared down to give an extremely low propeller RPM. In the case of a diesel engine a low propeller RPM permits the use of an engine with a high stroke/bore ratio and the combined effect of low RPM and high stroke/bore is to enhance both thermodynamic and hydro-dynamic performance.

We could now perhaps take a look at how the fuel performance of a typical VLCC has improved over the last 25 years or so. It should be mentioned that the service speed has been assumed to be 15 knots in each case. Service speeds do tend to alter somewhat based on the cost of fuel oil when the tanker was ordered. When fuel costs are high service speeds tend to be pitched around the 14 knots mark and when low, around the 15.5 knots mark. Also with the advent of first SBT and then the double hull design the overall dimensions of VLCCs have progressively increased for a given deadweight. These figures are only given as a rough guide (see Table 3).

We have previously mentioned that an SFC of 120 Gms/BHP/Hr is now achievable and it will be noted that the figure of 130 Gms/BHP/Hr is used in Table 3. The figure of 120 Gms/BHP/Hr is achieved by using what is called a power turbine whereby an additional exhaust gas turbocharger is mounted on the Main Engine and its power output added to that of the engine. It would appear that this somewhat complicated and expensive arrangement is not in general use and has therefore not been included, but owners of high powered

*Table 3. VLCC fuel costs*

|                      | 1970 STEAM | 1970 DIESEL | 1980 DIESEL | 1996 DIESEL |
|----------------------|-----------|-------------|-------------|-------------|
| Speed                | 15        | 15          | 15          | 15          |
| Fuel costs/tonne     | 100       | 100         | 100         | 100         |
| SFC @ 9,600 K Cal    | 210       | 167         | 136         | 130         |
| Annual cost $M       | 4.69      | 3.73        | 3.04        | 2.90        |
| Basis 1996 %         | +62       | +28         | +5          | 0           |

ships such as VLCCs or container ships always have the opportunity of this power turbine scheme.

It will be noted that the main improvements took place first when diesel replaced steam and second when the 1973 fuel crisis motivated the engine licensors into action. Future significant improvements over the 1996 figure would appear unlikely at present.

Because of their operational requirements it is most important that the reliability of the propulsion plant for oil tankers is maintained at the highest level. Immobilisation of the Main Engine for any reason is not normally allowed at either the loading port or discharge terminal. It was mainly for this reason that the inherently trouble free steam turbine was preferred for the propulsion of large tankers. Steam turbines require little maintenance between statutory surveys whereas diesel engines do need regular maintenance, leading to immobilisation of the engine.

The reliability and interval between overhauls of the modern diesel engine has now improved to such an extent that it is not now considered to be a serious factor affecting choice. The steady increase in output per cylinder of a typical VLCC having similar horsepowers can be illustrated using models from the MAN/B & W stable:

*Table 4. VLCC Main Engines*

|             | 1970 | 1980 | 1996 |
|-------------|------|------|------|
| Type        | K FF | L GF | SMC  |
| Bore MM     | 980  | 900  | 800  |
| Cylinders   | 9    | 8    | 7    |
| Stroke/bore | 2.2  | 2.4  | 3.8  |
| RPM         | 100  | 90   | 80   |
| SFC         | 167  | 136  | 130  |
| BMEP        | 10   | 15   | 18   |

If we assume that the thermodynamic loading is represented by the BMEP, the progressive increase in this parameter will be noted. Also the progressive reduction in the number and diameter of the cylinders will be noted. This reduction in the diameter and number of cylinders has a twofold advantage for the shipbuilder in that the length of the engineroom and weight of the engine are reduced, so that the cargo carrying volume can be increased and the lightship weight reduced, leading to an increase in deadweight for a similarly dimensioned vessel.

What might be called inconsiderate increases in thermodynamic loading was bad news for shipowners when the ever-decreasing number of 2-stroke licensors were jockeying for position as league leaders or simply trying to maintain their market share. Examples of this over the last four decades or so leading to the demise of many licensors have been documented elsewhere.

One of the first symptoms that occur when thermodynamic overloading takes place is observed at the piston ring/cylinder liner interface. The increase in temperature and pressure in this finely balanced critical area within the combustion chamber as cyclic conditions become more severe can lead to excessive liner wear or even thermal cracking of the cylinder liner.

Of course the performance of the majority of engines is satisfactory, but recent events have highlighted that in the larger bore engines, as used in large tankers and container ships, the incidence of failure in the more thermally stressed areas is higher than that experienced previously.

In the case of smaller tankers, diesel propulsion has been the first choice for many years and the owners of these vessels have a selection of engines on offer which do not call for special mention. For these tankers the power requirements are usually within the capabilities of a single screw 4-stroke medium speed engine as well, of course, as the slow speed 2-stroke.

It would appear that the majority of tanker owners choose low speed 2-stroke engines except for the really small tankers who usually go for the medium speed 4-stroke designs.

However, it must be said that in recent years small bore slow speed 2-stroke engines have been introduced to satisfy the demands of certain owners of small tankers who were not enamoured with the performance of their medium speed engines when on arduous tanker duty. This was probably as a result of operating with poor quality fuel oil and the questionable ability, felt by some owners, of the medium speed engine to perform satisfactorily with this fuel.

## 5. CONTAINER SHIP PROPULSION

The recent advent of the so-called post Panamax container ship, with a container capacity of over 6,000 TEUs and a speed of around 25 knots, has taxed the ingenuity of both shipbuilder and enginebuilder in providing such a vessel with a single propulsion unit. The largest diesel engines ever designed will be used to propel these proposed vessels.

As in the case of large tankers, the original choice of propulsion for the early container ships was steam turbine and even then it was necessary to provide twin screws for the larger higher speed models. There is usually a draught restriction on container ships occasioned by the water depth at the terminals, and for this reason the propeller diameter is also subject to some restriction and the low RPM engines used on large tankers are therefore not suitable.

A different engine is therefore necessary for container ships and in the case of the post Panamax size the RPM will probably be in the region of 100. The increase in hydrodynamic performance gained by the use of a larger diameter propeller is not a factor on container ships because of the aforementioned draught restriction. In addition, the thermodynamic performance of the higher RPM engine is slightly reduced in part due to the reduced stroke/bore ratio.

The output of the engine proposed for the post Panamax ship is around 90,000 horsepower developed by 12 cylinders, a quite staggering performance in anybody's eyes, thought impossible a few years ago. It is not possible to compare the performance of these innovative vessels with previous models for obvious reasons. However, as a matter of interest, the annual fuel savings between a 90,000 BHP diesel and 900,000 SHP steam turbine would be in the region of $4.4m basis fuel $100/tonne. The commercial performance of the post Panamax ship, based on the economy of scale concept, has obviously influenced their owners to design such vessels.

The steady improvement in container ship fuel performance and engine output for what might be called conventionally sized models, having a similar cargo carrying capacity, would follow a similar pattern to that already given for tankers and need not to be repeated here.

## 6. PASSENGER SHIP PROPULSION

In similar vein to container ships and VLCCs, diesel engines have wrested away from steam turbines their former dominance in the propulsion of the prestigious passenger ship. However, it is not the slow speed 2-stroke which has heralded the success of the diesel engine in this field but rather the medium speed 4-stroke.

The thermodynamic performance of the modern large bore medium speed 4-stroke is now almost equal to the slow speed 2-stroke but it would appear unlikely that the slow speed engine will penetrate the passenger ship market. The most favoured engineroom layout appears to be with four medium speed engines coupled via gearboxes to twin screws; however, some owners have opted for diesel electric propulsion, so dispensing with the gearboxes. Either of these systems offer numerous operating combinations to suit the vessel's speed requirements.

The reliability performance of a modern passenger ship is nowadays considered to be extremely high based on the redundancy factor offered by the multi-engined configuration and its many operating combinations. Most of the larger passenger ships are now engaged in the expanding cruise market and speeds between ports and also the length of each cruise can show considerable variation.

By having multi-engined diesel propulsion the required power output can be met by employing the appropriate number of engines to match the ship's speed. The popular father and son concept, for example, using an 8-cylinder and a 6-cylinder engine, with otherwise identical parts, coupled to each propeller via a gearbox, optimises power selection. This is especially so if a scheme incorporating shaft generators doubling as propulsion motors is included and these are electrically connected to the auxiliary power source so allowing power to flow either way.

The increase in performance using this sophisticated arrangement when compared with the previously used twin screw geared turbines is quite remarkable. Steam turbines have an extremely poor part load performance and whilst the standard arrangement was quite adequate when passenger ships were employed on regular runs at full speed, the advent of variable speed cruising represented a serious fall-off in performance for the steam turbine passenger ship.

A multi-engined diesel propulsion plant ensures that whatever ship's speed is required the engines chosen can be operated at near optimum output and efficiency. It would be expected that for a 50,000 horsepower plant the annual fuel savings by using diesel instead of steam propulsion would be in the region of $2.2m basis fuel at $100/tonne.

In the case of passenger ships engaged on the short sea trade, for example cross-channel or inter-island ferries, there appears to be a rising trend in the use of so-called HSS ships (High Speed Ship), see Fig. 6. Conventional ferries have speeds of around 20 knots and multi-engined medium or high-speed diesels geared to fixed or controllable pitch propellers usually cater for their propulsive needs.

The HSS ships probably have service speeds in the region of 35–45 knots and for the larger vessels now becoming popular the propulsive arrangements used on conventional ferries as mentioned above are not considered adequate in that the number of engines required and the use of conventional propellers would rule this out.

It would appear that the preferred propulsive method for the HSS ship is by the use of water jets, the pumps of which are driven by gas turbines in the larger ships and diesel engines in the smaller versions (see Fig. 6). The smaller HSS ships can also use super cavitating propellers as an alternative to water jets.

The various unique hull forms used by the HSS ships differ from the more or less standard hull form used in the typical ferry and include catamaran, semi-planing monohull (SPMH) and small waterplane area twin hull (SWATH) to name but a few.

Propulsive powers employed by the larger HSS ships are quite remarkable and bear no relation to those used in conventional ferries of equivalent size. For example, a conventional ferry may have an installed propulsive power of 20,000 BHP compared with up to 100,000 BHP for an HSS. Using the empirical cube law approach a doubling of ship's speed (20 to 40 knots) requires an eightfold increase in power, so that the power required by a conventional ferry to increase its speed from 20 to 40 knots would be around 160,000 BHP.

However, by using the unique hull forms mentioned earlier, these allow many of the HSS designs to lift out of the water at service speed so reducing the wetted area and of course the frictional resistance, not forgetting the apparent reduction in displacement tonnage.

The hydrodynamic performance of the HSS ship by using one of these hull forms is much improved over that of a vessel with a conventional hull and the factor of eight can be significantly reduced. There would appear to be no firm plans to incorporate the HSS concept into a conventional long-haul cargo or passenger ship, but various projects, for example the Fastship container ship project mentioned elsewhere, are presently being looked at. The future cost of fuel oil would obviously make an important contribution to the decision-making process if and when such a ship is built.

The efficiency of a conventional screw propeller as used in the relatively small sized ships we are discussing is probably in the order of 70%, not forgetting that the use of a slow RPM large diameter propeller is excluded for obvious reasons. The current performance of a water jet is also perhaps 70%, but the use of a unique hull form and its enhanced hydrodynamic performance at speed gives it the edge for this particular application.

The re-introduction of gas turbines for marine propulsion purposes would have seemed an unlikely development just a few years ago. One of the few applications of the gas turbine that survived concerned a large Baltic ferry. Because of the high cost of the fuel used by gas turbines (some form of distillate), conventional diesel engines were added to the propulsion system to cater for a reduced output when operating on the low speed winter schedules. The current revival of the gas turbine for merchant ship propulsion could therefore be mainly attributed to the development in underwater hull forms as used by many of the HSS vessels.

## 7. BULK CARRIER PROPULSION

Bulk carriers have traditionally been propelled by diesel engines, since diesel replaced steam many decades ago. The majority of bulk carriers use a single low speed 2-stroke diesel engine directly coupled to a fixed pitched propeller. Medium speed 4-strokes are still propular with owners of the smaller tonnage but the small bore slow speed 2-stroke appears to be making inroads into this comparatively small sector of the market.

Bulk carriers built before the fuel crisis of 1973 were invariably provided with diesel engines which would nowadays be considered to be vastly overpowered. Service speeds were then pitched above the 16 knots mark, which led to the need for these comparatively large Main Engines.

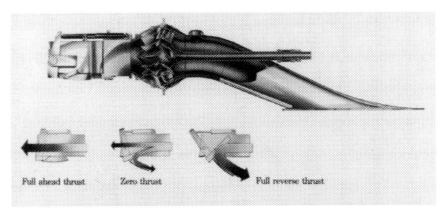

Full ahead thrust        Zero thrust            Full reverse thrust

*Fig. 6. High speed ship (HSS) and water jet* (courtesy KaMeWa)

In the case of a Panamax sized bulker built in the early 1970s, the performance of a typical Main Engine compared with a 1996 Panamax would be as shown in Table 5.

**Table 5.  *Panamax Main Engines***

|               | 1970   | 1996   |
|---------------|--------|--------|
| Type          | K EF   | L MC   |
| Bore MM       | 840    | 600    |
| Cylinders     | 7      | 5      |
| Service power | 15,750 | 10,000 |
| RPM           | 110    | 120    |
| SFC           | 167    | 135    |
| Service speed | 16.5   | 14.0   |

Because of the large reduction in service speed for bulkers over the last 25 years or so it is difficult to draw any firm conclusions from these figures, but the 24% or so reduction in fuel consumption is real.

## 8. OTHER PROPULSION SYSTEMS

Gas turbines made a brief appearance in the merchant ship propulsion field several decades ago. With the possible exception of the Baltic ferry mentioned previously, the vessels originally provided with gas turbines have either been re-engined with diesels or phased out. Their future use would appear to lie with the HSS vessel whose power requirements could not be met by conventional diesels without seriously reducing the vessel's payload.

The Japanese, amongst others, are attempting to develop an electro-magnetic propulsion system whereby an electric current passes through a powerful magnetic field created by a battery of super-conductive magnets so creating a thrust directly propelling the vessel forward. The principle is similar to that used by the linear motor now increasingly used in industry and, if successful, it would obviate the need for a propeller or water jet, so revolutionising marine propulsion.

Fuel cells have recently been suggested as a means of marine propulsion. Fuel cells have been successfully used in space vehicles where cost is presumably not an insurmountable problem. Fuel cells are not yet available in sizes suitable for marine propulsion and at this time are not very efficient. In the long term, they may well prove to be a challenge to the diesel engine although the electric current produced would probably drive a propeller or water jet.

Several sail-assisted and sail propelled vessels were built in the 1980s but the idea does not appear to have caught the imagination of the shipping industry, probably on account of the labour intensive activity in a cost conscious area, and it is not felt that sail-assisted vessels will become a factor in the future.

As already mentioned nuclear propulsion is used by several of the world's navies. There are also some Russian icebreakers which use nuclear propulsion. Several experimental merchant ships were built with nuclear propulsion some years ago. One of these was the Japanese flag "Matsu", which has never actually sailed due to a serious defect in a containment vessel and it would appear unlikely that "Matsu" will ever enter service. It would also appear extremely unlikely that a nuclear merchant vessel operating under normal commercial competitive terms will enter service in the foreseeable future.

## 9. SUMMARY OF CHAPTER TWO

Based on the current level of technological development the propulsive performance of a modern vessel is considered to be rather high and any significant improvement in the short to medium term appears unlikely. The derated Main Engine is not currently popular on account of its high cost, and fully rated engines designed for specific ship types are now the vogue, for example large bore slow RPM engines for VLCCs.

There has been quite a remarkable improvement over the last 25 years in conventional propulsion system performance and in the long term we would possibly have to look to unconventional propulsion systems for any further significant improvements.

# CHAPTER THREE

# FUELS

## 1. CRUDE OIL

Most, if not all, of the oil in shipboard use is derived from crude oil; this includes heavy residual fuel used in the Main Engine, distillate or blended fuel used in the generators and even the lubricating oils and greases used to lubricate practically all machinery on board. The performance of a ship's machinery is directly affected by the quality of fuel oil, so various factors concerning its use will be examined in this chapter.

Crude oil is a naturally occurring substance found beneath the earth's crust in various parts of the world, notably the Middle East, USA, Russia and, more recently, the North Sea. It probably has its origins in decayed animal organisms from the wilderness of prehistoric times.

Contrary to popular belief, it is a comparatively light substance with an average specific gravity of around 0.8 kg/litre. On reflection, this is not surprising as it does contain petrol, kerosene and diesel oil as well as the heavy fuels and lubricants used aboard ship. The main components of crude oil are hydrogen and carbon, which exist in various chemical compositions, depending on the geographical source of the crude.

In modern times, crude oil was first found in Pennsylvania in the 1850s and, after distillation into kerosene, was used as lamp oil. As industry expanded oil became the source of energy, first for steam boiler furnaces then for diesel engines during the early years of the twentieth century.

Quality and supply aspects remained fairly stable in the crude oil industry until 1973 when unnatural pressures were exerted to interrupt this stability, for mainly political reasons. The situation worsened progressively until the end of 1985, but since then there has been a move to return to some sort of stability in the supply and demand situation, which, of course, affects the cost of shipboard fuels. It would, however, be very difficult to foresee the middle- and long-term prospects for the stability of crude oil prices.

It is unlikely that crude oil reserves will last as long as 50 years, so some sort of alternative fuel for ship propulsion will eventually have to be found. Whether this alternative can compete with present-day crude oil prices will probably determine the medium- to long-term price of crude oil. Whereas there has been a recent encouraging downward trend in the price of crude oil from late-1980s levels which automatically affects bunker costs, there has been no such improvement in the quality of bunkers—nor is there any likelihood of this happening. The reason for this is partially on account of the 1973 crisis but also the oil industry's long-term economic strategy to obtain more product from the crude barrel. This inevitably has the effect of lowering the quality of residual fuel for shipboard use.

## 2. REFINERY PROCESS

Crude oil is converted to distillate and residual fuel in the refinery process and a simple flow diagram is shown in Fig. 7. In modern refineries secondary methods incorporating catalytic crackers and viz breakers perform the function of obtaining more product from the crude barrel. Certain areas, notably the Middle East, still have older refineries without these expensive secondary units,

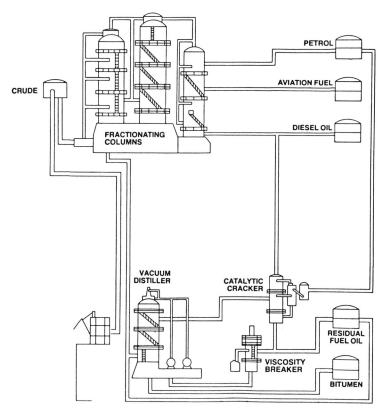

*Fig. 7  Refinery flow diagram*

and fuel quality, as expressed by the specific gravity, is rather good. In the natural order of things, these older refineries will eventually disappear and fuel bunkers worldwide will probably have similar properties, particularly from a specific gravity point of view.

The high quality of aviation and automobile fuels is sacrosanct and quite rightly so as it would be quite dangerous to lower standards in these industries for obvious safety reasons. This leaves only residual and so-called diesel oil as the targets of the oil industry's goals.

A simple description of the refinery process begins when heated crude is fed into the fractionating columns, in which vapourised products are led off at appropriate levels in relation to their boiling temperatures. This primary stage deals with the light ends—namely, petrol, kerosene and gas oil. Heavy products from the fractionating columns are then fed into the vacuum distiller, which is the last chain in the primary process. The products are then fed into the cracking or secondary section in which further light ends are extracted to the detriment of the residual components' quality. This is only a very simple explanation of what is a very complicated process and many more items of equipment are installed in a modern refinery. An illustration of a modern refinery complex is shown in Fig. 8.

There are some modern refineries on stream which do not have any residual fuel left in the final process. There remains only petcoke which cannot presently be used for shipboard fuels.

*Fig. 8. Refinery complex* (courtesy of elf lub marine uk Ltd)

It has been calculated that less than 5% of all crude oil is actually used as fuel aboard ships. This probably had an input in the oil majors' decision-making process for upgrading oil refineries to the deteriment of this low-volume consumer's quality.

## 3. RESIDUAL FUEL OIL (HEAVY OIL)

Heavy oil is a mixture mainly of hydrogen and carbon but also consisting of naturally occurring impurities such as sulphur, sodium, vanadium, water and ash. Its heat or energy content is directly related to its specific gravity, or density as it is nowadays called. The higher the density—the lower the heat value, for reasons now explained. Hydrogen has the higher heat value but lower density, conversely carbon has the lower heat value but the higher density. Carbon is the major constituent of fuel oil, accounting for over 80% of the total. It follows that the higher the density the greater the carbon content and, therefore, less heat content.

Sulphur also has a rather low heat value but this constituent on average has only around 3% of the total content, but it should be taken into account when calculating the heat value. During the combustion process any sulphur in the fuel is converted to SOx and as such is environmentally damaging when discharged into the atmosphere along with the exhaust gas. The level of SOx allowed to be discharged will probably be controlled by MARPOL regulations in the near future, as discussed in Chapter Eight. Apart from water, the other impurities do not affect the heat value to any significant extent.

Heavy oil when using primary refining processes had a density of around 0.96. Nowadays it is controlled to 0.991 to tie up with ISO 8217 (87) for fuels normally used aboard ship.

Actually, the density of the residual as delivered by a modern refinery is over 1.00. But, mainly because of present shipboard operational problems in using this residual, it is cut back to 0.991 before being sold as heavy fuel oil in the marine market—now predominantly diesel propelled. No restriction on density is necessary for steam powered plants, and the few steamers still remaining (also land based steam plants) use fuel of 1.00 density or even higher as steam plants can generally tolerate small amounts of water in fuel.

Modern purifying equipment can remove water from fuel oil even when it has a density above 1.00. So, in the short- to medium-term, fuel which has a density or around 1.01 may be available as vessels with this equipment enter service or existing vessels are retrofitted, but at present (1996) it has not appeared in the marine market place. The quality of fuel oil delivered to a vessel is also expected to be controlled by MARPOL regulations in the near future. These regulations will be aimed at reducing the amount of hazardous substances being dumped into fuel oil in certain parts of the world.

## 4. DISTILLATE FUEL (DIESEL AND GAS OIL)

The quality of distillate fuel using primary refining processes used to be stabilised at a density perhaps of around 0.85 with no measurable contaminants contained in the delivered fuel. Gas oil quality marginally exceeded that of diesel oil, mainly on account of its superior combustibility properties necessary for very high speed diesel engines. Both these fuels were referred to as straight-run distillates. Secondary refining processes have almost eliminated these straight-run distillates from the marine market, although they are available for special purposes at a much higher cost.

Density of fuel, now delivered as diesel oil, is approaching 0.90 and certain contaminants are found. Even so, most diesel generators can burn this fuel without any problems. One could argue that diesel oil, as supplied from the old refineries was, in fact, of too good a quality in the vast majority of cases. A fact not overlooked by the oil majors when their future plans were being formulated.

## 5. VISCOSITY

Historically, all marine fuels have been sold on a viscosity basis. The origins of this are not exactly clear, unless fuel was so cheap in the pre-1973 era that all other properties had no apparent contribution to its saleable value.

In Europe the unit used to measure viscosity was Redwood No. 1 at 100°F. In the 1970s this was changed to centistokes at 50°C for residual and at 40°C for so-called distillate fuels. It is also expressed as centistokes at 100°C in various specifications but in general terms it is usually ordered on the basis of centistokes at 50°C. For the benefit of readers, charts showing the new fuel type designations are shown in Figs. 9 and 10.

The viscosity of a fuel determines at what temperature it can be handled and burnt in the engine. It is a measurement of resistance to flow, and increasing the temperature of a fuel reduces its viscosity as it becomes thinner or less viscous.

It is very important that fuel is burnt in a diesel engine at the engine builders' recommended viscosity. At normal temperature a typical fuel will have a viscosity of around 1,400 cst and this will fall to around 380 cst at 50°C and 15 cst at 130°C, at which temperature it is usually burnt in most modern diesel engines. These modern engines are capable of burning fuel of up to 700 cst at 50°C, which requires a temperature of around 140°C at the engine, but this 700 cst fuel has not yet appeared in the market place, probably as a result of the present abundant supply situation and the reticence of most owners to use this extremely viscous fuel oil.

For existing vessels it should be emphasised that only fuel with a viscosity falling within the installed heating capability should be used. However, it can be

**Requirements 1990 for distillate fuels for diesel engines (as delivered)**

| Characteristic | Related to | CIMAC | limit | DX | DA | DB | DC[2] |
|---|---|---|---|---|---|---|---|
| Designation: | ISO 8217 | F- | | DMX | DMA | DMB | DMC |
| Residual inclusion | | | | none | none | some trace | allowed |
| Density at 15°C | kg/m³ | | max | — | 890 | 900 | 920 |
| Kinematic viscosity at 40°C | cSt[1] | | max<br>min | 5.5<br>1.4 | 6<br>1.5 | 11<br>2.5 | 14 |
| Flash point | °C | | min | 43 | 60 | 60 | 60 |
| Pour point winter[5]<br>summer | °C | | max<br>max | —<br>— | -6<br>0 | 0<br>6 | 0<br>6 |
| Cloud point | °C | | max | -16 | | | |
| Carbon residue Ramsbottom on 10% res.<br>Microcarbon | % m/m<br>% m/m | | max<br>max | 0.20 | 0.20 | 0.25 | 3.00 |
| Ash | % m/m | | max | 0.01 | 0.01 | 0.01 | 0.03 |
| Sediment by extraction | % m/m | | max | — | — | 0.02 | — |
| Total sediment | % m/m | | max | — | — | — | 0.05 |
| Water | % V/V | | max | — | — | 0.30 | 0.30 |
| Cetane number[4] | | | min | 45 | 40 | 35 | 35 |
| Visual inspection | | | | clear[3] | clear[3] | may be black | |
| Sulphur | % m/m | | max | 1.0 | 1.5 | 2.0 | 2.0 |
| Vanadium | mg/kg | | max | | | | 100 |
| Aluminium + Silicon | mg/kg | | max | | | | 25 |

[1] 1 cSt = 1 mm²/sec.
[2] Note that although predominantly consisting of distillate fuel, the residual oil proportion can be significant (see section 8)
[3] See 6: visual inspection
[4] Cetane index may be used if no cetane improvers are applied (not for DC)
[5] Applies to region and season in which fuel is to be stored and used (upper value winter quality, bottom value summer quality)

*Fig. 9. Distillate fuel classification* (courtesy CIMAC)

**Requirements (1990) for residual fuels for diesel engines (as delivered)**

| Characteristic | Dim. | Limit | CIMAC A 10 | CIMAC B 10 | CIMAC C 10 | CIMAC D 15 | CIMAC E 25 | CIMAC F 25 | CIMAC G 35 | CIMAC H 35 | CIMAC K 35 | CIMAC H 45 | CIMAC K 45 | CIMAC H 55 | CIMAC K 55 |
|---|---|---|---|---|---|---|---|---|---|---|---|---|---|---|---|
| Related to ISO 8217 (87): | | | RMA 10 | RMB 10 | RMC 10 | RMD 15 | RME 25 | RMF 25 | RMG 35 | RMH 35 | RMK 35 | RMH 45 | RMK 45 | RMH 55 | RMK 55 |
| Density at 15°C | kg/m³ | max | 950 | 975 | 975 | 980 | 991 | 991 | 991 | 991 | 1010 | 991 | 1010 | 991 | 1010 |
| Kinematic viscosity at 100°C[1] | cSt[2] | min[4] | 6 | | | | 15 | | | | | | | | |
| | | max | 10 | 10 | 10 | 15 | 25 | 25 | 35 | 35 | 35 | 45 | 45 | 55 | 55 |
| Flash point | °C | min | 60 | 60 | 60 | 60 | 60 | 60 | 60 | 60 | 60 | 60 | 60 | 60 | 60 |
| Pour point | °C | max | 0 / 6[3] | | 24 | 30 | 30 | 30 | 30 | 30 | 30 | 30 | 30 | 30 | 30 |
| Carbon Residue | % (m/m) | max | 12 | 12 | 14 | 14 | 15 | 20 | 18 | 22 | 22 | 22 | 22 | 22 | 22 |
| Ash | % (m/m) | max | 0.10 | 0.10 | 0.10 | 0.10 | 0.10 | 0.15 | 0.15 | 0.15 | 0.15 | 0.15 | 0.15 | 0.15 | 0.15 |
| Total sediment after ageing | % (m/m) | max | 0.10 | 0.10 | 0.10 | 0.10 | 0.10 | 0.10 | 0.10 | 0.10 | 0.10 | 0.10 | 0.10 | 0.10 | 0.10 |
| Water | % (V/V) | max | 0.50 | 0.50 | 0.50 | 0.80 | 1.0 | 1.0 | 1.0 | 1.0 | 1.0 | 1.0 | 1.0 | 1.0 | 1.0 |
| Sulphur | % (m/m) | max | 3.5 | 3.5 | 3.5 | 4.0 | 5.0 | 5.0 | 5.0 | 5.0 | 5.0 | 5.0 | 5.0 | 5.0 | 5.0 |
| Vanadium | mg/kg | max | 150 | 150 | 300 | 350 | 200 | 500 | 300 | 600 | 600 | 600 | 600 | 600 | 600 |
| Aluminium + Silicon | mg/kg | max | 80 | 80 | 80 | 80 | 80 | 80 | 80 | 80 | 80 | 80 | 80 | 80 | 80 |
| Ignition properties | | | see appendix, section 3 | | | | | | | | | | | | |

[1] Approximate equivalent viscosities (for information only):

| | | | | | |
|---|---|---|---|---|---|
| Kinematic viscosity (cSt) at 100°C | 6 | 10 | 15 | 25 | 35 | 45 | 55 |
| Kinematic viscosity (cSt) at 50°C | 22 | 40 | 80 | 180 | 380 | 500 | 700 |
| Sec. Redwood I at 100°F | 165 | 300 | 600 | 1500 | 3500 | 5000 | 7000 |

[2] 1cSt = 1 mm²/sec.

[3] Applies to region and season in which fuel is to be stored and used.
(upper value winter quality, bottom value summer quality)

[4] Recommended value only. May be lower if density is also lower.

*Fig. 10. Residual fuel classification* (courtesy CIMAC)

commercially attractive to upgrade certain older vessels, enabling higher viscosities to be used.

Viscosity of distillate fuels is not normally a problem and is in the range of 4–10 cst at 40°C, which is easily burnable without heating—except in Arctic-type conditions or in extreme known incidents when high-pour diesel oil was delivered.

## 6. DENSITY

We have already touched upon typical figures for expected densities of modern fuels, namely 0.991 and 0.900, respectively, for heavy and diesel oil—both of which are measured at 15°C.

If heavy fuel above 0.991 is supplied to vessels not equipped with the latest purification plant, water removal becomes impossible and main engine operational problems can be expected, with reduced performance being one of the results. Most fuel is sold by weight but measured by volume in the tanks of the bunker supplier's barge or at his pipeline meter.

To convert volume to weight requires an accurate knowledge of the density at the delivered temperature, which is usually converted to density at 15°C and then to weight. It is not unknown for unscrupulous suppliers to manipulate the density figures with obvious financial benefit to themselves. Very considerable sums of money can be involved, particularly in areas where low density fuels are still available and the delivery note density when manipulated higher by the supplier still does not approach that regarded as dangerous by the vessel's staff. It is therefore rather important that ships' staff are encouraged to check the density of the fuel as delivered. Lloyd's Register and DNV also offer a service which includes checking the density of the fuel oil delivered.

## 7. COMPATIBILITY

One of the most difficult properties to determine of a fuel is its compatibility, either inherent or when mixed with other fuels. It is unlikely that inherently incompatible fuel would be supplied to a vessel, but rare cases of this happening are on file. Mixing of fuels from different sources is a dangerous practice which can give rise to incompatibility and an important risk is eliminated if mixing of fuels in bunker tanks aboard ship is not allowed.

When using blended fuels in diesel generators a possibility exists of incompatibility problems arising and little can be done if the blended fuels are in fact incompatible. This, however, would not appear to be a major problem in practice.

A fuel is incompatible when it cannot hold the asphaltenes in solution. These come out of solution and form sludge, which can cause catastrophic problems with the fuel system, leading to complete immobilisation in extreme cases.

There is a simple method of checking for compatibility, called the spot test, which involves diluting a sample of oil to be tested with a distillate oil and allowing a drop of the mixture to dry on a type of blotting paper. The dried spot is compared with a reference list of five spots having a rating of one to five. Rating one is good and incompatibility problems are unlikely. The spot test is not entirely reliable and a more reliable test is the total sediment after ageing (potential) test, which gives an indication of a fuel's stability and cleanliness after storage and heating onboard.

## 8. CALORIFIC VALUE

The calorific value of a fuel is, in effect, its heat or energy content. When measuring the performance of an engine the results have to be referred back to the calorific value.

As mentioned earlier—the heavier the fuel, the lower the calorific value. Also mentioned earlier, fuel is sold on a viscosity basis which has no direct connection with energy. When discussing the performance of heavy oil and distillate fuels there is a difference between both viscosity and calorific value, but when unit cost is added to the equation the results may surprise some readers. Nowadays, calorific value is measured in megajoules per kilogram (mj/kg) whereas formerly the units of Kcals/kg or BTUs/lb were in general use. By adopting the unit cost approach to examine the energy performance of various fuels we get the following results (Table 6) based on actual examples (mid-1995 costs).

**Table 6. Energy performance of variance fuels**

| Fuel type | Viscosity | Density | Calorific value | Cost/ tonne $ | Unit cost |
|---|---|---|---|---|---|
| Heavy oil "A" | 380 | 0.991 | 40.00 | 100 | 2.50 |
| Heavy oil "B" | 180 | 0.950 | 40.50 | 101 | 2.49 |
| Diesel oil | 10 | 0.900 | 42.42 | 150 | 3.54 |
| Straight-run distillate | 5 | 0.860 | 42.92 | 160 | 3.73 |

The relative cost of diesel oil and straight-run distillate compared to heavy oil has narrowed over the last few years but even so it will be seen that the unit cost approach does illustrate value for money between different fuels.

Using heavy oil in Main Engines only became generally adopted in the 1950s when the unit cost approach showed that even at the low fuel costs ruling then ($14 heavy and $27 diesel) it was commercially attractive to pay the high conversion costs. It should be noted that diesel oil was then nearly double the cost of heavy oil whereas today it is only about 50% more and this has had a marked effect on schemes which previously exploited the large difference in cost between the fuels.


## 9. QUALITY TESTING

It is frequently mentioned that the quality of fuels has deteriorated in recent years and we have attempted to qualify what this means in quantitative terms. Apart from those already mentioned, there are other aspects to consider. One of these is the presence of catalyst fines in the delivered bunkers, probably caused by bad housekeeping in the refinery.

Several organisations, mainly associated with Classification Societies, exist which will test fuel samples submitted to them and give results with recommendations within several days of them being sent from the vessel.

Catalyst fines are only one of the dangerous contaminants looked for. Should these abrasive fines enter the fuel system, rapid wear on all the metallic surfaces in contact will occur. They are now identified by measuring the aluminium plus silicon content, the limits for which are shown as a maximum of 80 mg/kg in the ISO 8217 specification (see Fig. 10). Other contaminants found in fuel oil are calcium, iron and lead occasioned by dumping of used automobile lubricants into the refinery's crude supply. There have even been cases whereby chemicals have allegedly been dumped this way. In an extreme case naphthenic acid was allegedly the cause of extremely rapid wear on fuel pump plungers necessitating emergency repairs in a port of refuge. Normal quality testing would not identify contaminants such as this, but knowing the effect of the fuel on the fuel pumps gave certain leads which made identification that much easier.

Vanadium is a naturally occurring contaminant in the crude source which is not eliminated in the refinery process or the shipboard treatment plant. Excessive vanadium has a fouling effect in the steam generating sections of water tube boilers and, more importantly, on the exhaust valves of four stroke engines where it deposits itself to the detriment of the valves' efficiency.

Sodium can occur naturally in the crude supply or it can be introduced by contamination during its passage through the distribution network. If not removed by the purification plant, it can cause fouling of the turbochargers and gas passages within the Main Engine and on the heating surfaces of the economiser. The level of carbon residue is also given, which is indicative of the combustibility of the fuel. Several cases in which fuel pump plungers seized were attributed to a higher than usual carbon residue content. Another undesirable feature is the presence of wax, which leads to high pour point fuels, and this can cause problems transferring and handling the fuel if temperatures are allowed to fall close to the pour point and the wax solidifies.

All these and several other contaminants are looked for in each sample.

Additionally, a check on the density and viscosity is given to ensure the specification is met. We must not forget water, which is often found in fuel oils and can reach up to 1%, the recognised commercial limit. Shipowners are very reluctant to pay $100 per tonne for water and some suppliers have been suspected of adding water to the fuel for financial gain.

There are test kits suitable for shipboard use on the market. These, naturally, do not give the full range of tests available from the shore-based organisations but can be used as a screening device to decide if sufficient evidence exists to send the fuel to the experts for a full analysis. The test kit most familiar to the author is shown in Fig. 11. The tests incorporated in this kit are:

1. Density.
2. Viscosity.
3. Water content (fresh or salt).
4. Compatibility.
5. Carbon residue.

The oil majors have quite tight contracts when it comes to acceptance of their delivered quantities, but a quick test on density with a shipboard kit could avoid lengthy discussions later. Samples must be taken at each bunkering, whether or not it is intended to send them for analysis or test them aboard. Ideally, the samples should be made by a controlled drip using one of the inline sampler devices available to ensure they are representative and should be held aboard for several months. Not only will this action help prove if the fuel is unsuitable in the event of problems developing, but it will help defend any claim made for oil pollution against a vessel under MARPOL regulations. In a recent arbitration it was held that the suppliers of fuel oil were responsible for mechanical damage to a vessel's Main Engine which had used fuel oil

*Fig. 11. Fuel oil test kit* (courtesy elf lub marine uk Ltd)

---

## INTERNATIONAL CHAMBER OF SHIPPING
### RECOMMENDED BUNKER DELIVERY NOTE

| | |
|---|---|
| 1. Product name or general designation | |
| 2. Quantity in tonnes | |
| 3. Viscosity (cSt) at 50°C (residual fuels) or 40°C (distillate fuels) | |
| 4. Relative Density at 15°C | |
| 5. Flash Point (P-M) Closed Cup (°C) | |
| 6. Water Content Volume (percentage) | |
| 7. Pour Point (°C) | |
| 8. Conradson Carbon Residue (percentage weight) | |
| 9. Sediment (percentage weight) | |
| 10. Vanadium (ppm) | |
| 11. Sulphur (percentage weight) | |
| 12. Cetane Number (distillate fuels only) | |

*Note:* Specific energy (calorific value) (MJ/kg) can be calculated from the known density and sulphur.

Different bunker delivery notes may be recommended by various organisations.

---

*Fig. 12.  Bunker delivery note*

containing contaminants exceeding those given in the ISO 8217 specification. Fortunately, samples of the off specification fuel had been retained onboard.

## 10. DOCUMENTATION

Considering the amount of money involved in the purchase of fuel, very little documentation exists. In a move to regularise the situation, the International Chamber of Shipping (ICS) developed a Bunker Delivery Note in 1979 which contained all the information necessary to enable the shipowner to decide if what he had received was satisfactory and was as had been ordered. This delivery note, a copy of which is shown in Fig. 12, has not proved to be a success. Only a concerted effort by shipowners and their representative organisations will make this useful document internationally acceptable.

ICS in conjunction with BIMCO drew up a Bunker Quality Control clause some time ago in an attempt to apportion responsibility in the event of bunkers giving unsatisfactory performance being supplied. Since this clause was introduced, the market has been decidedly poor, which makes it difficult for shipowners to have this clause accepted by charterers. The author was a member of the committee which formulated these documents and it is sad to see all the efforts that were made being unacceptable due to current market conditions. An extract from the BIMCO clause is appended:

*BIMCO Bunker Quality Control Clause for Time Charters*

(1) The Charterers shall supply bunkers of a quality suitable for burning in the Vessel's engines and auxiliaries and which conform to the specification(s) mutually agreed under this charter.

(2) At the time of delivery of the Vessel the Owners shall place at the disposal of the Charterers, the bunker delivery note(s) and any samples relating to the fuels existing onboard.

(3) During the currency of the Charter, the Charterers shall ensure that bunker delivery notes are presented to the Vessel on the delivery of fuel(s) and that during bunkering, representative samples of the fuel(s) supplied shall be taken at the Vessel's bunkering manifold and sealed in the presence of competent representatives of the Charterers and the Vessel.

(4) The fuel samples shall be retained by the Vessel for 90 (ninety) days after the date of delivery or for whatever period necessary in the case of a prior dispute and any dispute as to whether the bunker fuels conform to the agreed specification(s) shall be settled by analysis of the sample(s) by ( ... ) or by another mutually agreed fuels analyst whose findings shall be conclusive evidence as to conformity or otherwise with the bunker fuels specification(s).

(5) The Owners reserve their right to make a claim against the Charterers for any damage to the Main Engines or the auxiliaries caused by the use of unsuitable fuels or fuels not complying with the agreed specification(s). Additionally, if bunker fuels supplied do not conform with the mutually agreed specification(s) or otherwise prove unsuitable for burning in the ship's engines or auxiliaries, the Owners shall not be held responsible for any reduction in the Vessel's speed performance and/or increased bunker consumption, nor for any time lost and any other consequences.

## 11. COMBUSTIBILITY

To define a heavy fuel oil's combustibility or ignition quality is rather difficult, as no internationally approved method is in existence. This is not the case for distillate fuels for which a cetane number is available. This gives a very good idea of the fuel's combustibility under test running conditions. Some oil majors have attempted to rectify this situation and Shell have introduced what they call the Calculated Carbon Aromacity Index (CCAI), which appears to have success when defining ignition quality of residual fuels.

CCAI is given as a non-dimensional number in the range 750–975. Below 850 is considered to be a very good reading, probably giving trouble free combustion, whereas above 875 is considered to be a poor reading, giving rise to poor combustion. As an example of its use, we could choose grade RMH 35 from ISO 8217 with a density of 0.991 and a viscosity of 35 cst at 100°C. This gives a CCAI of around 852 more or less in the middle of the range. Even the fuel of the future with a 1.01 density and a viscosity of 55 cst at 100°C gives a CCAI of 865.

Returning to the first example—namely grade RMH 35—if we substitute 25 cst at 100°C for 35 cst at 100°C we get a CCAI of around 860, a somewhat worse reading for what might appear to be a better fuel on paper.

Certain rather old four-stroke engines experience combustion problems when operating on modern fuels. In an actual example, fuel of 15 cst at 100°C, with a density of 0.980 gave problems, even though the CCAI was 860. The specification was changed to 15 cst at 100°C with a density of 0.960 and no further trouble was experienced; the CCAI of this new fuel being 840.

It would appear that some engines do have a CCAI threshold limit, but published data is hard to come by.

A nomograph is shown in Fig. 13 for the benefit of readers. Major bunker suppliers also produce programmable calculators which give all manner of functions which can assist in evaluating bunker quality. These include:

- Specific energy
- Viscosity
- CCAI
- Blending ratio
- Density/temperature corrections

## 12. FUEL ADDITIVES

The use of chemical additives in fuels has been commonplace for many years. Its origin probably goes back to pre-1950 when survey of oil fuel storage tanks at every special survey was a classification requirement. Chemicals were then used to reduce or eliminate the amount of sludge left in these tanks, thus reducing cleaning costs and off-hire time. These very inconvenient surveys

## NOMOGRAPH
## CALCULATED CARBON AROMATICITY INDEX
### Based on equation CCAI = D − 141 loglog (V + 0.85)−81

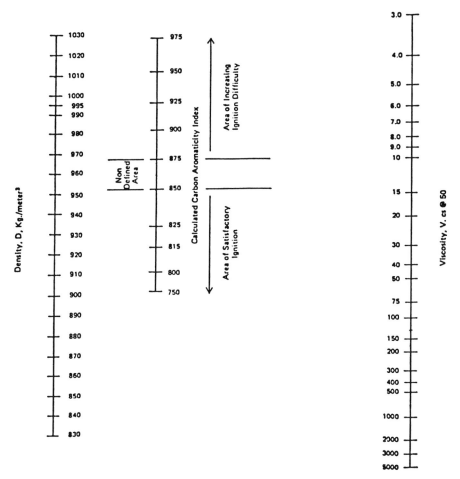

*Fig. 13. Nomograph for determining CCAI*

have now lapsed, but chemical additives received a new lease of life when fuel quality started deteriorating in the 1970s.

When chemicals are used for sludge-breaking purposes, before the combustion process has taken place, it would appear that they have a certain amount of success. They would also appear to have a contribution to make in improving the scavenge space cleanliness on certain loop scavenged engines. Their effectiveness as a combustion improver on an energy content basis is open to discussion. To conduct a shop test, in an attempt to prove this aspect, would be very costly in the case of even a moderately powered engine. This course of action would appear to be the best solution for those wishing to pursue the claims of their products, which could then be backed up by some sort of guarantee.

Water has also been introduced into fuel in a controlled amount and then emulsified before injection into the cylinders. Various shop tests have been conducted, and claims of fuel consumption improvements of around 3% have been made; also claims of improvement in engine cleanliness and reduction in NOx (nitrogen oxide) emission. One problem which could be expected when using this emulsified fuel is in the slow steaming mode, when extremely low exhaust gas exit temperatures occur and dew point corrosion problems rear their ugly head. Also, the modern engines have rather low exhaust gas exit temperatures and the question of dew point corrosion must be considered.

## 13. QUANTITY AUDIT

Several organisations will offer to carry out a bunker audit to check if the vessel is receiving the amount of fuel shown on the receipt note. The surveyors carrying out this task are very experienced in this type of work and have the advantage of being well trained and are supported by a specialised organisation at their head office. The author's experience is that the money recovered from the bunker supplier for shortage in supply matched the fee charged by the audit company. When bunkering in areas where serious shortage problems have been experienced, the occasional use of a bunker audit could prove to be a deterrent.

## 14. COST CONTROL

Depending, of course, on unit cost, fuel oil represents a major part of most vessels' operating costs. When heavy oil approached $200 per tonne, fuel costs accounted for over 50% of most vessels' operating budgets. At $100 per tonne it probably equals the total manning cost on our typical vessel even when slow steaming was practised.

Bunker purchasing is a specialised subject requiring very experienced personnel who ideally should be aware both of the technical aspects discussed in this chapter as well as the purely commercial aspects. The unit cost of energy should figure in any calculations made in determining the favoured supplier. Even credit terms should be taken into account when making a selection. Associated charges, such as for barging, are not always indicated when suppliers make quotations and due allowance should be made for comparison purposes.

The strategy of deciding the amount and supply location of bunkers is of utmost importance for spot voyage charters. A classical example is a Panamax vessel loading New Orleans for Japan and requiring bunkers before arrival at the discharge port. The main inputs to the equation are costs of fuel at loading port, fuel costs at a West Coast, USA, port and the freight rate.

If freight rates are high, it is normally more attractive to maximise cargo deadweight using maximum available draught through the canal, and pick up bunkers at Long Beach where costs are usually very competitive.

If freight rates are low and the differential in fuel costs between New Orleans and Long Beach is greater in Long Beach's favour than the freight rate, it is also more attractive to bunker at Long Beach. The only attraction in bunkering at New Orelans or another bunker port before the canal would be if freight rates were low and fuel cost difference in New Orleans favour greater than the freight rate. The difference in sailing distance by calling at Long Beach for bunkers is negligible if using a great circle route.

Should the vessel be coming off or on hire in a high cost area, for example Japan, it is commercially attractive for the shipowner to fill her with bunkers in a low cost port such as Long Beach to obtain the Japanese fuel costs if this is allowed in the charterparty. Conversely, if a vessel is coming off or on hire in a low fuel cost port it would pay to sail from a high cost port with minimum allowable bunkers on board.

Ship's staff should be encouraged to give accurate bunker requirements when requested to submit figures. Not only does this mean that optimised quantities at beneficial costs can be taken advantage of but also that any fuel turned away because the ship's tanks are full, does not incur a cost penalty from the supplier. Alternatively, if insufficient fuel has been ordered, a penalty may be incurred by the barge having to make a return trip to make up the shortfall.

Regarding the actual cost of bunkers, *Lloyd's List* gives a weekly rundown on worldwide costs which are an extremely useful guide. There are many specialised firms who will buy your bunkers for you based on their vast experience and commercial clout.

## 15. SUMMARY OF CHAPTER THREE

Fuels costs in recent years have become more stable. Whether this is temporary or not remains to be seen. We will have to find an alternative energy source in the medium- to long-term, although the emphasis on doing this will no doubt subside due to the recent stabilisation of costs. Shipowners will have to prepare themselves for the quality of fuel oil expected in the medium term. It is hoped that this chapter will have alerted them to the various issues involved, not forgetting that MARPOL will soon become involved in its quality.

CHAPTER FOUR

# PERFORMANCE MONITORING

## 1. MEASURING METHODS USED

Performance monitoring systems can extend to very comprehensive systems using sophisticated equipment such as Doppler logs and cathode ray tubes. Questions that should be asked by any prospective user are: what is expected of the system, will it be cost-effective and do the people entrusted with its use fully understand the basic principles involved?

Probably the most important parameter is the ship's speed, both over the ground and through the water. Most ships now have Satnav, so speed over the ground is available on demand or at least when a satellite is in a suitable position. Speed through the water is a little more difficult and a Doppler log gives very accurate results at high capital cost. Cheaper electric magnetic or venturi type logs are available but are not as accurate as the Doppler log.

Next in importance is the developed horsepower of the main propulsion system. The classical method is to take indicator cards from each cylinder and calculate the mean indicated pressure and thence the indicated horsepower using a Planimeter. When used by an expert, a Planimeter is fairly accurate but suffers from the effects of any shipboard vibration and requires a steady hand. The mechanical efficiency of the engine has to be known so that brake horsepower can be calculated and the whole operation, perhaps, has a 5% measurable tolerance. It should be mentioned that most 4-stroke engines and one of the few remaining 2-stroke designs do not have facilities for taking indicator cards.

Torsionmeters are available for measuring shaft horsepower and can be coupled with a strain gauge for measuring thrust. Accuracy within a 2% tolerance is a reasonable target for this type of equipment. By replacing the indicator with a cathode ray tube, it is possible to obtain a more accurate measurement of the indicated horsepower, possibly within a 2% tolerance.

Main Engine revolutions are accurately measured on most vessels using comparatively simple equipment. This parameter is probably the easiest of all to measure and is very useful in determining trends, as will be discussed later.

Next we come to fuel consumption which, being directly related to horsepower, is rather important. In the case of the performance of chartered vessels, fuel consumption and speed are the two most used parameters in determining if a vessel is performing to charterparty warranties or not.

Fuel consumption can be measured by flowmeters or simply by tank soundings and although this latter method is subject to large daily fluctuations it is reasonably accurate over a period. In the case of charterparty off-hire surveys tank soundings are still the only method used. Using flowmeters has its uses, particularly when Main Engine performance is being monitored, but they are of only limited use for charterparty purposes. A point to remember is that in the case of modern fuels usually containing amounts of sludge and water the flowmeter does not measure these contaminants removed by treatment on board, so using a flowmeter only would result in a deficit when trying to balance fuel consumed with the closing stock.

The measurement of weather is important as this arguably has the greatest impact on a vessel's performance. Apart from wind speed and direction instruments (anemometers), very little instrumentation exists and reliance on visual observations is the norm.

Various pressures and temperatures in the propulsion machinery systems are also measured using standard thermometers, pyrometers and pressure gauges to enable laid down limits to be observed.

These then are the parameters requiring measurement and the means generally used aboard ship to accomplish this. Some comments on the practical aspects of each follow.

## 2. SHIP'S SPEED

The movement of a ship through the water is subject to many actions. First, we have the frictional resistance of the hull surfaces and the resistance imposed by wave and eddy making. The sea itself is far from being stationary and ocean currents as well as swell must be taken into account. Even air resistance has to be considered, especially on high-sided car carriers, container vessels and the like.

Using Satnav can give a reliable speed over the ground which is satisfactory for practical purposes. Most charterparty warranties use speed over the ground and sea trial speed runs also measure speed over the ground. Measurement of speed through the water requires a more technical approach, and if no extraneous forces were acting on the hull, speed through the water would be the same as over the ground for all practical purposes. By comparing speed through the water with speed over the ground we can calculate the effect of ocean currents on the vessel. We would still be unable to decide the strength and direction of the current, only its resultant effect.

Most ships are equipped with Ocean Routeing Charts from which the prevailing current speed and direction and also the wind force/direction can be obtained. These are based on historical data and are in a monthly form covering the most frequently used trade routes. There are also the weather services to turn to if up-to-date weather patterns are required for either present voyage planning or past performance analysis.

It will be seen that there are various options for determining if speed over the ground is being affected by extraneous forces. If this is not the case, and the ship's speed is down, then it can be assumed in most instances to be due to hull fouling.

## 3. HORSEPOWER

Horsepower is transmitted to the propeller from the Main Engine cylinders via pistons, connecting rods, crankshaft and, finally, the propeller shaft. Horsepower is normally measured by means of an indicator or cathode ray tube which measures pressure within the cylinders over a full working cycle. The resulting pressure volume diagram is converted first to mean indicated pressure and then indicated horsepower.

This is the power developed in the cylinders and it must be converted to brake horsepower, which is the indicated horsepower less the frictional losses in the transmission system—notably piston rings against liner wall. Some modern engines have actually reduced the number of piston rings to increase the mechanical efficiency, which is the same as reducing frictional losses. Mechanical efficiencies of around 93% are claimed for these modern engines.

To be strictly correct, the propeller horsepower should be used in hydrodynamic calculations. These take into account the losses between the brake, normally taken at the flywheel, and the propeller. Frictional resistance in the shaft bearings, stern tube bearing and sealing glands are included in this calculation; these probably amount to around 1½%, which must be deducted from the brake horsepower.

Torsionmeters are sometimes used to measure horsepower and work on the principle of the degree of twisting in the intermediate shaft being proportional to the torque. When the measured torque is multiplied by the RPM, the brake horsepower can be derived.

## 4. REVOLUTIONS/SLIP

Revolutions are indicated in analogue form by means of a tachometer, which gives a visual indication of the revolutions being turned. The average revolutions shown in the abstracts and logs are measured by an integrating counter which gives rather accurate results.

The engine speed is derived from multiplying the average revolutions by a propeller constant. This constant is calculated by the propeller designer and is obtained from the mean face pitch. When multiplied by the average revolutions this gives the theoretical advance of the vessel, and when compared with the vessel's speed over the ground gives the apparent slip as:

$$\frac{E - S}{E}$$

where E is the engine speed and S the ship's speed over the ground.

Hydrodynamicists generally use the true slip in their calculations and, in the above formulae, S becomes the ship's speed minus the wake speed. For practical purposes wake speed is not measurable with any degree of accuracy, and apparent slip is favoured in this study.

Actually, the calculation of mean face pitch can give rise to some discussion. From the author's experience, vessels built in the Far East generally have lower apparent slips than European-built vessels when measured on sea trials. This is not to say they are more efficient, but different methods of calculating mean face pitch are presumably used. The important thing is that apparent slip is used for detecting trends rather than for vessel comparison purposes. Apparent slip has a very important input to the bottom line in a ship performance audit. A 1% change in slip is equal to a 3% change in fuel consumption, based on cube law considerations at constant ship's speed.

## 5. FUEL CONSUMPTION

On a typical vessel there are usually three main consumers of fuel, namely, main propulsion, boilers and diesel generators. In some installations, the main propulsion, boiler fuel and diesel generator fuel comes from the same service tank, which can lead to measurement problems if this is not apportioned correctly.

Measurement of fuel flow to the main propulsion system is usually by flowmeter. Due to the complexity of the modern fuel system, placing of the flowmeter is rather important otherwise the amount of fuel in circulation will be measured. This is around three times the actual fuel consumed and, if this were measured, it would be meaningless.

We will trace the path of the fuel from bunker barge to engine so that the practical problems in accurately measuring fuel consumption are realised. The fuel being bunkered passes through the supplier's meter or by checking the soundings of his barge, and the quantity agreed by supplier and ship's staff. In some cases agreement cannot be reached but, in general, it would appear that, providing ship's-staff take care and, more important, show interest, no marked differences occur between supplier's and the ship's figures.

Delivered fuel is then directed to various storage tanks around the vessel, usually double bottom or deep tanks. Ship's staff take soundings to check if the delivered quantity compares with the supplier's figures. Problems immediately arise because of various factors. For example, if double bottom storage tanks are being used then soundings are subject to large corrections in trim effect, which may not be easy to accurately determine. The temperature of the delivered fuel may well be known and can be easily measured, but its temperature in the double bottom tank can only be estimated. This would also apply to the density if it has been mixed with other fuels, although mixing fuels is a practice now frowned upon by most shipowners.

At sea, the fuel in the storage tanks is pumped to the settling tank and allowed to stand to enable water and sludge to settle out. These are drained off and a loss from the delivered quantity immediately arises depending, of course, on the amount drained off. The fuel is then fed into the service tank via the purification system, in which further amounts of water and impurities are removed by the extremely high gravity forces in the centrifugal purifiers. It has been estimated that as much as 1% of the total fuel delivered is lost during its passage from storage tanks to the engine.

The fuel is then fed into the engine via a flowmeter, if fitted. A certain amount of fuel leaks from parts of the system, notably fuel pumps and injectors; the amount of leakage is dependent on the condition of these delicate parts. This leakage must be deducted from the reading taken from the flowmeter if we are conducting a performance test.

The alternative method of measuring fuel consumption is simply by tank soundings, which may be by hand-held tapes or by pressure transducers with a direct reading to a gauge. Experienced ship's staff will be able to determine fuel consumption reasonably accurately using this equipment over a voyage, but for accurate daily consumption intended for performance analysis a flowmeter is obviously more accurate.

When time-chartered vessels are subjected to on-hire and off-hire surveys the moment of truth arrives when independent surveyors check the quantity of fuel remaining aboard. Ideally, this should check out with the amount of fuel remaining in the abstracts, which, presumably, will have been analysed on the assumption that the daily fuel consumptions shown are in fact correct. However, some quite startling differences have been noted when off- and on-hire survey results have been compared with remains shown on the abstracts. Historically this can be traced back to the now discouraged practice of the chief engineer having fuel up his sleeve.

An exercise was recently undertaken by the author spanning a 12-month period covering 16 time-chartered vessels. The result showed a total book difference of around 325 tonnes or 0.057 tonnes per day per ship, which would exceed the accuracy of most flowmeters.

We could say that over a period fuel consumption by tank soundings gives reasonable accuracy but, for performance monitoring purposes, a flowmeter would obviously be more suitable.

## 6. WEATHER

When weather is mentioned, most seafarers immediately think of wind force as expressed by the Beaufort Scale, which for reference purposes is given hereunder:

**Table 7.  Beaufort Scale**

| Number | Description | Wind speed—knots |
|--------|-------------|------------------|
| 1 | Light Air | 2 |
| 2 | Light Breeze | 5 |
| 3 | Gentle Breeze | 9 |
| 4 | Moderate Breeze | 13 |
| 5 | Fresh Breeze | 19 |
| 6 | Strong Breeze | 24 |
| 7 | Near Gale | 30 |
| 8 | Gale | 37 |
| 9 | Strong Gale | 44 |
| 10 | Storm | 52 |
| 11 | Violent Storm | 60 |
| 12 | Hurricane | Above 64 |

We must also consider in which direction the wind is blowing, as obviously a wind force 4 on the bow will have a completely different effect on a vessel to a wind force 4 on the stern. For some unknown reason, standard charterparty weather conditions generally refer to the wind force only; not the direction.

Another weather factor affecting vessel performance is swell, which can be expressed by the following scale represented in order of magnitude:

**Table 8.  Swell represented in order of magnitude**

| | | Intensity | | |
|---|---|---|---|---|
| | | Low | Mod. | Heavy |
| Length | Short | 2 | 4 | 7 |
| with | Mod. | 2 | 5 | 8 |
| respect | Long | 3 | 6 | 9 |
| to ship's | | | | |
| length | No swell | | 1 | |
| No data | 0 | | Very heavy swell 10 | |

Ocean currents are another phenomenon affecting vessel performance, and these can readily be expressed as their speed in knots and direction.

To simplify the recording of these aforementioned parameters we can use a simple sector system for relating the relative direction of either wind force, swell or current to the ship's heading as in Fig. 14.

The log abstract or passage summary could then be simplified to a six figure entry as shown (see Table 9).

This will cover most of the weather conditions normally assumed to affect performance.

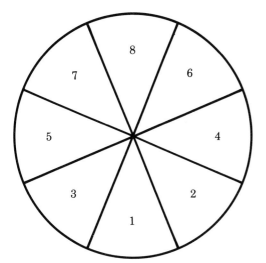

**Fig. 14. Simple sector system**

**Table 9. Log abstract or passage summary**

| Wind | | Swell | | Current | |
|--------|-------|--------|-------|--------|-------|
| Sector | Force | Sector | Force | Sector | Speed |
| | | | | | |
| | | | | | |

We can also introduce factors for determining what effect the weather is having on the vessel by adding a rating for pitching and rolling, also deck wetness. These important factors can be represented numerically in order of magnitude as follows:

*Pitch/roll*
1. None.
2. Slightly.
3. Easily.
4. Moderately at times.
5. Moderately.
6. Heavily at times.
7. Heavily.
8. Violently at times.
9. Violently.

*Fore deck wetness*
1. Dry.
2. Spray.

3. Wet.
4. Very wet.

All these criteria can now be recorded by a simple digital system on a daily basis as shown:

**Table 10. Single digital system for daily recording**

| | Wind | | Swell | | Current | | Pitch/ | Deck |
|---|---|---|---|---|---|---|---|---|
| Date | Sector | Force | Sector | Force | Sector | Speed | roll | wetness |
| 1.10.95 | 2 | 4 | 2 | 2 | 7 | 2 | 1 | 1 |
| 2.10.95 | 2 | 5 | 2 | 3 | 6 | 2 | 2 | 2 |
| 3.10.95 | 3 | 4 | 3 | 2 | 6 | 2 | 1 | 1 |
| 4.10.95 | 2 | 6 | 2 | 4 | 6 | 2 | 3 | 1 |

This represents only part of a typical voyage abstract or passage summary. Other data normally included such as RPM, position, course and various fuel consumptions will also be shown.

Although an improvement on the limited information normally given on a typical voyage abstract, it still has a disadvantage as it must rely on the accuracy of whoever is entrusted to enter the data. This arises when a weather pattern covering a 24-hour period has to be condensed into a single line entry. It is possible, of course, to split the day into watches in a similar manner as the deck and engine logs are filled in. This would be considered a retrograde step; abstracts were originally introduced to avoid the tediousness of examining the submitted logs. To return to this labour-intensive practice knowing that shore personnel are subjected to manning reductions in similar manner as their seagoing colleagues would not be popular.

Unless this proposed splitting of the day were confined to two distinct 12-hour periods, it is unlikely that it would be accepted under NYPE time charters for calculating heavy weather periods. Although it could possibly be used in some tanker charters at lesser periods than 12 hours.

Experience has shown that given proper instructions it is possible for seagoing personnel satisfactorily to enter data on a once per 24-hour period, which will adequately describe average weather conditions and its effect on the vessel.

## 7. PRESSURES—TEMPERATURES

Various critical pressures and temperatures affect the performance of the vessel, starting with atmospheric pressure and the ambient temperatures of sea water and outside air. It is normal to convert these to ISO standards when comparing actual results to those recorded at the shop or sea trials. The main effect of pressures and temperatures is, of course, on the main propulsion machinery, although it is important that auxiliary machinery and steam plant are given due consideration.

Pressures and temperatures in the Main Engine combustion cycle are the most important means of measuring the efficiency of the plant. The theoretical considerations governing ideal cycle efficiency are that heat is supplied as a single high temperature, T1, and rejected at a single low temperature, T2. It can be shown that maximum efficiency is achieved when T1 is as high as possible and T2 is as low as possible in the form

$$\frac{T1 - T2}{T1}$$

In an existing plant we can achieve this by keeping the maximum cycle pressure (P Max) to the shop trial figure and also keep the scavenge pressure, hence temperature, to shop trial figures having regard to ISO corrections. The mean effective pressure (P Mean) is that converted directly to the output in horsepower and must be kept as high as possible for obvious reasons. The ratio between P Max and P Mean is a more practical means of determining cycle efficiency, as it is rather easy to measure pressures but rather difficult to measure cyclic temperatures. The higher this ratio, the higher the thermo-dynamic efficiency.

Another pressure used to measure plant efficiency is the compression pressure (P Comp). This is the maximum pressure in the cylinder when the fuel is shut off; a comparatively easy measurement in practice. It can even be determined with the fuel kept on if accurate draw cards are taken with the PV indicator.

The relationship between P Comp and scavenge pressure (P Scav) gives a good guide to the condition of piston rings and amount of liner wear, which is, in effect, the gas tightness of the cylinder/piston configuration. By using this relationship we can monitor the condition of piston rings and liner whilst the engine is running, so that corrective action can be taken in port. Each engine type has its own P Comp/P Scav relationship and this is normally given in the instruction book.

Correct fuel injection timing is a prerequisite of optimised engine performance, and incorrect timing will almost certainly reduce the P Max with resultant loss of efficiency. Incorrect timing can also be determined with the use of the PV diagram or the cathode ray tube.

Each fuel will have its own combustion properties and, in an ideal world, the fuel injection timing should be checked and adjusted each time bunkers are taken. Modern engines are arranged so that injection timing can be adjusted when the engine is running, which makes this operation relatively simple. Different engines have their own mechanical or electronic means of accomplishing this and the equipment is nowadays known as variable injection timing (VIT).

So the difference between modern engines and older types is that the means of adjusting fuel injection timing is now done rather easily whereas it used to be a time-consuming task necessitating altering fuel pump cam position and/or adding/removing liners from the fuel pump housing.

This, more or less, covers the essential pressures in the combustion chamber, which leaves us with some of the more important temperatures to consider.

One of the most important is the temperature of the fuel as it is injected into the cylinders. Actually, it is the viscosity we are really concerned about and it is normal nowadays to provide viscosity controllers, usually called viscotherms, to monitor this function. Viscotherms avoid the necessity of operators converting the viscosity of whatever fuel is in use to temperature. Bunker receipt notes are notorious for describing the viscosity of the fuel as it was ordered and, in practice, it is generally less. For example, 380 cst at 50°C may turn out to be 320 cst at 50°C.

There is also the problem of using fuel of different viscosities, the result of which may be difficult to determine. The viscotherm takes care of these difficulties and heats the fuel to enable the preset viscosity to be maintained.

Jacket water temperatures are now kept much higher than they used to be, nominally 85°C against the 65°C previously used. This increases thermal efficiency slightly and has the added function of reducing acidic attack on the cylinder liners of modern long stroke engines.

Exhaust gas temperatures are also important. In the case of cylinder outlet temperatures these represent T2 in the ideal cycle referred to earlier. In the case of impulse turbo-charged engines, cylinder outlet temperatures did not have any significant contribution except, perhaps, for determining trends. Constant pressure turbo-charged engines have a more discernible contribution and differences in individual cylinder outlets can indicate unequal power distribution, which should be verified by indicator diagrams. Exhaust gas temperatures vary with the engine room ambient temperature and the scavenge air temperature. Any increase in these will manifest itself in increased exhaust gas temperatures. To ensure that the correct amount of combustion air is delivered to the cylinders, the scavenge temperature should be kept at the engine builders' recommended figures, so optimising efficiency.

However, by increasing the scavenge air temperature the exhaust gas temperature is also increased, and heat recovery from the economiser likewise increased. This should be borne in mind on plants having large exhaust gas recovery systems incorporating a turbo-alternator. At certain Main Engine loadings, a slight increase in scavenge temperature can mean an extra 20–30kW output from the turbo-alternator.

## 8. MONITORING SYSTEMS

So how do we monitor all these numerous measurements and present them in some sort of simple understandable form?

There are very sophisticated Main Engine monitoring systems already on the market and more are being developed. As this book is aimed at a representative readership, it is not intended to discuss fully these highly technical systems beyond saying that most of the basic considerations have been explained in this chapter. It might interest readers to know that some of these sophisticated systems are more technologically advanced than those used on most engine builders' test bays where, unlike ship's staff, most participants have achieved high academic standards.

The author has developed a rather simple manual system, which is illustrated in Fig. 15. It has been dubbed a manual system to distinguish it from a computerised system, which is the subject of a later chapter.

The vessel shown is a 1982-built Panamax with a rather conventional hull form. Improved vessels with a superior engine performance and far better hulls are, of course, now available but the general principles involved in producing such a system is basically the same. RPM has been chosen as the base, mainly because this is probably the most accurate of all the many variables included in the study. Starting at the top curve on the graph and working downwards we start with P Max as recorded at the sea trial when running on heavy oil. This should give a reasonable comparison against service results taken in good weather and, if too far adrift from the sea trial figure, further investigation is called for. In an actual example involving serious damage to a propeller, this part of the system was used to identify the resultant drop in speed caused by the damaged propeller. As engines age and fuel oil quality deteriorates P Max has a tendency to drop, and it should be maintained at the recommended level, always providing the engine condition is satisfactory.

The next set of curves represents the loading on the Main Engine caused mainly by the resistance of the vessel through the water and partially by the ruling weather conditions. Normal rating of the Main Engine as tested at the shop trial is the basis of the 100% curve. At sea trials it is normal for service power to be developed at around 103% service revolutions, so that a margin for future increased resistance is built into the propulsion system.

As resistance increases in service, so the absorbed load on the Main Engine increases irrespective of the actual output. To avoid problems identifying the output in terms of horsepower, fuel consumption has been used and the means of converting RPM to horsepower thence consumption is shown in the table. More modern engines using VIT will have improved SFC at reduced outputs to those shown here.

The loading curves may not be accurate in absolute terms but they are very useful in determining trends, especially when operating in sea areas promoting underwater growth. Once the absorbed load rises above 115% a careful watch

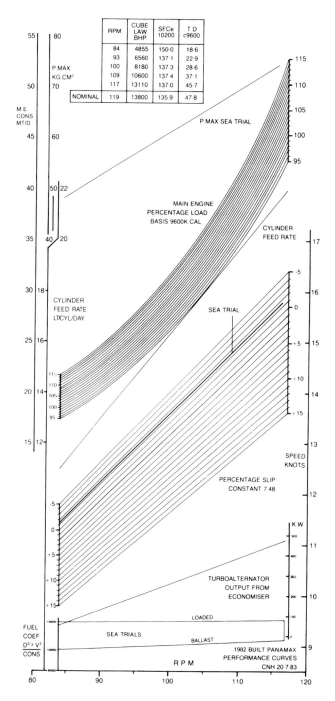

| | RPM | CUBE LAW BHP | SFCe 10200 | T D c9600 |
|---|---|---|---|---|
| | 84 | 4855 | 150·0 | 18·6 |
| | 93 | 6560 | 137·1 | 22·9 |
| | 100 | 8180 | 137·3 | 28·6 |
| | 109 | 10600 | 137·4 | 37·1 |
| | 117 | 13110 | 137·0 | 45·7 |
| NOMINAL | 119 | 13800 | 135·9 | 47·8 |

*Fig. 15. Manual ship performance monitoring system*

should be instituted until the vessel can be scrubbed or dry docked. A word of caution when using these curves with derated Main Engines; unless the derated horsepower and revolutions are used the results will show that in all probability overloading is taking place even though this is not strictly true.

The next curve shows cylinder lubricating oil feed rate, which gives guidance on the consumption of this rather expensive commodity. It should not be used in isolation, but other factors must be considered. For example, cylinder wear rate and physical condition of the scavenge spaces with respect to its oily or dry appearance.

Curves showing apparent slip percentage are directly under the cylinder feed rate curve. These are useful for giving an instant slip percentage reading without the trouble of carrying out the calculation. They are very useful for determining trends and also for predicting future performance.

The vessel depicted in the example is fitted with a steam turbo-alternator and the next curve shows the expected kW output over the range of revolutions. Should this be below expectations, further investigation is called for. For example, the dump steam valve may be open or excessive steam is being diverted to other less essential consumers.

Finally, the fuel coefficient—as calculated on the sea trials, which, of course, were in rather good weather—is shown. Due allowance must be made for weather conditions when service results are being compared with these sea trials results.


## 9. SPEED VERSUS CONSUMPTION

The most important consideration of all performance aspects is the vessel's speed against consumption, both in laden and ballast conditions. All other parameters mentioned in this chapter are simply vehicles used in arriving at what might be called the bottom line of ship's performance. The manual graphic system, described in the previous section, does not cater for the speed and consumption relationship, and a further graphic system is necessary, as shown in Fig. 16, which indicates the predicted loaded and ballast speed/consumption curves.

As will be seen, it is self-explanatory and is usually on the basis of fair weather. Actual service results can be shown and the author favours a recording method with all weather and fair weather corrected figures. Deviation from the curves can be indicated either vertically (as fuel consumption) or horizontally (as speed difference). They can be updated as and when differences in performance are such that the existing curves give unattainable performance. For example, if the vessel's bottom is fouled.

Sea trials performance, converted from horsepower to fuel consumption at the expected fuel quality, can be shown for reference and the sea margin easily calculated for predictive purposes.

For reference, a graphic illustration of four typical vessels giving fair weather service performance of modern designs compared with older designs showing the quite remarkable improvements that have been made in the intervening period is provided (see Fig. 17). Ship's speed does tend to follow fuel costs and whilst the curves reflect the increases in performance, the range of speeds may not reflect the actual figures.

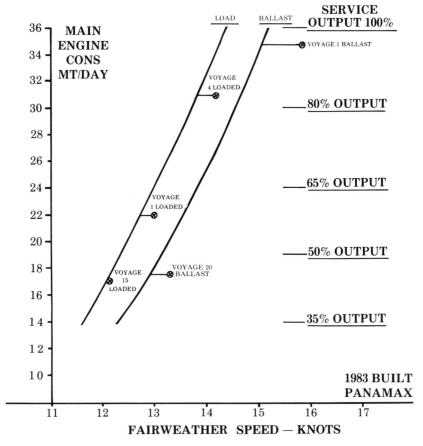

*Fig. 16  Speed and fuel consumption graph—Panamax*

## 10. SUMMARY OF CHAPTER FOUR

There are many expensive performance monitoring systems on the market and they no doubt do a good job. For those not wishing to spend any money on additional equipment, the simple method described here may suit their purpose. In a later chapter, a low cost computerised performance system will be described.

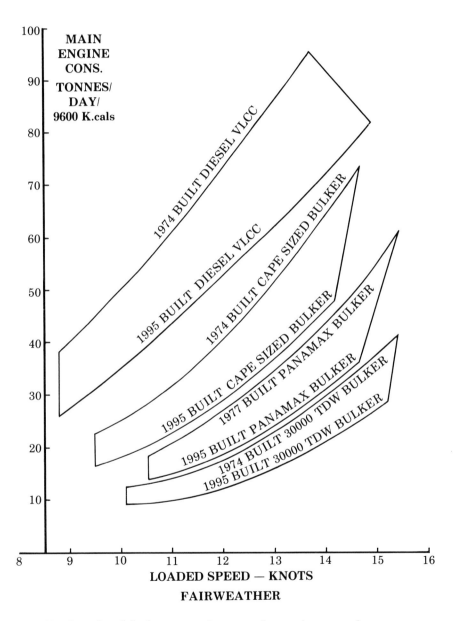

*Fig. 17.  Speed and fuel consumption growth—various vessels*

CHAPTER FIVE

# COMMERCIAL PERFORMANCE

## 1. INTRODUCTION

The technical performance of a ship mainly relates to its speed and fuel consumption and the various means available to ensure that optimum performance is achieved having regard to the capital outlay involved. In this chapter we will discuss the commercial performance of various popular ship types.

## 2. BULK CARRIERS

There are several sizes of bulk carrier currently in use which can be categorised, in ascending order, as handy sized, Panamax, Cape and VLBC, although other intermediate less popular sizes are also in use. Bulk carriers are usually built to the same general design, having a single hull, double bottom, hopper and topside tanks as shown in Fig. 18. This design is inherently self-trimming and its introduction four decades ago avoided the use of temporary centreline shifting boards, previously needed when bulk cargoes such as grain were likely to shift in bad weather when carried in conventional tween deckers.

Most bulk carriers are now built with what is called a B–60 freeboard, permitting them to operate with an increased draught and therefore a commensurate increase in cargo deadweight. In the case of a Panamax sized bulk carrier of around 60,000 TDW, for example, the assignment of a B–60 freeboard could result in an increase of cargo deadweight of perhaps 3,000 tonnes. Existing vessels of whatever size not having the benefit of this B–60 should seriously consider adopting this effective means of increasing cargo deadweight at what is usually a moderate conversion cost.

The commercial performance of bulk carriers could be described in simple terms as a measurement of their earning capacity in the market place, usually the Baltic Exchange. Those bulk carriers built with a long-term time charter in mind will, in all probability, have been provided with all the many features asked for by the charterer based on his expert knowledge of the proposed cargoes and anticipated geographical area of operation. For those owners who build a bulk carrier for operation on the spot market, they have to decide what features they should provide to enhance commercial performance based on their own experience.

One of the first considerations is whether or not heavy cargoes such as iron ore are to be carried. If, as seems likely in most cases, the answer is yes then the hull has to be strengthened and a classification notation given on the lines "Strengthened for Ore Cargoes. Nos. 2, 4, 6 and 8 holds may be empty". This notation is invariably applied to most bulk carriers in order to ensure cargo flexibility but in certain instances the expense of adding this notation can be avoided if, for example, a long-term grain charter is envisaged.

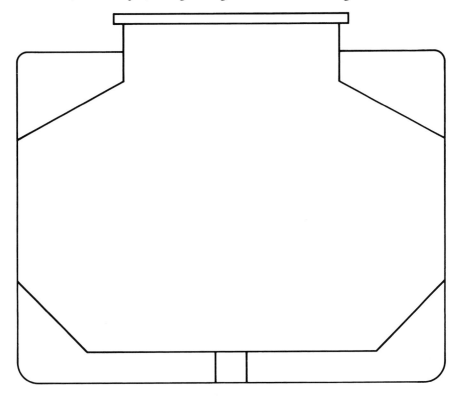

*Fig. 18. Typical bulk carrier*

In the case of a long-term grain charter or even perhaps a long-term alumina charter, it is highly desirable for the cargo hold spaces to be coated with an approved paint to facilitate pre-loading hold inspections by cargo surveyors or port authorities. A vessel with a heavy cargo classification notation but engaged in the grain trade for a lengthy period would soon find any paint coatings quickly removed and the hold steelwork damaged if it was then employed in the iron ore trade on completion of the grain charter. This is because chute loading of such heavy cargoes, its abrasive action on passage and the aggressive action of grabs, bulldozers and even pneumatic hammers whilst unloading, collectively have the effect of causing the aforementioned damage. The situation has reached serious proportions and the leading Classification Societies have recently highlighted the problems that bulk carriers are exposed to, particularly when carrying heavy cargoes over lengthy periods of time.

The loss rate of bulk carriers when carrying heavy cargoes is rather high and structural failure appears to be the highest single cause. So much so that the IMO is expected to introduce some, as yet undefined, regulations in the near future in an attempt to correct the situation. The loss of the UK registered "Derbyshire" is probably the incident with the highest profile and was the one which arguably caused most concern amongst regulatory bodies.

It would appear that if owners of conventional bulk carriers could steer away from carrying these high density, abrasive and sometimes corrosive cargoes they would greatly extend the commercial life of their vessels. High density cargoes are usually only carried in alternate holds, which increases the shear force and bending moments imposed on the hull, and in bad weather the acceleration and deceleration forces acting on the widely spaced heaps of heavy cargo will be superimposed, exacerbating the situation. Most bulk carriers are able to carry the full range of appropriate cargoes from light grain to iron ore and the variation between these extremes in specific gravity is around a factor of 10. This range of cargoes is imposed on owners by the commercial necessity of meeting the vagaries of the market place, which led to the long-standing design of the currently used bulk carrier that can handle most known cargoes.

One solution to the problem of carrying high density ore was the introduction of the ore carrier several decades ago. Most of these vessels could also carry oil but they were not popular and none have been built recently, probably on account of their high cost. It would appear that the problem of carrying such cargoes as iron ore in a conventional bulk carrier is far from resolved and may lead to drastic changes in the near future. One possible solution might be the introduction of a double hull similar to that already incorporated into tanker design following OPA 90 regulations to be discussed.

To extend the range of cargoes capable of being carried by the modern bulk carrier certain measures can be taken by the owner. One of the most popular is the provision of $CO_2$ in the cargo spaces. By fitting a total flood $CO_2$ fire extinguishing system such cargoes as coal, seed cake pellets, and direct reduced iron, as well as other cargoes susceptible to spontaneous heating, can be carried, so enhancing commercial performance.

The provision of deck cranes on the smaller size of bulk carrier of up to, say, 35,000 TDW is more or less standard. Some of the larger sized bulk carriers have also been provided with deck cranes, more especially those of Panamax size. Unless the owner has some firm commercial reason for doing so, the provision of deck cranes on the larger bulk carriers does, on the face of it, seem an unwarranted expense, probably in the region of $3.5m.

Sophisticated self-unloading equipment has also been provided on several bulk carriers of around the Panamax size. This equipment can achieve unloading rates of around 6,000 tonnes per hour and must not be confused with standard deck cranes, traversing deck cranes or other above deck arrangements. These self-unloaders are usually of the continuous moving belt variety, located at tank top level with either a scoop or belt elevating the cargo to deck mounted chutes and thence to the quayside stockpiles. They are particularly suited to the transportation of lighter cargoes to ports without discharge equipment and again firm commercial reasons are a prerequisite for their provision. Early vessels of this type had a single large hold but recent classification regulations now require transverse bulkheads to be fitted in most instances.

The smaller sized bulk carriers can have an alternative design to that already mentioned. One of these is the fully open bulk carrier, as shown in Fig. 19, whereby continuous longitudinal bulkheads form squared-off hold spaces suitable for the carriage of timber, packaged forest products or other such break bulk cargoes. When provided with container fittings on tank top and hatch covers, these vessels are suitable for the carriage of containers, especially empty containers when a cargo imbalance occurs in the currently flourishing container trade and space is at a premium on the regular ships.

These fully open bulk carriers are usually provided with large hatch openings, making them suitable for the carriage of long lengths of pipe, a popular cargo in recent years. These vessels do tend to command a higher freight rate than that received by a comparatively sized bulker of conventional design. However, they invariably have a centreline box girder at hatch coaming level and are not popular with bulk cargo shippers due to restrictive operation when using grab discharge methods.

The smallest type of ship occasionally used in the bulk cargo trade is the multi-purpose vessel, usually of somewhat smaller deadweight than the handy sized bulk carrier. There are many versions of the multi-purpose vessel, which, as its name suggests, can carry many types of cargo dependent on the shipbuilding specification. A traditional bulk carrier will rarely carry any cargo on the return leg of a loaded voyage and is usually ballasted back to the next loading port. Over a period of around 100 ship years' experience with bulk carriers, the author can only recall one return voyage whereby cargo was carried instead of ballast and this involved a cargo of limestone from Japan to Australia. The multi-purpose vessel was primarily designed to avoid non-revenue earning voyages but their popularity was not as first predicted and they are not currently fashionable in the dry bulk sector.

Another type of vessel designed to obviate non-revenue earning ballast voyages was the combination carrier, the most common version being the OBO (ore bulk oil).

There are other types of combination carrier in use including the ore bulk oil carrier already mentioned. The concept of the combination carrier was commercially sound but it turned out, in the eyes of many observers, to be

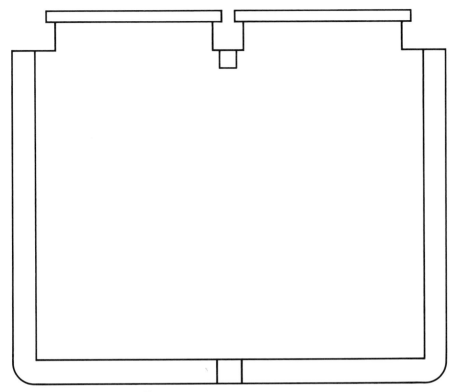

*Fig. 19. Fully open bulk carrier*

technically flawed. Apart from safety considerations, the inter-cargo cleaning operations often taxed the resources of those onboard and usually precluded the use of low-cost crews from developing countries. Because of their rather poor safety record, OBO vessels are not acceptable to many of the major charterers. This is probably due to a series of accidents affecting these vessels some years ago, allegedly due to explosive vapours from a previous oil cargo entering a ballast space with predictable catastrophic results. The recent introduction of OPA 90 by the US Government has also dealt a serious blow to the survival of those combination carriers built without a double hull.

General cargo vessels are still being built, usually, but not necessarily, for use by developing countries. Prior to the introduction of the self-trimming bulk carrier the general cargo vessel carried all the bulk cargoes, albeit not very effectively. For example, when carrying a grain cargo they had to be provided with portable shifting boards rigged on the centreline of each hold, an extremely labour-intensive activity.

This covers most of the various types of vessel used to carry bulk cargoes. The ongoing research into the high loss rate generally affecting the larger sized bulk carriers may result in a fundamental design change, possibly the adoption of a double hull at the vulnerable side shell area within the cargo hold, which is presently of only a single hull configuration. This will be discussed more fully in Chapter Seven.

Equipment thought necessary to enhance the commercial performance of the bulk carrier should also be considered by owners intending to operate this type of vessel. We have already discussed $CO_2$, the provision of which increases the portfolio of cargoes capable of being carried. Australian hold ladders of the approved design are also a highly desirable feature as most bulk carriers will almost certainly visit Australia during their lifetime.

The carriage of grain in the topside tanks of conventionally designed bulk carriers of the larger size is often resorted to if the hold capacity is insufficient to achieve maximum cargo uplift. It is normal to arrange what are called bleeding connections between the topside tanks and the cargo hold so that the grain in the topside tanks can gravitate into the hold whilst unloading. Various problems can arise with this arrangement, the most common being cleaning the topside tanks prior to loading and after discharge of cargo. This cleaning can be made less labour intensive by arranging the tank stiffeners inside the hold rather than inside the tank. Another problem is maintaining the covers forming the bleeding connection in a watertight condition when carrying ballast water in the topside tanks on the ballast leg.

On the larger bulk carriers it is recommended that drop valves are fitted to the topside tanks. These valves enable the ballast water in the tanks to be dumped overboard quickly and independently from the main ballast system. Cargo loading rates at some terminals can be as high as 15,000 tonnes per hour, which usually exceeds the capacity of the main ballast pumps, therefore risking the possibility of the vessel touching bottom at the loading berth. It is not unknown for vessels to be placed off hire if the cargo loading rate has to be reduced or even suspended because water ballast cannot be discharged quickly enough, and the provision of drop valves greatly reduces the risk of this happening.

The larger bulk carriers sometimes have problems with air draught, for example in achieving sufficient sinkage to enable the loading chutes to reach the hatch openings or to enable the vessel to pass under bridges in such rivers as the Mississippi or the Plate en route to the loading terminals down river. To reduce a vessel's air draught the height of the masts of course should be made as low as possible. Provision of the necessary piping to make it possible to fill certain holds temporarily with sea water and therefore enable deeper sinkage should be considered. This course of action extends the number of loading ports a vessel can visit and adds to its commercial performance. It also avoids the distinct possibility of a vessel being turned down by the charterer on arrival at the port if it cannot meet the air draught requirements at the berth.

Ice strengthening is another feature that can improve the commercial performance of a vessel, which can then accept a charter to the high Arctic or to other geographical areas having natural resources of the type shipped in bulk carriers. The demand for ice class bulk carriers is not high but freight rates are usually much more attractive than those in the conventional trade.

## 3. TANKERS

The range in standard tanker sizes is somewhat similar to those of bulk carriers and is described in ascending order of size as Parcel, Panamax, Aframax, Suezmax, VLCC and ULCC. In general terms there are three basic types of cargo carried in tankers, namely crude oil, refined products and chemicals.

Until quite recently, crude oil tanker design followed similar lines, and consisted of a single hull without double bottom, two continuous longitudinal bulkheads and seven or so staggered transverse bulkheads depending on the number of cargo tanks. Crude oil tankers started to increase in size after the end of the Second World War until they reached the ULCC of over a half million tonne TDW size in the late 1970s. These ULCCs proved to be commercially unpopular and no such vessels have been built in recent times.

VLCCs of around 280,000 TDW now appear to be the commonest size of large crude oil tanker now being built. As a direct result of OPA 90 regulations, most crude oil tankers are now being built with a double hull configuration. This is a commercial decision in that in order to trade to the US a double hull is essential even though IMO approved alternative designs would be suitable for trade to most other countries. Apart from environmental issues discussed in Chapter Eight, the adoption of a double hull design greatly assists tank cleaning operations in that the cargo tanks are virtually free from internal stiffeners and the smooth bulkheads allow free drainage of oil to the pump suctions, leaving very little residue.

The increase in ballast tank capacity of crude oil tankers occasioned by the introduction of, first, MARPOL Segregated Ballast Tanks (SBT) and, secondly, OPA 90 regulations, has increased their dimensions compared with earlier tankers of equivalent deadweight tonnage. Ship's length is the most expensive dimension to increase and shipbuilders therefore tend to increase beam or depth when increased cubic capacity is required. This does tend to lead to a ship having a reduced length/breadth ratio and with it an associated reduction in hydrodynamic performance. This has been compounded by the advent of higher RPM Main Engines and the unpopularity of derated engines in an attempt to reduce or stabilise first cost.

The lightship weight of crude oil tankers has been reduced in recent years in part due to optimised design involving finite element techniques and other computerised methods employed by the various Classification Societies, coupled with the increased use of high tensile steel. This reduction in lightship weight is primarily due to shipbuilders attempting to reduce the cost of a new crude oil tanker. Over the last 20 years the cost of a new VLCC has risen from around $40m to $85–$90m, although it must be said that this in part is due to

MARPOL requirements, for example SBT, COW and, more recently, double hulls. If this reduction in steelweight had not taken place the cost of a new VLCC would have been much higher, not forgetting that the introduction of the double hull design added around 7% to the cost. In some quarters it is felt that the reduction in steelweight could lead to what has been called the throwaway design and with it a shorter commercial life for the ship.

As mentioned, the current cost of a new VLCC is around $85–$90m and to service the debt on this amount requires perhaps $50,000 per day, to which must be added operating costs of $12,000 per day making $62,000 in all. It will easily be seen that the major expense involves the initial cost and any significant improvement in commercial performance must be directed here. A 10% reduction in propulsive or operating performance would only equate to a corresponding reduction of around 2.4% in capital debt servicing. Average spot market charter rates for 1990s built VLCCs for the 4th quarter of 1995 were about $25,000 per day, leaving most independent owners of this tonnage in financial difficulties.

For this reason the quest for any improvement in performance has now switched from technical to commercial, usually as expressed as the capital cost or debt financing arrangements. Most crude oil tankers appear to share this extremely poor outlook and only those tankers owned by the oil majors appear to be largely unaffected by the current situation.

However, the current market for product or parcel tankers is in slightly better shape than that employed in the crude trade. The average product tanker is around 30,000 TDW but the oil majors occasionally build much larger units for their own account. One of the most important decisions a prospective owner of a product tanker has to make is the choice of tank coating and it cannot be emphasised too strongly that this should receive his very careful attention. On this decision rests the future commercial performance of the vessel, affecting as it does the number of cargoes which can be carried.

The second important decision is that of cargo separation relating to the number of grades of cargo that can be carried simultaneously. A basic product tanker will have perhaps a four grade separation with a conventional pumproom housing four cargo pumps. The more sophisticated product tanker will be equipped with one deepwell cargo pump for each cargo tank and, assuming the necessary piping is arranged, the tanker can carry as many different grades as there are tanks; an extremely attractive arrangement which maximises commercial performance. By including various other items of a technical nature certain chemicals of a low safety and pollution profile can be carried on these tankers so further improving their commercial performance.

Dedicated chemical tankers are a rather special breed of vessel which require expert personnel both afloat and ashore to operate in a commercially satisfactory manner and this is one of the most important aspects of their operation. The usually high value of the numerous cargoes capable of being carried plus their inherent dangers make it absolutely essential that only experienced personnel are involved in the operation of these specialised vessels. For this reason it is exceedingly rare that crews from developing nations with their low cost benefits are appointed, mainly because of lack of suitable training facilities.

Again tank coatings and cargo separation arrangements are of prime importance and in many instances stainless steel is used not only for piping and valves in the cargo handling system but also for the tank boundary bulkheads, leading to a very expensive vessel as reflected by the high freight rates commanded by these specialised vessels.

In the case of both parcel and chemical tankers, the propulsive performance takes second place to the commercial performance as reflected by the grade and number of cargoes capable of being carried. The capital cost of these vessels does not appear to be under the same sort of pressure as that seen in the crude oil sector. This is almost certainly because any reduction in cost could adversely effect the specification and hence the commercial flexibility of these high technology vessels.

## 4. CONTAINER SHIPS

The container carrying capacity of these ships is gradually increasing and is currently pitched at the 6,000 TEU mark. The previous cut-off point was at the Panama beam restriction of 32.2 metres, which equated to a TEU capacity of around 3,500. Once this physical/commercial barrier was breached the so-called post Panamax container ship arrived with no apparent limit on future increases apart perhaps from those concerning port facilities.

Some of the early container ships had speeds in excess of 25 knots but the high fuel costs in the late 1970s made this high speed difficult to maintain. It was at this time that the original high powered twin screw steam turbines were replaced with lower powered single screw diesel engines with a typical speed reduction from 25 to 20 knots. Now that fuel costs have apparently stabilised the speeds of recently ordered container ships are back at the 25 knot level. Thus, those early re-engined ships would now appear to be at a commercial disadvantage due to their low speed and it would be interesting to know the current thoughts of the owners regarding their re-engining philosophy.

Recent developments in container ship design concern the introduction of the coverless container ship whereby the provision of hatch covers is dispensed with. This greatly assists container handling operations in that the removal and stowage of hatch covers is eliminated and the container cranes can devote all their time to container movements, thus reducing inport time. Another benefit of the coverless container ship is the elimination of the costly maintenance needed to retain the watertightness of the hatch covers. Coverless container ships have to be provided with enhanced drainage arrangements and large

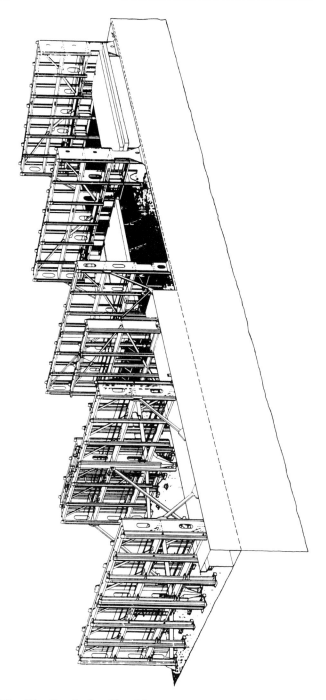

*Fig. 20.  On deck cell guides*

capacity drainage pumps in order to maintain seaworthiness but the commercial benefits are considerable.

Another development in container ship design is the ondeck cell guide arrangement, usually but not necessarily associated with the coverless design. This idea eliminates the complex container lashing systems comprising various rods, lashings and interlocking devices and avoids the previous labour intensive activity previously needed to rig the lashings after cargo was loaded and before the vessel could proceed to sea. Inport time is therefore reduced, leading to an improvement in commercial performance (see Fig. 20).

Economy of scale has certainly been a big factor in keeping container transportation costs down and, with the technical developments mentioned earlier, has assured that the commercial performance of the modern container ship is good. In many of the established container trades the so-called box rate is at the same level it was several decades ago. Because of the high capital value of especially a large container ship and the insignificant contribution that manning costs have on the overall economics it is unusual to employ crews from outside the flag state, which in many cases is that of the beneficial owners. The high value of many of the goods shipped in containers makes it extremely important that sailing schedules are strictly adhered to and in some instances shippers may have to choose between airfreight or container ship to meet critical deadlines.

In an effort to entice some of this high value cargo away from the airfreight competition, a so-called Fastship project has recently been announced whereby a drive on container ship with a 1,800 TEU capacity and a speed of 40 knots will attempt to reduce passage times by half. The hull of this proposed vessel is apparently not of the semi-planing type so that the propulsion power needed would be extremely high and recourse to gas turbine driven water jets would appear to be the only possible solution. This propulsion system is extremely sensitive to fuel costs—costs which previously saw the demise of other gas turbine propelled container ships some years ago.

## 5. PASSENGER SHIPS

One of the commercial success stories of the 1990s is the modern passenger ship, invariably used in the role of a cruise liner. The emphasis has been on the needs of the passengers and their comfort as opposed to essentially technical considerations.

It goes without saying that air conditioning, onboard entertainment and culinary delights have to be of an extremely high standard, dependent of course on the cost of the cruise selected.

The current size of a modern cruise liner is in the 70,000 GT range with a passenger capacity of between 2,000 and 3,000, the lower figure reflecting the higher cost end of the market. Because of the extensive list of ports likely to be visited on a worldwide basis it is commercially advantageous for the vessel to have as shallow a draught as possible so enabling those ports with a limited draught to be visited if selected by the cruise organisers.

One of the problems experienced when operating a large passenger ship is that of waste disposal, having regard to MARPOL Annex V garbage regulations, in view of the number of passengers carried. Much of this waste is incinerated onboard and the remainder processed into a suitable packaged form for collection inport without interruption to the ship's schedule. Several passenger ships have been heavily fined when environmentally motivated passengers have observed crew members throwing garbage overboard in restricted areas and adherence to the regulations is essential in order to avoid such fines.

The economies of scale commercial concept which briefly embraced the crude oil tanker market in the 1970s and is now practised by the container ship market has recently spread to the cruise liner sector. Several cruise liners of around 100,000 GT are on order and are expected to enter service in 1997. The often publicised "Phoenix World City" project involving a 250,000 GT cruise liner carrying 6,200 passengers has not yet been contracted for despite several false starts, but would appear to be the ultimate in cruise liner design if it ever sails.

What might be referred to as a typical 70,000 GT cruise liner costs in the region of $300m and, as in the case of other high cost ships, the commercial performance has a much bigger impact than that of propulsive performance in the overall scheme of things.

In the case of the smaller passenger ship, such as cross-channel and inter island ferries many of these are of the roll on roll off design essentially for the use of accompanied cars and trucks. Due to recent tragedies involving this type of vessel, it will in all probability soon become mandatory to provide very expensive transverse bulkheads on the vehicle decks with an estimated cost of perhaps $3m per vessel. Some of the older vessels may find it commercially unattractive to retrofit these bulkheads and the only option may be to send them to the scrapyard. Certain countries may not adopt the IMO regulations relating to transverse bulkheads and some of these older vessels could of course find their way there.

The opening of the Channel Tunnel has already affected the commercial viability of those vessels on this high density run and fitting these bulkheads has come at an inopportune time. Also a considerable amount of vehicle space will be lost especially on those vessels with hoistable car decks. The length of stay inport could also be lengthened by the erection and lowering of the transverse bulkheads so reducing the number of trips per day on the busier routes such as Dover–Calais.

Duty free sales are an important source of income on many of these vessels, especially those engaged between countries with high alcohol and tobacco duty. Any legislation introduced which restricts these sales would have a marked effect on the commercial performance of these vessels.

## 6. SUMMARY OF CHAPTER FIVE

The commercial performance of most vessels has recently assumed a more important role than that of their technical performance, which hitherto dominated the thoughts of most shipowners and shipbuilders when fuel costs peaked in the late 1970s.

Most owners now tend to focus on reducing capital cost or debt financing to the exclusion of energy saving measures, although these could of course come back if for some reason fuel costs escalate some time in the future.

Because of concern over the high accident rate of various classes of vessel, for example Ro Ro ferries, bulk carriers and tankers, the cost of these vessels is set to rise and in the case of tankers this has already occurred by the introduction of double hulls by those owners intending to trade to the USA.

# CHAPTER SIX

# FACTORS AFFECTING CHOICE OF A VESSEL, ITS MACHINERY AND EQUIPMENT

## 1. BASIC PHILOSOPHY

Shipowners intending to order new tonnage must consider every aspect in what should be a controlled decision-making process. In the real world this seldom happens and new vessels are, in many cases, ordered for seemingly obscure reasons. A lot depends on whether the proposed newbuilding is for a long-term time charter, arranged coincident with signing a newbuilding contract, for speculative time charters or for operating on the spot market or even for an affreightment contract. It could even be for bareboat charter purposes.

Each possibility will be discussed on its merits, but it is assumed that no prior agreement with any shipyard has been made. It is also assumed that the shipowner has already made a choice of the basic type of vessel he requires. Other aspects will also be considered which affect the vessel's operational performance.

## 2. LONG-TERM TIME CHARTER

This type of agreement used to be popular especially with Japanese trading houses, who would arrange both the shipyard and charterer. In recent years these agreements have fallen from favour and are unlikely to reappear until freight rates are restored to profitable levels.

The charterer will usually make all the major decisions regarding cargo gear, speed, type of cargoes, cubic capacity, range and geographical area of operation. The shipowner will make decisions relating to Main Engine and auxiliary machinery selection, flag state, Classification Society and various other items. For the purpose of our study, we will assume that the choice of shipyard has been left to the shipowner without any interference from the charterer.

The technical department of the shipowner should, ideally, be aware of all shipyards capable of building the proposed vessel and a telexed enquiry giving outline particulars, delivery requirements and asking for a price indication will be sent to those shipyards. About 20 shipyards are usually circulated and, in the current climate, most will reply giving particulars of their standard design closest to the shipowner's outline. From these replies a shortlist of three will probably be drawn up, based on previous experience with the shipyard or at least in the country where it is located. This will normally give an indication of the financial terms available and the workmanship expected.

At this stage, the shipowner's special requirements will be introduced to the shortlisted shipbuilders. High on the list will be the performance of the vessel, both in technical and commercial terms. On the technical side propulsion efficiency will receive priority, also auxiliary energy consumers, especially if a product carrier or a crude tanker is involved. As an example of this we could examine the operating scenario of a typical product carrier. If the shipowner's/charterer's chartering department is efficient, a very low percentage of the vessel's sea time will be spent in the ballast condition. Emphasis must, therefore, be given to efficient tank cleaning systems and cargo tank heating requirements; both high energy consumers. Cargo discharge operations must also figure high on the list for this type of vessel to reduce inport time.

A modern product carrier will almost certainly have an electro-hydraulic centralised system supplying the needs of both cargo pumps and deck mooring machinery. The improvement in performance using this type of auxiliary equipment over the previous method of using a conventional pumproom housing steam-driven cargo pumps and with steam mooring winches is quite dramatic. A cargo discharge operation on a 30,000 TDW product carrier, using the conventional system, consumes around 50 tonnes heavy oil; a modern electro-hydraulic system, perhaps 12 tonnes of blended or heavy fuel oil. Also, energy for the system is immediately available at the touch of a button instead of waiting until a boiler is flashed, itself an energy waster.

In the case of Panamax bulkers, there is no possibility of such ancillary system saving. Even so, centralised electro-hydraulic deck machinery systems have been commonplace for many years on Panamax bulkers and it was a logical development to extend their use to tankers.

Returning to our product carrier, cargo heating requirements can be rather high and are not normally subjected to charterparty performance warranties. However, it is in owner's and charterer's interest to minimise fuel consumption in this critical area. One means of achieving this is to provide the largest possible exhaust gas economiser so that surplus heat in the exhaust gases can be converted to steam and directed to cargo heating purposes at sea. Any extra cost for the provision of this additional plant would be the subject of a financial agreement between shipowner and charterer, not forgetting that such plants are not now popular on account of the limited amount of surplus heat produced by a modern Main Engine.

Regarding charterparty speed and consumption warranties, the figures agreed between shipowner and charterer will determine the horsepower requirements. In the case of a bulk carrier using a standard NYPE form, it is usually specified that the warranted performance is in fairweather conditions.

Shipowners, therefore, have an opportunity of using a lower sea margin to calculate the vessel's horsepower requirements. By using a sophisticated self-polishing underwater paint system, the hull-fouling contribution to the sea margin can theoretically be somewhat reduced, although legislation will restrict the use of this paint if it contains TBT.

We could say that if a NYPE charterparty is involved the horsepower requirements could be downgraded by a contribution of the fairweather clause and the use of self-polishing paint. It is becoming increasingly popular to define weather conditions in an additional clause forming part of the charterparty as a further protection to owners against performance claims.

So, instead of using, say, a 20% sea margin for an unqualified performance, the shipowner could perhaps opt for a 10% sea margin. This represents a very considerable saving in the vessel's construction costs, reflected by having a much smaller Main Engine. A smaller Main Engine means less space required for the engine room, as well as smaller pumps, generators, even smaller pipes, electric cables and a host of other items—not forgetting the benefit of increased cargo deadweight.

Should the proposed vessel not have the benefit of a fairweather clause in the charterparty, the advantages mentioned above would not, of course, apply. The shipowner, based on his own experience, would have to decide what percentage sea margin should be included and most shipbuilders will produce simple graphs showing speed and consumption with various sea margins as shown in Fig. 21.

## 3. SPECULATIVE CHARTERS AND SPOT VOYAGES

In the case of this type of operation, the shipowner will not be able to rely on the protection of a fairweather clause unless standard NYPE charterparty terms are envisaged throughout the vessel's economic life. The shipowner does, however, have a good opportunity to decide what size Main Engine he should specify. We have seen the advantages of having a smaller Main Engine, and an actual example of this is now given.

If we take a typical Panamax bulker—ordered in 1974 and delivered in 1977—it was then the vogue for this type of vessel to be rather highly powered. In the example under review the installed horsepower was provided by a 17,000 BHP Main Engine, which was not uncommon. The vessels (two were ordered) entered service and immediately commenced slow steaming, as their entry into service coincided with a trough in the Panamax market. They slow steamed at around 6,000 BHP until 1981 and throughout that year operated at 65% power—equal to around 11,000 BHP. During 1982 they reverted to slow steaming, and operated this way until they were sold in 1988.

In 1981, when the Panamax market looked promising, four additional Panamax bulkers were ordered. The first two were, more or less, standard

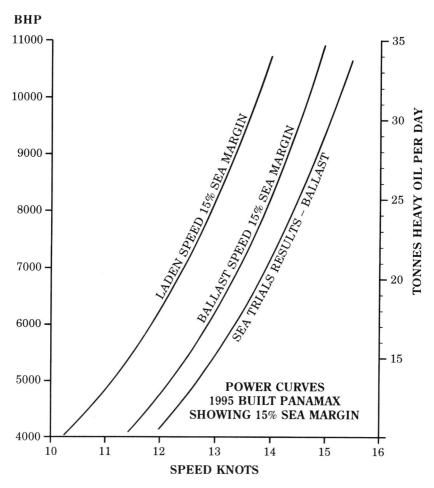

**Fig. 21. Speed and consumption graph showing sea margin**

designs and were provided with 14,000 BHP Main Engines. It was not possible to reduce the size of the engine nor was it possible to obtain the latest derated engine. The opportunity presented itself to take this course of action with the later vessels, and 11,000 BHP derated long stroke engines were provided. This, more or less, tied up with the horsepower requirements during the good year of 1981.

The arrival in service of these four Panamaxes also coincided with another trough in the market (1982–83). All four of these additional vessels slow steamed at various reduced outputs until they too were sold in 1988. So that even the 11,000 BHP Panamaxes were overpowered during this period. Panamax bulkers recently ordered appear to have Main Engines of around 10,000 BHP giving a service speed of about 14 knots with a 15% sea margin.

Indications are that a service speed of 14.5 knots will become fashionable if fuel costs remain as they are.

Derating is nowadays only rarely applied to Panamax bulkers, the emphasis being on smaller higher revolution (hence cheaper) Main Engines. This has a marked effect on both the hydrodynamic and thermodynamic performance and a present day Panamax will not be as efficient as a vessel ordered, for example, 12 years ago.

By having Main Engines of reduced output it is possible to eliminate the forward bunker tanks and their sometimes troublesome heating and transfer systems.

Although we have concentrated on the Panamax bulker in this section, the comments made would apply to other vessels involved in such charters.

## 4. CHARTER OF AFFREIGHTMENT

In a very simplistic charter of affreightment contract, a shipowner will ship an agreed quantity of cargo from A to B on an annual basis over a period of time. If the period is sufficiently long a newbuilding may be the most cost-beneficial solution to the problem, especially if existing vessels are not ideally suitable. The shipowner has a good opportunity to build the most suitable economic vessel if this course of action is justifiable, given the length of contract.

The project can be approached using a selection of vessels with varying cargo deadweights and installed power plants. The loading and discharging port physical restrictions will probably be a limiting factor, unless some interport restriction, i.e. canal transits, overrides the port restrictions. There may be a necessity to use a port state registry, which could greatly affect operating costs, and this aspect must be carefully examined.

Shipbuilding costs, like freight rates, follow some unpredictable cyclic pattern—as do fuel costs. It is, therefore, very difficult to arrange things so that all financial aspects fall into place to the benefit of the owner or charterer. An exercise undertaken some time ago at the ruling shipbuilding, operating and fuel costs is given in Table 11 and updated figures are shown for comparison.

The basic requirement of this particular charter of affreightment was that the annual quantity shipped was 300,000 tonnes over a total distance per voyage of 12,660 miles. Six different combinations of deadweight and horsepower were included in the study; only the best and worst are shown in Table 11. The study illustrates that the cost of speed is rather high and the largest deadweight, smallest powered vessel was the most cost-effective—even though large differences in fuel costs are taken into consideration. Each shipowner will have his own ideas for arranging finance; those shown may have to be adjusted on whatever terms are currently available in the country where the shipyard is located.

### Table 11. Charter of affreightment calculations

|  | 1982 study | | Updated to 1996 | |
| --- | --- | --- | --- | --- |
|  | Vessel A | Vessel B | Vessel A | Vessel B |
| Cargo deadweight | 37,500 | 33,500 | 37,500 | 33,500 |
| Service BHP | 7,600 | 12,800 | 7,600 | 12,800 |
| Service speed | 13.75 | 15.75 | 13.75 | 15.75 |
| Vessel cost | $22.4M | $23.2M | $24M | $25M |
| Fuel cost per tonne $ | 175/300 | 175/300 | 100/150 | 100/150 |
| Daily fuel cost— 365 days $ | 4,230 | 6,580 | 2,350 | 3,675 |
| Daily finance cost $ | 13,360 | 13,801 | 14,304 | 14,900 |
| Daily operating cost $ | 3,760 | 4,000 | 2,500 | 2,700 |
| Total daily cost $ | 21,350 | 24,381 | 19,154 | 21,255 |
| Required freight rate | $26 | $29.70 | $23.3 | $25.9 |

## 5. BAREBOAT CHARTER

It is rather difficult to formulate any positive policy with regard to bareboat charters. Whoever puts up the finance gets his return on investment and is not directly concerned with performance during the period of the charter. The ship operator is concerned with the performance of the vessel but does not control the specification of the vessel to the extent he would if it were his own.

Bareboat charters are generally arranged with fixed business in mind and, providing the ship performs within the warranted speed and consumption, no problems should arise.

Any additional features required by the operators would have to be passed on to them, presumably in the form of increased hire.

## 6. CARGO RELATED OPERATIONS

To enhance the performance of any vessel it is important to minimise the amount of off-hire time when performing essential cargo space cleaning operations. Dealing first with bulk carriers employed in the grain trade, it is quite common for the hold spaces to be turned down by a surveyor from a cleanliness point of view. Some of these decisions are questionable, but the shipowner's stance should be to make sure there is no room for argument by spending sufficient time and effort on the cleaning operation. In certain parts of the world, for example Australia, it is not permitted for crew members to clean holds—in the event of these being turned down by a port official. Shore labour has to be used and is very expensive in that part of the world.

Reduced crew numbers do not help matters, and every assistance should be given them in the execution of this task. Portable, even permanent, hold cleaning machines using water and compressed air are available on the market.

To assist in removing the washed-down residues permanent piping to the upper deck can be installed so that a mucking-out pump is quickly connected without having to haul long lengths of hose around. Small portable davits for each hold access opening to assist in handling the mucking out pumps and drums used for final cleaning operation are more or less essential.

For bulkers carrying grain in topside tanks it is a good idea to arrange the longitudinal stiffeners in the hold rather than in the tank with the standing flange positioned downwards, sloping in such a way as to avoid trapping any grain. This action will greatly speed up cleaning operations and will also help avoid build-up of mud in the topside tanks, which usually leads to the start of serious corrosive action. If carrying Petcoke, the introduction of a chemical into the washing water has proved successful.

Bilge wells in cargo spaces can be arranged with a duplex well having a weir interposed to reduce cleaning out operations and also to help to keep residues out of the bilge piping system. The capacity of the bilge pumps must meet classification rules, but should also be capable of dealing with large quantities of hold cleaning water.

To improve the flexibility of bulk carriers, consideration should be given to the provision of special equipment for carrying cargoes of a dangerous nature. Direct reduced iron (DRI) comes into this category, and from time to time enquiries are received for vessels fitted with special nitrogen or $CO_2$ blanketing arrangements, enabling this product to be carried.

Various seed cakes and pellets also require to be protected by either a fixed $CO_2$ total flooding system or, in some instances, a portable high expansion foam generator—depending on the physical characteristics of the cargo. The carriage of sulphur requires special precautions, and many shipowners exclude this cargo when drawing up a charterparty. Contact with water, especially sea water, is to be avoided and hold spaces should ideally be protected by paint and then limewashed before loading.

MARPOL Annex 1 regulations cover the tank cleaning of crude oil carriers, and the advent of crude oil washing and more recently the introduction of double hulls has greatly simplified tank cleaning operations aboard these vessels.

Product carriers and similar types of vessel generally have different cleaning requirements in that commercial considerations outweigh MARPOL regulations. The standard of cleanliness to meet charterers' inter-cargo requirements is high, and efficient tank cleaning equipment must be of the highest calibre. In the case of edible oil and similar viscous cargoes, the labour-intensive operation of "sweeping out" can be lessened by the introduction of inboard tank surfaces being completely free from all stiffeners and heating coils. This is usually arranged by having a double bottom tank in which these stiffeners are located. Several recently delivered vessels of this type have the upper deck stiffeners mounted actually on the upper deck instead of in the tank, although they are sometimes located in a void space under the deck.

Heating coils can be eliminated by the provision of independent deck mounted heaters through which the cargo is circulated by means of the cargo pumps. This greatly reduces tank cleaning operations, but other aspects should be considered, for example running the cargo pumps at sea. An example of a modern product carrier is shown in Fig. 22 with an original design shown under.

Accessibility to the upper parts of tank structures has always been a problem for inspection purposes relating to both cargo and classification surveyors' requirements. There are "knock down" lightweight staging frames available which are capable of being passed through the tank entry opening and assembled *in situ*. Another possibility is to use a special raft which can be inflated on the tank bottom when empty and floated up when ballasting the tank to whatever level requires inspection. More recently the provision of fixed walkways and ladders integrated with access openings and manholes has become popular, especially on the larger vessels.

Chemical carriers have their own special cleaning requirements and pollution aspects are covered by the MARPOL Annex II regulations which entered force in April 1987. Tank structures have an even greater possibility of being arranged without internal stiffeners on these specialised vessels. On more sophisticated chemical carriers stainless steel is used extensively, as are deck mounted tanks.

## 7. LABOUR SAVING DEVICES

With the current trend to reducing the numbers of ship's staff for survival, let alone economic reasons, it is very important that the remaining staff can carry out labour-intensive operations efficiently. Mooring equipment is a case in point and, arguably, was the last obstacle to making any significant reduction in the deck manning level. Self-tensioning winches and remote centralised winch controls were introduced, as were large barrels which enabled mooring ropes to be permanently coiled on the winches rather than in underdeck lockers. Another feature gaining popularity is the bow thruster, which not only simplifies mooring operations but also makes a significant reduction in the number of tugs required each time the vessel enters or leaves port. Some vessels have a stern thruster as well as a bow thruster if frequent port visits are scheduled.

Easy access to store spaces using gantry type or radial cranes, instead of a rigged derrick, also saves many man hours. Some vessels on dedicated runs were able to use the container method of storing with some success. In this scheme, a full container is loaded at the home port and any remains in the landed container credited to the shipowner.

Access to the engine room and also within the machinery spaces to permit the easy handling of heavy parts is rather important nowadays. Tremendous

## THE DIFFERENCE

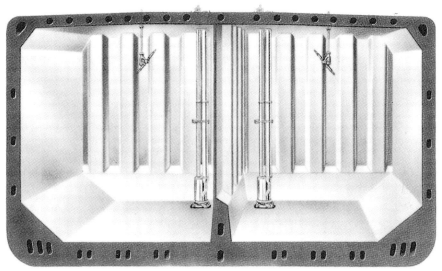

YOUR CHOICE

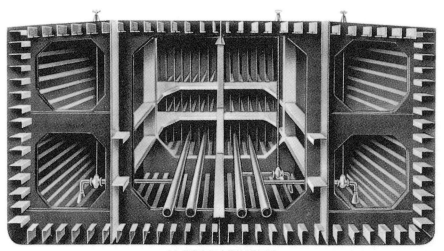

ALTERNATIVE???

*Fig. 22. Tank arrangement—modern product carrier*

advances have been made in the development of hydraulic and pneumatic tools permitting one-man operation for dismantling procedures which previously required a gang of men.

The use of superior materials in many machinery components leads to longer operational life and much less maintenance. This would also apply to the use of superior lubricating oils which extend operational intervals between piston overhauls. Now that installed Main Engine powers have dropped, it is possible to specify a smaller number of cylinders—the author was instrumental in using four cylinder large bore engines, which reduces maintenance considerably.

The introduction of self-cleaning heavy oil purifiers also made the labour-intensive function of dismantling and cleaning purifiers by hand a thing of the past. In these days of poor quality fuel, self-cleaning purifiers have come into their own, not only from a labour-saving point of view but also from consideration of the problem of hygiene.

Unmanned engine rooms are now standard and the main benefits are to release engine room personnel from tedious watchkeeping duties and redeploy them in carrying out essential maintenance functions as well as allowing reductions in complement. It is important to see that engine room workshops are properly equipped and ship's personnel adequately trained in workshop and welding techniques so as to be able to take advantage of the increased amount of time available for maintenance functions.

Planned maintenance, if carried too far, can be counterproductive in that increased spare parts consumption can rise dramatically to meet the sometimes excessive demands of the maintenance schedules. When freight rates are high off hire must be avoided, when they are low it is, of course, not so important. Planned maintenance became popular in the heady days of high freight rates and its significance as part of the overall strategy is somewhat reduced, and will continue to be so until freight rates recover.

Maintenance of steelwork is an area which should receive care, preferably at the vessel's construction stage. Paint coatings such as zinc silicate can virtually reduce fabric maintenance of the upper deck steelwork to zero. Members of the deck crew can then be employed in maintaining the cargo spaces and associated equipment, which are revenue related, as opposed to fabric maintenance, usually a cosmetic, time-consuming chore.

Tank coatings should also receive careful consideration in relation to their required duty. This would apply to cargo tanks, ballast tanks and cargo holds. Cathodic protection in ballast tanks is an added insurance against corrosion. This develops rapidly in coated tanks when small coating breakdowns direct all the available potential onto the unprotected area, which experiences rapid deterioration in the form of deep pits. The extensive use of plastic-type hardwearing accommodation bulkheads avoids the repainting of these spaces over a normal vessel's lifespan and, therefore, makes a useful contribution to labour saving.

## 8. REGISTRY AND MANNING CONSIDERATIONS

The commercial performance of any vessel is closely related to the country of registry and nationality of the officers and crew. We have learnt, in previous chapters, of the possible improvements in overall vessel performance expressed in miles per tonne of fuel used, and there is little scope for any further dramatic improvements. This is not the case with respect to registry and manning, and the attention of shipping economists has been transferred from the technical scenario to these important aspects.

Historically, vessels were registered in the port in which the owner was located and crewed by personnel residing in or close by. The emergence of the Panamanian and Liberian registers changed all that and there are very few vessels left which operate in the traditional manner. There are, however, still some countries which apply protectionist policies to their shipping industries, but these are not within the scope of our study.

It is, therefore, assumed that the shipowner has a fairly flexible approach to registration and manning and is not inhibited by too many constraints. The first decision is, probably, whether to manage the vessel himself or to enter into a management contract with one of the large number of specialised companies now existing and growing at an increasing rate. These management companies will give various management options such as crew only, officers and crew, full operational and, finally, operational and chartering management.

The shipowner may have his own staff capable of carrying out all these functions himself and may choose this option. Management companies do have access to low-cost officers and crew and a shipowner may not have such access. They also have the possibility of arranging bulk discounts on all manner of purchases; again the shipowner may not have this option, purely on account of the reduced size of his fleet. All management companies give their shipowner customers regular computerised accounts, showing actuals against budget and accrual rate for all the various operating expenses.

In order to remain competitive with a management company there are various measures a shipowner can take. For example, he can encourage his officers to sign an "offshore" agreement whereby the officer is responsible for most, if not all, of those additions to his salary normally borne by the shipowner. The main benefit in this scheme is the reduced amount of leave taken, with a corresponding reduction in repatriation costs and coverage of the rank. In extreme cases this has risen to two personnel per rank but can be stabilised at much less than this under the "offshore" agreement.

There are many crewing agencies who will supply crew members only and, providing they speak the same language as the officers, no problems normally arise.

It is unlikely that European owners can reduce manning costs to those available using a management company employing, for example, Far Eastern officers and crew. Some charterers, however, have objections to using this type of crewing operation and this could be a stumbling block to their wholesale use.

For shipowners having a rather large fleet it is possible to give one or two vessels to a management company on a trial basis, so that results can be monitored and compared with existing sister ships. This has an added attraction in that the original staff will produce their best endeavours to show they are capable of matching the opposition. It should be mentioned that the IMO will shortly be introducing the ISM (International Safety Management) code (due to become mandatory as of 1 July 1998), which will apply to all shipowners who manage their own ships as well as to management companies. (See Chapter Seven.)

Choice of registry also has an input to the equation. The main benefits in registering in a so-called flag of convenience country are well known and no further comment is called for.

Normally the port of registry will not affect the cost of a newbuilding as most shipbuilding nations are signatories to the IMO Conventions governing safety, pollution and other such matters. This is not the case with respect to manning, especially the actual numbers of officers/crew to be accommodated aboard, although the ISM code will for the first time introduce safety and pollution related procedures into operational practices. Not so long ago, a total complement of 40 would be aboard our standard vessel. This has gradually been eroded and now probably averages around 25 on a worldwide basis and very considerably less in specially designed newbuildings. The size of the accommodation deckhouse can be considerably reduced to meet the needs of the smaller number of crew members, with a resultant saving in building costs.

## 9. SECONDHAND TONNAGE

Purchase of secondhand tonnage is rather restrictive with regard to performance aspects, although previous chapters will give an idea of how to judge expected performance based on examination of the vessel's logs. The results can then be compared with data given earlier for the various types of vessels, particularly the fuel coefficient. It is possible to provide some of the performance improvers, should this course of action be deemed desirable after studying the previous performance results.

One of the most important aspects when contemplating the purchase of a secondhand vessel is to spend some time perusing the logs, abstracts and work books. If these have been filled in correctly, a wealth of information relating to the vessel's performance can be extracted. This would also apply to the cargo record book, which can give valuable information for the use not only of the buyer's sea staff but also the chartering department.

Classification records will give details of the various surveys carried out both for regulatory and damage purposes, which will give a good idea of the vessel's condition and expected performance reliability in service.

A very useful service is provided by Lloyd's Intelligence at Colchester, UK, who, for a nominal fee, will give all reported incidents to any vessel under consideration for purchase.

## 10. COMMERCIAL ASPECTS

Given the cyclic nature of the shipping industry, it is very important that the timing of any shipbuilding contract is judged correctly. When the market is buoyant, shipyard order books are full and the time-span between signing a contract and taking delivery of a new vessel can be three years. This is an almost impossible commercial restriction for any shipowner to be faced with when attempting to arrange a time charter so far in advance.

The question of escalation also rears its ugly head and, in the situation described, shipbuilders either close their order books or insist on an escalation clause, usually related to steel and manpower costs.

In a depressed market the ball game changes completely and the time span between signing contract and accepting delivery can be as short as one year. It is at these times that the speculators move in to sign contracts for ships at about half the cost of that ruling in the buoyant period. Panamax bulkers ordered in 1981 and delivered in 1983 cost around $30m each and probably required a daily charter rate of $16,000 to give a reasonable return on this amount of investment. This type of vessel, if ordered in 1984, could have been obtained for around $18m. Several Panamaxes delivered in 1983 were, in fact, sold by the banks, who had repossessed them, for around $9m "as is where is" in October 1985. Panamax bulkers ordered in 1995 are nearly back at their 1981 cost of $30m.

Such are the vagaries of the sale and purchase market, also the newbuilding market, which are obviously not for the faint-hearted. When the time between contract and delivery is as short as one year it follows that, with the current shipyard capacity available, any but the most unforeseen recovery will be short-lived. If a new vessel has been contracted for with favourable credit or finance terms, it has been found extremely useful to include all additional spare parts, lubricating oil and even bunkers into the first cost if cirumstances allow.

## 11. SUMMARY OF CHAPTER SIX

The approaches which can be made to the various types of charterparties are illustrated. Shipowners, in order to remain competitive, must provide the latest labour-saving devices to assist in reducing crew numbers. Manning costs are the current target for the economists, and management companies are the current fashion for reducing these costs, not forgetting that the ISM code will weed out those operators without sound operational procedures. Owners with large fleets can partially compete by arranging offshore agreements and employing low-cost ratings.

The timing of a shipbuilding contract is important; on balance vessels ordered at peaks in the market would appear to have the tremendous financial disadvantage of never repaying this cost over the vessel's life cycle.

CHAPTER SEVEN

# SAFETY PERFORMANCE

## 1. INTRODUCTION

The safety performance of vessels has in recent times come in for much criticism especially if lives are lost, for example when a passenger ship sinks or catches fire. Bulk carriers have also been in the news lately and their rather high loss rate is a cause for concern by the authorities.

In this chapter we will review various aspects of ship safety and identify those jointly responsible for performance in this crucial area.

## 2. INTERNATIONAL MARITIME ORGANISATION

Safety onboard vessels is regulated by the IMO (International Maritime Organisation) under the SOLAS (Safety of Life at Sea) Convention, which has dealt with all the numerous aspects of marine safety since 1948. The IMO is the United Nations agency charged with this task and its Marine Safety Committee (MSC) has particular responsibility for the technical aspects involved in the following subjects:

- Safety of Navigation
- Radiocommunications
- Life Saving Appliances
- Standards of Training and Watchkeeping
- Carriage of Dangerous Goods
- Ship Design and Equipment
- Fire Protection
- Stability and Load Line and Fishing Vessel Safety
- Containers and Cargo
- Bulk Chemicals
- International Safety Management.

Each of these specialised subjects is separately dealt with by a relevant sub-committee that regularly reports back to the MSC, which then makes periodic amendments to the SOLAS Convention based on the advice received.

The MARPOL Convention will be discussed in Chapter Eight and this essentially anti-pollution IMO Convention does have many safety aspects included, especially those related to oil tanker operations. It is a prerequisite to reducing oil pollution of the sea that a safely run tanker is essential and both Conventions share similar aims in achieving this goal.

For example, serious explosions took place aboard three large tankers several decades ago and led not only to a tragic loss of life but also to pollution of the sea by oil. The cause of these explosions was adjudged to be by electrostatic forces generated by tank washing machines then using seawater at the time. This led first to the introduction of inert gas installations and secondly to Crude Oil Washing (COW). Inert gas is a safety measure controlled by SOLAS and COW is an anti-pollution measure controlled by MARPOL, and their introduction has virtually eliminated the incidence of tanker explosions when cleaning tanks and has also been responsible for a reduction in the build up of sludge within the tanks.

SOLAS and MARPOL are the main IMO Conventions and they are constantly being updated as more operational and constructional problems are analysed and solutions introduced. IMO *per se* does not have the mandate or even the resources to enforce its conventions and this important aspect is left to the governments of member states party to the Conventions, the so-called flag states. The marine departments of these flag states, particularly those from the traditional seafaring nations, are usually well able to enforce the IMO Conventions.

With the emergence of so-called flag of convenience countries, and not forgetting that some countries have not signed the IMO Conventions, it is not always possible for these countries to exercise effective control of their ships to the same extent as that exercised previously by the traditional seafaring countries, and recent incidents have highlighted this shortcoming. To address this problem the IMO introduced what is called Port State Control, whereby surveyors representing the marine departments of member states conduct surveys and inspections on ships flying other flags which enter their ports.

This development in ship safety matters follows certain allegations, in many cases supported by facts, that the conditions found on some flag of convenience vessels were not in accordance with accepted safety standards as laid down in the IMO Conventions. The scope of these Port State Inspections has recently been extended to include operational safety procedures as well as the original inspections, which mainly concerned verification of the relevant certificates and spot checks on items of safety equipment. In the event of serious problems being found during these inspections the vessel will be detained until the attending surveyor is satisfied that the vessel is safe to proceed.

The MSC at the IMO has recently been embroiled in the safety of Ro Ro ferries following the "Herald of Free Enterprise" and "Estonia" disasters. Their main concern is the loss of stability in the event of seawater entering the vehicle decks and the lack of sub-division on these large open spaces allowing the free water to surge unrestricted, leading to sinking or capsize. We could say that the reason the seawater entered the car decks is a separate issue to that of the resultant loss of stability. In the case of the "Herald of Free Enterprise" the crew failed to close the bow doors and various measures, such as closed circuit television cameras, have been introduced to prevent this occurring again.

The "Estonia" incident was apparently the result of the bow doors being torn off by the force of the weather being experienced at the time. The measures taken following this case include a review of the locking arrangements on the doors and spot inspections of the door structure, usually by classification surveyors. The obvious solution to the problem is to avoid the loss of a Ro Ro vessel in the event of water ingress and this is presently being reviewed. In an attempt to improve the situation regarding some of the early Ro Ro ships, buoyancy sponsons were attached to the side shell to improve the damage stability criteria. It is expected that the eventual solution will be the introduction of transverse watertight bulkheads across the vehicle decks, so restricting the water to one area of the vehicle decks rather than the whole length of the decks.

The IMO is the recognised authority on fire safety and it constantly updates SOLAS regulations under the auspices of the Fire Safety Committee, which is responsible for this important aspect of safety performance under the guidance of the MSC. Recent developments in this area mainly concern passenger ship fires such as befell the "Scandinavian Star", allegedly caused by an arsonist. Regulations subsequently formulated include the provision of water sprinklers, smoke detectors, improvement of evacuation signs and in the closing mechanisms of fire doors.

In the case of engine-room fires these are in many cases caused by the leakage of hot fuel oil from defective high pressure pipes onto even hotter surfaces leading to ignition. The solution in this case was the introduction of double sheathed fuel pipes with a leakage alarm system incorporated giving ship's staff early warning of a potentially dangerous situation developing. As will be discussed in Chapter Eight, Halon is not now allowed to be used as a fire extinguishing medium and the use of water mist nozzles has recently been recommended in certain applications, not forgetting that $CO_2$ total flood is still the preferred fire extinguishing system for many.

A recent development at the IMO concerns the International Safety Management Code (ISM) relating to the safe operation of vessels by the ship managers. The code also includes pollution aspects as listed under in the 12 main categories:

1. Safety and Environment Protection Policy Ashore and Afloat
2. Name of Company and Officials with Contact Details
3. Designated Officials to Liaise between Ship and Shore
4. Master's Responsibility Defined
5. Qualifications and Fitness of Personnel
6. Plans of Shipboard Safety Operations

    7. Procedures for Emergency Preparedness
    8. Accident Reports with Analysis
    9. Maintenance of Ship and Equipment
  10. System Documentation
  11. Company Safety Audit
  12. Certificate Verification.

The ISM code is due to enter into force in 1998 but in the case of vulnerable vessels, such as passenger ships and Ro Ro ferries, many organisations, for example the European Union, will apparently bring forward the introduction of ISM to this year (1996).

Radiocommunications are also the responsibility of the IMO and it has recently introduced the Global Marine Distress and Safety System (GMDSS). This system does not require the use of morse code to transmit important information regarding such items as severe weather warnings and major accidents involving ships in the area concerned, and arranges close liaison with coastal stations to speed up help.

It will be seen that the IMO plays a leading role in the introduction of rules and regulations relating to the safe operation of vessels.


## 3. CLASSIFICATION SOCIETIES

The classification of vessels goes back hundreds of years and was originally introduced to give comfort to the owners and insurers of ships and their cargoes that the chosen vessel was itself in good condition and capable of safely delivering the cargo to its destination in a satisfactory condition; and this is basically the situation which exists even today.

Whereas the IMO SOLAS Convention relates to a vessel's safety equipment and operational requirements affecting the safety performance of a vessel and its crew, Classification Societies deal mainly with the constructional aspects of the vessel and its essential machinery. In addition, after a vessel has been built its hull and machinery are inspected by the Classification Societies' surveyors on a predetermined regular basis in order to maintain the vessel in class. There is a certain amount of cooperation between the Classification Societies and the IMO especially in respect of serious incidents, and many of the Classification Societies also carry out safety equipment surveys on behalf of various flag states for essentially logistic reasons.

If any vessel does not retain its classification it would be virtually impossible for it to obtain insurance cover and its future commercial operation would be in serious doubt. There are 11 major Classification Societies who collectively belong to an organisation called IACS (International Association of Classification Societies). IACS periodically issue unified rules and regulations covering the more important aspects of classification. However, at present it would appear unlikely that the Classification Societies will unite in similar fashion to the member states of the IMO.

There is little basic difference between the rules and regulations relating to ships' structures and machinery manufacture of the IACS societies, and these differences are being slowly eroded by the introduction of the unified rules mentioned earlier. Of course the interpretation of certain aspects of the rules is open to abuse during ship inspections by certain Classification surveyors who may be more tolerant than those from other societies. However, this would be difficult to prove and in any case most Classification Societies have legal clauses protecting them from the actions of their surveyors.

Until quite recently it was the practice of some unscrupulous shipowners to engage in a so-called class shopping activity whereby the owner of a vessel found to have a serious structural defect revealed by an astute classification surveyor would shop around until he found a more tolerant surveyor or Classification Society, usually from outside the IACS group. This course of action was of course to save the shipowner money by effecting a cheaper repair to the defect. This class shopping activity has been outlawed by IACS who report back any suspicious requests to the original Classification Society. Outside the IACS group there are many smaller societies whose activities are shrouded in mystery and of course these will take onboard many of the vessels blacklisted by IACS. Most reputable charterers, however, will only engage a vessel classed with an IACS member, although there are, no doubt, many vessels sailing the high seas whose safety gives grounds for concern.

Classification Societies have come in for criticism particularly when vessels are found in poor structural condition and in extreme cases shell plates have been known to become detached from the hull. In these isolated cases the shipowner must take his share of the blame in that ship's staff usually have ample time and opportunity to monitor the condition of their vessel and experienced shore staff also make periodic visits to the vessels under their control primarily to check such matters.

Contrast this to the classification surveyor who only visits a vessel when surveys are due, not forgetting that certain parts of a vessel's structure only require surveying at five-year intervals. Serious deterioration of the steelwork can take place over this rather lengthy period in the usually hostile marine environment. It is the shipowner's responsibility to draw the attention of his Classification Society to any damage or deterioration to the hull or machinery and this is normally a condition for retaining class. It follows that in many cases the shipowner was aware of a serious condition existing aboard one of his vessels but chose not to inform the Classification Society.

In similar fashion to the IMO Conventions, classification rules and regulations are regularly updated especially when repetitive failures or incidents are reported back from field surveyors. Recent examples of this are close up surveys of the internal structure of oil tankers, intermediate surveys of the holds in bulk carriers and the ballast tanks of tankers and bulk carriers, as well as regular inspections of the bow doors of Ro Ro car ferries.

Experience dictated that a five-year interval between surveys of those items mentioned above was inappropriate having regard to the amount of corrosion and mechanical damage likely to be suffered. In the case of large bulk carriers Lloyd's Register issued a booklet to the masters of all bulk carriers classed by them which clearly showed the areas of most concern and an extract is shown in Fig. 23. Lloyd's Register, in an effort to ease the situation, especially for those bulk carriers carrying heavy cargoes such as iron ore, also increased the scantlings and thickness of critical steelwork within the holds. In addition, the so-called corrosion allowance or diminution was reduced in these critical areas. It should be mentioned that both the IMO and a working group from IACS are working on the problems of bulk carriers, in particular their high loss rate from structural failure, which is shown in Fig. 24, courtesy of Lloyd's Register.

The steelwork within the seawater ballast tanks of all vessels is vulnerable to corrosion and in many cases the deterioration of this steelwork has led to the premature scrapping of vessels. Particular areas with high corrosion rates were those cargo holds of bulk carriers and the cargo tanks of pre-MARPOL tankers used for carrying seawater on the ballast voyages. Modern tankers with SBT or double hulls have extremely large capacity dedicated ballast tanks and it is very important that the internal steelwork is protected by a classification-approved paint coating. Access to these spaces should also be given priority so that regular inspections can be made and any breakdown in the coating rectified. Applying a paint coating to bulk carrier holds is counterproductive if cargoes such as iron ore are to be carried. This rather difficult situation is presently being looked at by IACS.

An illustration showing advanced corrosion in an unprotected ballast tank is shown in Fig. 25. It should be mentioned that ballast tank paint coatings have only been introduced into classification rules fairly recently, mainly as a result of such incidents.

Classification Societies used to allow continuous surveys of the hull structure whereby each part of the structure is seen at five-year intervals, but in the case of tankers, bulk carriers and combination carriers this is not now allowed, at least by Lloyd's Register, because of the aforementioned problems. On these vessels it is now necessary to examine vulnerable parts of the structure at each special survey, usually every five years, and also at an intermediate survey nominally at between two and three year intervals. These surveys increase in severity as the vessel's age and corrosion and fatigue problems become more likely.

In the case of machinery surveys, these are still usually carried out on a continuous basis by the majority of owners and it must be said that this arrangement has proved to be satisfactory in that it is unusual for a machinery breakdown to result in complete immobilisation of a well-maintained vessel. So much so that most Classification Societies allow the sailing chief engineer to

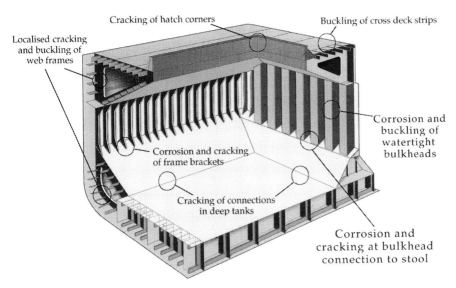

*Fig. 23. Bulk carrier structural problems*

carry out surveys of the machinery on their behalf. A recent development in this area is the introduction of diagnostic techniques to determine the performance of certain items of machinery, for example the use of vibration analysers to check the performance of pumps and compressors whilst running. This arrangement avoids dismantling items of machinery that are working to acceptable performance criteria and prevents the ingress of dirt, always a possibility in the close confines of a ship's engine room.

Boilers and pressure vessels are excluded from the chief engineers' scheme as they have inherent dangers not usually shared by other equipment in the engine room. As a safety measure all items of essential machinery are duplicated and most main diesel propulsion engines can be operated, albeit at reduced output, with one or more cylinders out of action. It is considered that the safety performance of ship's machinery is nowadays quite high.

It will be seen that Classification Societies do have an important part to play in the safety performance of vessels and they are constantly updating their rules and regulations to keep abreast of developments. Some of the recent innovations include the introduction of black box recorders as used in the aircraft industry for many years. These recorders are connected to various strain gauges and accelerometers arranged throughout a vessel's hull and can be used to determine forces being imposed on critical parts of the hull in bad weather at sea or during cargo operations in port. Although the IMO have recommended that owners fit these black box recorders it would appear that very few have actually done so.

In the case of Lloyd's Register, other recent innovations include computerised systems for Hull Condition Monitoring (HCM), Structural Design

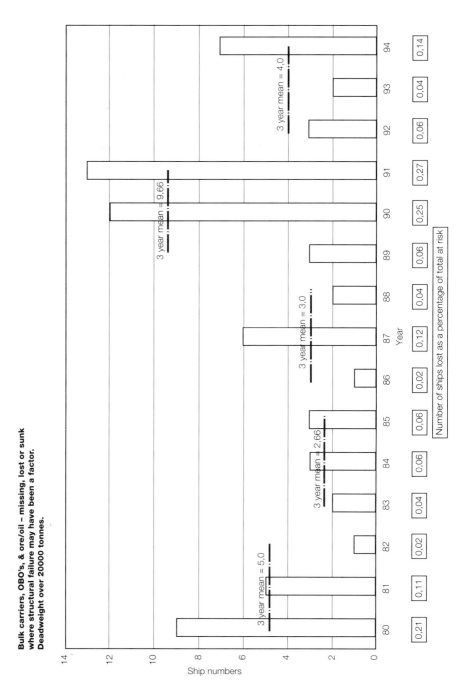

**Fig. 24. Bulk carrier loss rate**

Assessment (SDA), Ship Event Analysis (SEA) and other such aspects, all
included in what is called their "ShipRight" procedure and collectively aimed
at improving the structural safety of vessels.

*Fig. 25.  Corrosion in a double bottom tank*

## 4. SHIPOWNERS

Most shipowners operate their vessels in a safe and efficient manner, which is
not really surprising in view of the capital cost involved and the financial
necessity to maximise a vessel's effective life cycle. However, in certain cases
the reason why many ships are found to be in poor condition is purely for
short-term financial gain due to the owners deferring essential maintenance
when freight rates are low. These same owners then find that when freight rates
are high it is inconvenient to place the ship off hire in order to carry out this
maintenance. Whilst this scenario may not be typical it will strike a chord with
certain owners.

It has been postulated that around 80% of marine accidents are caused by
human error, itself a combination of negligence and poor judgment. The other
20% is composed of structural and machinery failures. We have seen how the
regulatory authorities have concentrated their efforts in their quest for
improved safety. In the case of the Classification Societies we could say that

they are mainly concerned with the structural and machinery aspects of safety and are not therefore directly involved in the majority (80%) of accidents affecting safety.

The IMO and the marine departments of the various flag states are primarily concerned with the design and installation of safety equipment aboard ships, but unlike the Classification Societies they do control the standards and qualifications of the personnel appointed to ships and are therefore concerned with those accidents arising from human error.

In recent years shipowners have been involved in many cost-cutting exercises in order to survive in a very competitive market, and one of the first measures taken was to switch from national flags to flags of convenience. Manning and registry costs can, in some instances, be halved by switching to a flag of convenience, which allows access to low-cost crews from developing nations. Coupled with, but independent of, this flag switch was a reduction in manning levels so that the situation with regard to safety existing aboard many vessels could be described as far from satisfactory.

It was mainly for this reason that the IMO introduced the STCW Convention (Standards of Training Certification and Watchkeeping) in an attempt to improve the calibre and safety consciousness of personnel engaged by owners to serve in their ships, observing that this was sometimes found to be lacking during spot checks. By employing crews of mixed nationalities speaking different languages the situation during an emergency situation could sometimes become extremely serious, especially if passengers speaking a different language to that of the crew were involved, as has in fact happened in several cases.

The ISM Code previously mentioned also has the intent of improving safety by making shipowners, or their managers, aware of their responsibilities with regard to the safe management of vessels under their control. Industry has for many years used a quality management system to qualify for ISO 9000 and some shipowners have already adopted ISO 9000 as a precursor to obtaining documents of compliance and safety management certificates for assessment in respect of the ISM code for both shoreside and seagoing staff.

Many shipowners belong to recognised organisations whose aim is to promote the safe and efficient operation of vessels in their members' fleets. These include INTERTANKO (International Tanker Owners), INTER-CARGO (International Cargo Owners), ICS (International Chamber of Shipping) and many other mainly national shipowning organisations. Most of these are represented at the IMO and they put forward their members' views during regular meetings of the various committees and sub-committees. It would be counterproductive for the IMO to introduce rules and regulations which the industry cannot meet and the major Classification Societies also have shipowner representatives on their technical committees to give constructive advice as to the practicality of introducing new rules.

Until quite recently it was unusual for a shipowner, or a management company employed by him to run his ships, to be prosecuted over a serious incident which had occurred aboard, and ship's staff were usually the only parties implicated if negligence or error of judgment was proved to be the cause. In recent years, however, there is an increasing trend also to apportion blame to ships' managers if they are adjudged to have played a contributory part in the accident, for example if they did not issue laid down procedures to ships' staff for all manner of contingencies.

The adoption of the ISM code will hopefully reduce the number of serious accidents that occur and lead to a safer and more environmentally friendly operation by eliminating those operators whose standards in these respects are considered far from satisfactory.

## 5. SHIP'S STAFF

As previously mentioned, the majority of maritime accidents have been attributed to negligence or human error on the part of ship's staff and it is the captain in his role as the shipowner's representative who has to shoulder the major part of any blame levelled against a ship involved in a serious accident. We could say that it is the activities of ship's staff that should receive priority attention from the regulators after they have made all possible efforts to improve the design and construction of ships in order to make them as safe as possible.

One of the most common accidents at sea is that involving a collision or grounding of a vessel, usually but not always in poor visibility. Most vessels are provided with so-called anti-collision radars and, in recent years, electronic charts. Also many other devices such as satellite navigational instruments and echo sounders are fitted as standard so that all possible means have been provided to avoid such accidents. A recent development is that of the one man on the bridge watchkeeper, which is possible providing certain additional items of a surveillance nature have been installed. At the moment it is not possible to operate with one bridge watchkeeper in the hours of darkness or in periods of poor visibility. Some of the more traditional flag states are not in favour of one man bridge operation, which they see as a retrograde safety step, a view no doubt influenced on account of the high incidence of accidents involving navigational error.

In recent years cases of alcohol and drug abuse have apparently been on the increase and this has led to serious accidents on vessels whose crews have been found guilty of these activities. When the ISM code becomes mandatory it will become compulsory for all safety-sensitive crew members to be regularly tested for alcohol or drug abuse. Every shipowner will then have a drug and alcohol policy document, which must be shown to every employee who must acknowledge acceptance before being accepted for employment. Certain countries, for example the US, already operate a random test regime for alcohol or drug abuse on the crews of visiting ships, especially those which pose a possible environmental danger, for example oil and chemical tankers.

What are referred to as human factors (HF) are becoming popular in most industries, especially those with a potential safety hazard such as in nuclear power generation. It has been proposed that the HF discipline could be extended to the shipping industry and the IMO and IACS are currently looking at the proposal. It is rare for Classification Societies to become involved in purely manning matters but it does make sense that a dialogue should exist between those who design the ship and its equipment and those who operate it.

Peculiar to the shipping industry are the long hours worked by many of the crew members. In the case of watchkeepers this is usually a 56-hour week, comprising seven days, each having two periods of four hour watches to which must be added time worked on essential maintenance. Also, in the case of bridge watchkeepers, it is not unusual for them to work around the clock supervising cargo operations in port and immediately proceed to the bridge, where they would be expected to navigate the vessel from port through the many dangers inherent in such operations. This type of activity is frowned upon by the authorities but no doubt it is still practised by unscrupulous owners and it certainly compromises safety.

Because of reduced levels of manning and the move towards developing nations for the supply of crews it is becoming increasingly difficult to train seagoing personnel for future senior appointments onboard ships. The situation could become more serious when the ISM code is introduced and extended training methods deplete the available supply of new entrants.

Accidents to personnel aboard ships is also an area causing concern in many quarters, not forgetting that a ship can be a very dangerous workplace, and it is important that appropriate safety precautions specifically aimed at seafaring activities are taken. In the case of those serious accidents mentioned earlier, for example the "Estonia" and "Scandinavian Star", many crew member as well as passenger lives were lost. Fires and explosions have also taken many seafarers' lives over the years but it must be said that safety measures taken to avoid such accidents appear to be effective.

Less serious accidents involving personal injury can be reduced by taking certain measures onboard ship by those serving aboard. For example, all UK registered ships must report all accidents involving injury to the Department of Transport, and other traditional seafaring nations have similar schemes, the purpose being to eliminate unsafe practices aboard ship.

UK registered ships also have to appoint a safety committee working under a safety officer who makes his suggestions to improve safety to the captain, acting as chairman of the committee. All accidents aboard ship are analysed by the safety committee and details entered in a safety record book for future analysis by the authorities. This course of action is followed by many traditional seafaring nations.

It must be said that a large number of shipboard accidents are as a result of ships' staff not wearing protective equipment and clothing, for example safety helmets, eye protectors and suitable footwear. Proceeding onto the open deck in bad weather without rigging safety lines and working aloft without a safety harness are other major sources of accidents onboard ship.

Finally, the UK Department of Trade has issued a Code of Safe Working Practices for Merchant Seamen, which covers most of the potential dangers met with by seamen in the course of their duties and it is highly recommended that this useful document is circulated amongst ships' staff.

## 6. SUMMARY OF CHAPTER SEVEN

It is mainly as a consequence of serious accidents that existing safety measures are improved or new measures introduced. Those issues presently under scrutiny in the marine sector are the safety of bulk carriers and Ro Ro ferries and no doubt other issues will arise from time to time. In the case of those vessels just mentioned the eventual solution may result in a fundamental design change.

The majority (80%) of marine accidents involving safety procedures are allegedly caused by human error and the impending introduction of the ISM code will hopefully reduce the number of accidents from this source.

CHAPTER EIGHT

# ENVIRONMENTAL PERFORMANCE

## 1. INTRODUCTION

Environmental issues have long exercised the minds of those who draw up regulations affecting the construction and operation of ocean-going ships. In the first instance, the Safety of Life at Sea, or SOLAS as it is usually referred to, was the regulators' primary concern. Even in these environmentally-sensitive days the safety of a ship and its crew assumes priority over pollution aspects in the event of a serious marine accident. The famous phrase of "pouring oil over troubled waters" was related to the age-old practice of such an operation carried out when abandoning a stricken ship in a raging sea. Technology has progressed and this archaic and rather dubious practice has ceased to be used and it would appear most unlikely that anyone performing this operation would nowadays escape prosecution.

Whilst oil pollution of the sea is still arguably the legislators' prime objective in improving environmental performance, other sources of pollution are being targeted and will also be reviewed.

## 2. OIL POLLUTION

What is referred to as operational pollution from oil tankers was considered to be the major culprit when, in 1954, the first International Conference on Oil Pollution was held in London. This conference was convened to examine all shipboard practices leading to pollution of the sea by oil and led to the introduction of the 1954 Oil Pollution Convention. Legislation has moved forward since this Convention was introduced and in the intervening 40 years, and the International Maritime Organisation (IMO), headquartered in London, now controls the performance of all pollution issues relating to the international seaborne transportation industry.

Environmental issues, usually concentrating on oil pollution, are regulated by what is called the MARPOL Convention. This was first introduced in 1973 and subsequently modified in what is a continuing process as we proceed up the learning curve. To date there are five Annexes to the MARPOL Convention summarised as follows:

- ANNEX I      Oil Pollution
- ANNEX II     Chemical Pollution
- ANNEX III    Harmful Substances in Packaged Form
- ANNEX IV     Sewage
- ANNEX V      Garbage.

There are currently moves afoot to include other environmentally-sensitive issues in the MARPOL Convention, primarily those related to gaseous emissions (discussed later) and possibly also those in the large portfolio of solid cargoes carried aboard bulk carriers, presently excluded from the MARPOL regulations.

Returning now to Annex I this is arguably the most important environmental issue, affecting as it does such horrific oil spillages as the "Torrey Canyon" (March 1967), the "Amoco Cadiz" (March 1978) and the "Exxon Valdez" (March 1989). These incidents are not included under the umbrella of operational pollution mentioned earlier but are classified as accidental discharges, usually following such calamities as a grounding, collision or explosion involving a laden tanker.

It is these accidental discharges that recently received the urgent attention of the IMO and, because of the "Exxon Valdez" incident, the US Government has acted unilaterally in an effort to appease its environmental activists by introducing the OPA 90 (Oil Pollution Act 1990) whose application has far-reaching repercussions.

Sometimes operational oil discharge is caused by crude oil tankers cleaning their cargo tanks at sea and then pumping the oily residues overboard. Included in this category is the pumping overboard of engine room bilges and sludge removed from fuel oil of ever-decreasing quality. A modern tanker built to the latest IMO MARPOL regulations will pump virtually no oil overboard during tank cleaning operations.

This is because the ballast water tanks and the cargo oil tanks are completely segregated in what is called the SBT (Segregated Ballast Tanks) design. Previously, seawater ballast was allowed to be carried in cargo tanks during a ballast voyage in order to immerse the tanker deeper in the water so as to enhance seakeeping qualities. It was the unavoidable mixing of ballast water with the remaining cargo oil and sludge left in the cargo tank after pumping out the oil that was primarily responsible for such terrible oil pollution.

Many beaches bear testimony to the effect that this oil contaminated ballast water had on the environment, and globules of tarry sludge and oil have ruined many articles of beach apparel, leaving bathers covered in an oily mess. What was called the load on top procedure was introduced as a stopgap method of reducing this pollution. It was based on the principle that when discharging the dirty ballast water the pumps were stopped before the really nasty stuff at the bottom of the tank was pumped overboard, and the next cargo simply loaded on top of the residues. As these residues mainly consisted of oil the environment was spared the horrors of their undoubted effect on aquatic life. Owners of tankers built before the introduction of SBT in 1982 were given the choice of either converting them to the SBT design or fitting what is called a Crude Oil Washing (COW) system. Very few owners chose the SBT conversion route because of the large capital cost involved and also the considerable loss of revenue caused by the reduction in cargo carrying space. Those tanks previously used for the alternate carriage of ballast water and cargo oil could not thereafter be used for cargo, which on a VLCC of around 250,000 TDW, could represent a direct loss of 20% in revenue earning space.

By comparison, the majority of owners choosing the COW route lost no cargo space but were still faced with perhaps a $1m cost for retrofitting the COW equipment—a far better solution than the $2m needed for blasting and recoating the internal surfaces of those cargo tanks then designated to carry the more aggressively corrosive ballast water.

The principle involved in COW is based on the fact that crude oil possesses quite good cleaning properties. This is not surprising as crude oil does contain the so-called lighter ends of the barrel, which of course includes petrol and paraffin, for example. By directing jets of crude oil onto the internal structure of a cargo tank whilst it is being discharged, most of the more tenacious ingredients which have settled out of the cargo and deposited themselves on the horizontal surfaces of the tank are discharged along with the cargo.

This has a twofold effect in that it avoids a build-up of sludge on these horizontal surfaces and it ensures that the cargo tank is in a fairly clean condition to receive the ballast water loaded for the return trip to the loading port. By a combination of calculation and measurement, it can be demonstrated that the amount of oil then pumped overboard from properly COW cleaned tanks when the ballast water is being pumped out, is less than 0.0033% of the total oil carried. This is a much improved situation to that existing before the advent of COW, and as previously mentioned this will be completely eliminated when SBT tankers are eventually the only type of tanker allowed. It will take about 10 years before most existing COW tankers are phased out due to their increasing age and, with it, costly repairs.

It has been estimated that the amount of oil entering the seas from operational discharges since COW and SBT have been introduced has been reduced from around 600,000 tonnes in the 1970s to perhaps 60,000 tonnes per year in 1995. This will be further reduced as the COW tankers are progressively scrapped and eventually there should be no pollution from tank cleaning operations.

As already mentioned, engine room bilges and fuel oil sludge are also included under the umbrella of operational discharge. These discharges have also been reduced by a combination of improved performance from filtration and separation equipment, the use of onboard incineration, increased tank storage capacity coupled with improved shoreside reception facilities for these noxious pollutants. It should be mentioned that in special sea areas such as the Mediterranean, Baltic and Black Seas, it is prohibited to discharge any oil whatsoever into the sea.

Returning now to accidental oil discharge, the "Exxon Valdez" incident caused much consternation to the environmental pressure groups, which is not surprising in view of the devastation caused and the deaths of around 400,000 sea birds and 5,000 mammals. Just when the battle against operational pollution was beginning to be hailed as a victory, it was a thorn in the sides of the IMO to see all this good work undone by the "Exxon Valdez" catastrophe. As a direct result of this dreadful accident, it is now more or less mandatory under the MARPOL Convention for all new tankers to be built with a double hull, so minimising the amount of oil escaping in the event of the tanker suffering a grounding or collision.

However, not everyone agrees that a double hull will reduce the amount of accidental oil pollution in the event of a repeat incident such as befell the "Exxon Valdez". For example, it has been postulated that if the "Exxon Valdez" had been provided with a double hull, the amount of oil entering the sea would actually have been much greater and in addition the tanker could have become a total loss. This is based on the probably correct assumption that such was the force of the impact with the reef that the "Exxon Valdez" suffered, it would have pierced both the outer and inner skin. This would have allowed seawater and cargo oil to enter the empty ballast tanks and so impale the vessel further onto the reef and with it a distinct possibility of the vessel capsizing.

Notwithstanding the above, the several alternatives to the double hull tanker have been rejected by the US, although the MARPOL Convention will accept an equivalent design if it can be demonstrated that it offers the same amount of protection as the double hull design. It is doubtful if many owners will go to the trouble of building one of the several alternatives on offer knowing that it will not be acceptable to the US, who, as mentioned earlier, are acting unilaterally on this matter. These alternatives include the mid-deck tanker, coulombi egg tanker and the hydrostatic balanced loading method for existing single hull tankers.

Strenuous efforts to improve safety have been made by introducing vessel separation schemes, improved port control and communications, as well as drug and alcohol testing of ships' personnel. In spite of all these measures a tanker called "Braer" caused massive oil pollution when she went aground off the coast of Scotland in 1993. The cause of the accident was due to a complete loss of power, itself caused by seawater entering the fuel service tanks via an air pipe damaged by an unsecured piece of equipment breaking loose in heavy weather. No doubt other such uncategorised incidents, for example, the "Sea Empress", leading to accidental oil pollution will still occur from time to time.

## 3. CHEMICAL POLLUTION

Annex II of the MARPOL Convention relates to NLS, or Noxious Liquid Substances, invariably referred to as chemicals when carried aboard ships, themselves known as chemical carriers. Whereas oil has only one identifiable pollution hazard profile, chemicals have been allocated four, based on the severity of the probable pollution effect. These are categorised as follows:

A  Highly toxic to aquatic life
B  Moderately toxic to aquatic life
C  Slightly toxic to aquatic life
D  Practically non-toxic to aquatic life.

Dependent on which pollution category the substance to be carried is placed, so the amount allowed to be pumped into the sea is determined. This varies from nil for a category A substance to no practical limit for a category D substance.

An added complication with the seaborne chemical trade is that three ship types are available based on the safety (not environmental) aspect of the chemical being carried. This in turn determines the allowable size of cargo tank and its distance from the outer shell. It does not follow that the most dangerous cargoes (Ship type I) are the most noxious pollutant (category A). Creosote is a case in point; it is in the highest pollution category of A yet can be carried aboard a type III ship having the lowest safety profile.

The pollution aspects of, particularly, new chemicals are constantly under review at the IMO and all incidents involving pollution are monitored so that the regulations can be tightened up if loopholes are revealed. It must be said, however, that large chemical spills are fortunately quite rare and they do not give environmentalists the same sort of ammunition that oil spills invariably do. The reason for this rather good environmental performance is almost certainly due to the expertise of those employed in the chemical trade, coupled with the advanced design characteristics of chemical tankers.

## 4. HARMFUL SUBSTANCES

Annex III relating to harmful substances carried in packaged form aboard ships only entered into force in July 1992 and its impact on the environment has yet to be measured. It is arguably the most difficult Annex to enforce in that dishonest shippers could conceal the true identity of the contents of a package if they so desired. This of course would lead to prosecution if the culprit was ever caught and a recent incident in which a Ro Ro ferry capsized has revealed just such an improper procedure. It must be emphasised that these wrongly described substances played no part in the capsizing of the vessel but pollution of the surrounding sea was invariably compromised.

Many environmentally-damaging substances are shipped in packaged form aboard ships and amongst them could be included PCBs, pesticides and even pharmaceutical poisons. If any of these were allowed to enter the sea in any significant amount a serious environmental incident could quite easily arise. Immediate search and recovery operations for such lost packages are of course very important in view of the difficulties in searching the seabed, or sea surface, from a logistic point of view.

This, and the correct packaging, labelling and description of the goods being shipped from an environmental aspect, are seen by the IMO as the best way forward in improving performance and therefore reducing the likelihood of possible damage to aquatic life from this source.

## 5. SEWAGE

Annex IV on Sewage has not yet entered into force and there would appear to be no compelling need to make it mandatory. Ships in port have for many years been forced by local regulations to have either a sewage treatment plant or retention tank so that sewage is not allowed to enter their waters. There would appear to be very few ships without these facilities and the environmental position is not normally an issue with the various pressure groups.

## 6. GARBAGE

Annex V on Garbage entered into force in December 1988 but it is doubtful if it will materially effect the environment except perhaps for those beaches and coastlines close to a busy shipping route on which the resultant flotsam and jetsam are eventually deposited. One of the main objectives of Annex V was to prohibit the disposal of non-biodegradable material, such as plastic, into the sea under any circumstances. In sheet form plastic was in many instances drawn into the seawater inlets supplying the machinery services of many ships both large and small.

This has caused much damage due to overheated machinery and in severe cases has resulted in complete immobilisation of the ship. Plastic in line or rope form has a propensity of being drawn into propeller shaft seals causing severe damage and even emergency dry docking in some cases. There are regulations included in Annex V which permit disposal overboard of non-plastic garbage subject to it being passed through a grinder if the ship is more than three miles from land, otherwise the ship must be more than 12 miles from land.

In the special areas mentioned earlier, it is not permitted to discharge garbage overboard and seaports located within the special areas have an obligation to arrange regular garbage collection from ships in their ports. This is an attempt to discourage diposal of garbage overboard until the ship has left the special area.

## 7. GASEOUS EMISSIONS

A recent target of environmentalists is the emission of gaseous substances into the atmosphere and the Montreal Protocol of 1987, which entered into force on 1 January 1989, covers such substances, of which many are damaging to the environment. With respect to ozone depletive substances used aboard ships, these are refrigerants containing chlorine (usually Freon) and the fire extinguishing media Halon, both of which are identified as being in this category. Both these substances will be phased out in accordance with the time scale agreed under the Montreal Protocol.

A replacement refrigerant containing much less chlorine than Freon has recently been developed but it is likely to have a rather high unit cost as reflected by its lengthy development. Ammonia and $CO_2$ have also been suggested as replacements for Freon and work is proceeding, although both these gases were in common use before the advent of Freon.

Exhaust gas emissions from main and auxiliary engines will also be defined by future MARPOL regulations. The substances involved are nitrous oxide and sulphur dioxide, which are formed in the combustion process whether the engines be steam or diesel. The technology already exists for reducing nitrous oxide by selective catalytic reduction (SCR) but the process is expensive and labour intensive to operate. Sulphur dioxide can also be removed from the exhaust gas but here again the equipment is rather expensive, and there is a school of thought that it is better to remove the sulphur from the fuel at the refinery rather than aboard a ship. An SCR plant is shown in Fig. 26. Emissions from shipboard incinerators will also be controlled by restricting the type of material allowed to be incinerated having regard to the emissions produced in the process. Fuel oil supplied to ships will also be subject to future MARPOL controls relating to any harmful products they may contain.

Oil and chemical tankers also emit volatile and carcinogenic vapours if the cargoes being loaded also possess these properties. It is becoming increasingly common for harbour authorities to demand vapour return lines when environmentally-damaging substances are being loaded aboard a ship in a port under their jurisdiction. These vapour return lines ensure that no vapours can escape and damage the local environment. IMO is expected to introduce its own regulations regarding vapour return lines in the near future and they are likely to involve shipowners in considerable expense.

All these gaseous emissions are expected to form part of a new Annex VI to the MARPOL Convention in the not too distant future.

## 8. ANTI-FOULING PAINT

A recent study at the Sullom Voe oil terminal off the coast of Scotland has indicated that certain types of molluscs were being poisoned by tin leaching out

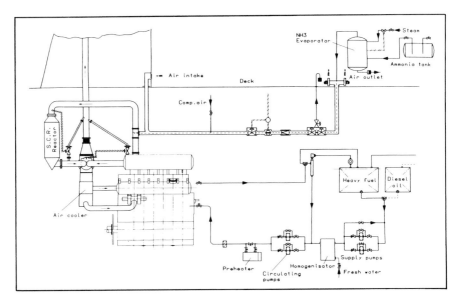

*Fig. 26. Selective catalytic reduction plant (SCR)*

of the anti-fouling paints normally applied to the underwater surfaces of visiting tankers. This tin is in the form of TBT (Tributyltin) and its purpose is to discourage the attachment of molluscs onto the underwater hull of a ship. Such is the toxicity of paint containing TBT that it is obviously attacking non-targeted organisms, in this case the Sullom Voe molluscs.

Other likely sufferers are oyster beds and fish farms in the vicinity of terminals and seaports handling all the various types of ship using this popular underwater paint. This paint owes its popularity to its ability to extend the interval between dry docking and in addition it prevents a fall off in a ship's performance. At present no really satisfactory alternative, giving a similar interval between dry dockings, has been developed but of course it is only a question of time. It is expected that MARPOL will eventually introduce regulations controlling the allowable toxicity of underwater paint applied to ocean-going ships on similar lines to those already adopted by pleasure craft. Several countries, notably Japan, have also banned the use of TBT paint, no doubt to protect the interests of their fishermen.


## 9. SUMMARY OF CHAPTER EIGHT

These then are the main environmental issues being faced by the shipping industry. The "Exxon Valdez" incident has caused much consternation to environmental groups, with atmospheric pollution running a close second. "Exxon Valdez" was only two years old and complied with the most recent

MARPOL regulations, having protectively located SBT and COW in the cargo tanks. The owners were a long-established shipping company flying the US flag employing their own nationals and it was not a so-called flag of convenience operation.

Arguably, the incident would never have happened if the major oil companies serving the Alaskan port of Valdez had not persuaded the local authorities to relax local navigational regulations which governed tanker movements in poor weather conditions and the hours of darkness. These local regulations have, of course, been reintroduced along with many others governing tanker traffic in the area. In spite of this, the regulators have decided that double hulls are now mandatory even though, as previously mentioned, a similar incident could possibly have been even more horrific if a double hull had been provided on the "Exxon Valdez".

Atmospheric pollution in the shipping industry should perhaps be viewed against the vastness of the world's oceans and the extremely insignificant effect ship emissions would have on the overall scheme of things. It is very doubtful if this will sway the regulators when they eventually introduce regulations governing such emissions into the MARPOL Convention.

The shipping industry is not in a particularly good shape at the moment and unlike many other industries it cannot increase the price of its product to meet the expenses involved in future environmental regulations. It has been estimated that a double hull tanker costs about 7% more than a single hull model and even single hull tankers cannot, at present, recoup their financial costs, let alone their running costs. The subject of cost is never even mentioned when the industry regulators hold their regular meeting in their quest for safer and more environmentally friendly ships.

However, it will be seen that the environmental performance of the merchant fleet has vastly improved over the years, due mainly to the efforts of shipowners and the effects the increased regulations have had on the initial cost and subsequent operation of their vessels.

# CHAPTER NINE

# CHARTERPARTY PERFORMANCE CLAIMS

When the freight market is depressed charterparty performance claims abound, especially when the vessels concerned have been fixed at a high rate and the charterers try to retrieve the situation. It can become a little complicated when vessels are sub-chartered and the sub-charterer claims from the head charterer who then claims from the shipowner. Each basic type of charter, bulker and tanker has different approaches to the question of performance claims and these will be reviewed.

## 1. BULK CARRIERS

A large number of bulk carriers are chartered under the New York Produce Exchange form (NYPE) and the latest revision has recently been issued, which is entitled NYPE 1993. This latest version has the following clause relating to performance: "Speed about ... Knots fully laden in good weather conditions up to and including maximum force ... on the Beaufort wind scale, on a consumption of about ... long/metric tons of ...."

It will be seen that the legal interpretation of the word "about" would figure highly in any claim for underperformance. Regarding the vessel's speed, it would appear that "about" has been arbitrated as being within half a knot tolerance. With respect to fuel consumption, it is not widely published what the tolerance is but 3% seems to be a figure frequently used, although cases of 5% have been known.

With regard to the interpretation of good weather this would be for negotiation between owner and charterer but in general terms force 5 is the usual figure included in the space provided on the form. As will be discussed later, owners should be made aware of the penal effect of agreeing too high a Beaufort number or even accepting no restriction on weather, i.e. an all weather situation.

So how are these underperformance claims calculated? If we take a straightforward example to start with, a vessel on a voyage from New Orleans to Rotterdam averaged 11.62 knots on 28 tonnes of heavy fuel oil and 2.2 tonnes of diesel oil per day. The NYPE charterparty speed and consumption was 12.5

knots on 27 tons of heavy fuel oil and two tons of diesel oil. It should be noted that the vessel used metric units of measurement and the NYPE form used imperial units. It is not unknown for American units (short tons) to be used and whilst the differences are small, they must be taken into consideration.

We can start by converting the charterparty figures to metric as under:

27 tons = 27 × 1.01605 = 27.43 tonnes

2 tons = 2 × 1.01605 = 2.03 tonnes

Passage distance = 5,000 nautical miles

Charterparty speed = 12.5 knots − 0.5 allowance = 12 knots

$$\text{Charterparty time} = \frac{5,000}{12} = 416.67 \text{ hours}$$

$$\text{Actual time} = \frac{5,000}{11.62} = 430.29 \text{ hours}$$

Loss of time = 13.62 hours

Hire rate = $2.60

Deadweight = 60,460 tons

$$\text{Hourly hire rate} = \frac{60,460 \times 2.6}{30.4 \times 24} = \$215.45$$

In this case, the average of 30.4 days per month is used, which appears to be standard for time charters of six months or more. In the example under review, the underperformance claim for increased passage time would therefore be:

(1) 13.62 × 215.45 = $2,934.43

We must also consider the additional fuel consumed both by virtue of the increased passage time and, in this particular case, the increased daily consumption over that warranted in the charterparty. This is calculated as follows:

$$\text{Charterparty H.O. consumption (with 0.5 knot and 3\% fuel)} = \frac{5,000}{12 \times 24} \times 27.43 \times 1.03$$
$$= 490.50 \text{ tonnes}$$

$$\text{Actual consumption} = \frac{430.29}{24} \times 28 = 502 \text{ tonnes}$$

(2) Additional fuel consumption = 11.5 tonnes

The same applies for diesel oil and in this particular example would be:

$$\text{Charterparty D.O. consumption (with 0.5 knot and 3\% diesel)} = \frac{5,000}{12 \times 24} \times 2.03 \times 1.03$$
$$= 36.3 \text{ tonnes}$$

$$\text{Actual diesel consumption} = \frac{430.29}{24} \times 2.2 = 39.44 \text{ tonnes}$$

(3) Additional diesel consumption = 3.14 tonnes

One further point we should take into account is a refund on brokerage relating to the time element only. We are now in a position to calculate this claim and we will assume the brokerage was 3.75% of the cost of heavy oil at $100 and of diesel oil at $150 per tonne. The calculation will then become:

|  |  | $ |
|---|---|---|
| (1) | Excess hire | 2,934.43 |
|  | 3.75% address commission | (110.04) |
| (2) | Excess heavy oil 11.5 × $100 | 1,150.00 |
| (3) | Excess diesel oil 3.14 × $150 | 471.00 |
|  | *Total* | $4,445.39 underperformed |

This example describes what might be called a typical case of a Panamax bulker bringing a cargo of grain from New Orleans to Rotterdam. It would be extremely unlikely that a passage of this nature would be performed in good weather conditions as described in the NYPE charterparty. We must, therefore, adjust the above claim by including some heavy weather and, in order to explain the procedure fully, an abstract covering the voyage in question is shown in Table 12.

### Table 12. Passage summary—all weather

| Date | Distance | Time | Speed | Wind force | RPM | H.O. | D.O. | Remarks |
|---|---|---|---|---|---|---|---|---|
| 1.10.95 | 292 | 24.00 | 12.17 | 2 | 93.2 | 28.0 | 2.44 | |
| 2.10.95 | 287 | 24.00 | 11.96 | 3 | 93.1 | 28.0 | 2.2 | |
| 3.10.95 | 299 | 24.00 | 12.46 | 3 | 94.1 | 28.0 | 2.2 | |
| 4.10.95 | 237 | 24.00 | 9.87 | 7 | 90.6 | 27.5 | 2.2 | |
| 5.10.95 | 238 | 24.00 | 9.92 | 7 | 90.5 | 27.5 | 2.2 | |
| 6.10.95 | 242 | 24.00 | 10.08 | 5 | 91.2 | 27.5 | 2.2 | |
| 7.10.95 | 252 | 24.00 | 10.50 | 5 | 93.1 | 28.0 | 2.2 | |
| 8.10.95 | 293 | 23.00 | 12.74 | 3 | 93.8 | 27.0 | 2.2 | Clocks advanced |
| 9.10.95 | 285 | 23.00 | 12.39 | 2 | 92.7 | 27.0 | 2.0 | Clocks advanced |
| 10.10.95 | 298 | 23.00 | 12.96 | 1 | 93.4 | 27.0 | 2.0 | Clocks advanced |
| 11.10.95 | 282 | 23.00 | 12.26 | 4 | 93.1 | 27.0 | 2.0 | Clocks advanced |
| 12.10.95 | 294 | 23.00 | 12.78 | 4 | 93.6 | 27.0 | 2.0 | Clocks advanced |
| 13.10.95 | 271 | 23.00 | 11.78 | 5 | 92.4 | 26.5 | 2.0 | Clocks advanced |
| 14.10.95 | 259 | 24.00 | 10.79 | 6 | 91.8 | 27.5 | 2.2 | |
| 15.10.95 | 301 | 24.00 | 12.54 | 4 | 92.7 | 28.5 | 2.2 | |
| 16.10.95 | 253 | 24.00 | 10.54 | 6 | 91.3 | 28.0 | 2.2 | |
| 17.10.95 | 272 | 24.00 | 11.33 | 5 | 91.7 | 28.0 | 2.2 | |
| 18.10.95 | 292 | 24.00 | 12.17 | 4 | 93.1 | 28.5 | 2.2 | |
| 19.10.95 | 53 | 4.18 | 12.32 | 4 | 93.4 | 5.5 | 0.6 | |
| Totals | 5,000 | 430.18 | | | | 502 | 39.44 | |
| Averages | | | 11.62 | | 92.8 | 28.0 | 2.20 | |

This is the complete voyage showing every day's performance, and we can show the fairweather figures by eliminating those days during which the average wind force exceeded Beaufort 4 as follows:

Returning now to the all weather calculation, we can substitute the fairweather averages as indicated below.

### Table 13. Passage summary—fairweather

| Date | Distance | Time | Speed | Wind force | RPM | H.O. | D.O. | Remarks |
|---|---|---|---|---|---|---|---|---|
| 1.10.95 | 292 | 24.00 | 12.17 | 2 | 93.2 | 28.0 | 2.44 | |
| 2.10.95 | 287 | 24.00 | 11.96 | 3 | 93.1 | 28.0 | 2.2 | |
| 3.10.95 | 299 | 24.00 | 12.46 | 3 | 94.1 | 28.0 | 2.2 | |
| 8.10.95 | 293 | 23.00 | 12.74 | 3 | 93.8 | 27.0 | 2.2 | |
| 9.10.95 | 285 | 23.00 | 12.39 | 2 | 92.7 | 27.0 | 2.0 | |
| 10.10.95 | 298 | 23.00 | 12.96 | 1 | 93.4 | 27.0 | 2.0 | |
| 11.10.95 | 282 | 23.00 | 12.26 | 4 | 93.1 | 27.0 | 2.0 | |
| 12.10.95 | 294 | 23.00 | 12.78 | 4 | 93.6 | 27.0 | 2.0 | |
| 15.10.95 | 301 | 24.00 | 12.54 | 4 | 92.7 | 28.5 | 2.2 | |
| 18.10.95 | 292 | 24.00 | 12.17 | 4 | 93.1 | 28.5 | 2.2 | |
| 19.10.95 | 53 | 4.18 | 12.32 | 4 | 93.4 | 5.5 | 0.6 | |
| Totals | 2,976 | 239.18 | | | 93.4 | 281.5 | 21.04 | |
| Averages | | | 12.44 | | | 28.23 | 2.11 | |

Actually, there is another factor to be taken into account based on arbitrations, which effectively means that if a vessel is underperforming in fairweather it would similarly underperform in heavy weather. We must, therefore, apply the average fairweather performance to the whole voyage. As it happens, the example we have chosen does not clearly indicate this point, as the vessel was overperforming in fairweather. However, we will calculate the performance claim just to illustrate how it is done:

$$\text{Fairweather time} = \frac{5,000}{12.44} = 401.93 \text{ hours}$$

$$\text{Charterparty time} = \frac{5,000}{12} = 416.67 \text{ hours (as original)}$$

Using the ½ knot tolerance, the vessel clearly overperformed and no claim would arise with respect to time lost.

The H.O. fuel consumption will also be calculated:

$$\text{Fairweather consumption} = \frac{401.93}{24} \times 28.23 = 472.77 \text{ tonnes}$$

Charterparty consumption = 490.50 tonnes (as original)

The vessel clearly underconsumed H.O. and no claim would be forthcoming from charterers. In the event of the loss of time being considerable it can be offset by savings in fuel consumption, but this is clearly not the case here.

D.O. will likewise be calculated:

$$\text{Fairweather consumption} = \frac{401.93}{24} \times 2.11 = 35.33 \text{ tonnes}$$

Charterparty consumption = 36.3 tonnes

Again, the vessel underconsumed and no claim would be expected.

It will be seen that by applying the good weather clause, an underperformance claim of $4,445.39 can be reduced to nothing.

As a point of interest, we can calculate the amount of underperformance if no good weather clause was used nor were the ½ knot and 3% tolerances applied:

Charterparty time $= \dfrac{5,000}{24}$ 400 hours

Actual time = 430.29 hours

(1) Loss of time = 30.29 hours

Charterparty H.O. consumption $= \dfrac{5,000}{12.5 \times 24} \times 27.43 = 457.17$ tonnes

Actual H.O. consumption = 502.00 tonnes

(2) Additional H.O. consumption = 44.83 tonnes

Charterparty D.O. consumption $= \dfrac{5,000}{12.5 \times 24} \times 2.03 = 33.83$ tonnes

Actual D.O. consumption = 39.44 tonnes

(3) Additional D.O. consumption = 5.61 tonnes

The calculation then becomes:

| | | |
|---|---|---|
| (a) Excess hire 30.29 × 215.45 | = | $6,525.98 |
| 3.75% address commission | = | ($244.72) |
| (b) Excess heavy oil 44.83 × $100 | = | $4,483.00 |
| (c) Excess diesel oil 5.61 × $150 | = | 841.50 |
| Total | | $11,605.76 |

We can now examine what all this means in terms of charterparty clauses and its effect on the shipowner using the voyage described earlier as the basis in Table 14.

**Table 14. Summary of charterparty clauses**

| Summary of clauses | Fuel costs $ | Daily hire $ | Under-performance claim $ | Cost/day $ |
|---|---|---|---|---|
| All weather, no speed or speed allowances | 100/150 | 5,170 | 11,605.76 | 647 |
| All weather, half knot and 3% fuel allowance | 100/150 | 5,170 | 4,445.39 | 248 |
| Good weather, half knot and 3% fuel allowance | 100/150 | 5,170 | Nil | Nil |

Should fuel costs have been at their early 1980s level the situation would, of course, have been much worse. If, as sometimes happens, shipowners are obliged to accept an all weather clause and/or guaranteed speeds and consumptions it will serve as a reminder of what sort of claims they are liable for. The highest underperformance claim under an all weather clause seen by the author in recent years amounted to $67,152 on a single voyage—Australia to Europe. Should the shipowner have had the benefit of a good weather clause there would have been no underperformance claim, as the vessel was within the warranted figures. Instead, a claim amounting to $1,160 per day had to be settled by the owner.

On occasions, a voyage may be performed at two distinct speed settings at charterers' instructions, and the calculations should be on the basis of two separate voyages, not on the average of the whole. Should more than two speed settings be used, it may be in the shipowner's favour to discount this voyage.

On other occasions vessels are asked by charterers to perform the voyage at a fuel consumption figure between those specified in the charterparty. The underperformance claim is then submitted at a fuel consumption specified in the charterparty. This is a potentially dangerous situation in financial terms, and an example of how the unsuspecting shipowner can incur a penalty is given.

Charterparty warranted performance:

13 knots on 48 H.O. × 2.0 D.O.
12 knots on 38 H.O. × 2.0 D.O.
Actual fairweather average: 11.44 knots on 43.3 H.O. × 1.2 D.O.

As will be seen, this is between two consumption settings.

The voyage in question was 5,597 miles and the hire rate was $288 per hour and fuel costs $182/$250, which were typical at the time in question. Charterers chose the 38 T/D performance to calculate the claim.

**Charterers' calculations**

$$\text{C/P time} = \frac{5,597}{11.5} \times 486.7 \text{ hours}$$

$$\text{Actual time} = \frac{5,597}{11.44} = 489.2 \text{ hours}$$

(1) Excess = 2.5 hours

$$\text{C/P H.O.} = \frac{486.7}{24} \times 38 \times 1.03 = 793.8 \text{ tonnes}$$

$$\text{Actual H.O.} = \frac{489.2}{24} \times 43.3 = 882.6 \text{ tonnes}$$

(2) Excess = 88.9 tonnes

$$\text{C/P D.O.} = \frac{486.7}{24} \times 2.0 = 40.6 \text{ tonnes}$$

$$\text{Actual D.O.} = \frac{489.2}{24} \times 1.2 = 24.5 \text{ tonnes}$$

(3) D.O. savings = 16.1 tonnes

| | | |
|---|---|---|
| (a) 2.5 × $288 | = | $720 |
| Commission | = | ($27) |
| (b) 88.9 × $182 | = | $16,180 |
| (c) 16.1 × $250 | = | ($4,025) |
| Net underperformance | = | $12,848 |

**Owners' calculations**

Fairweather average 11.44 on 43.3/11.2, corrected for 38 T/D using cube law:

$$\sqrt[3]{\frac{11.44^3 \times 38}{43.3}} = 10.95 \text{ knots}$$

C/P time = 486.7 hours

Actual time $= \dfrac{5,597}{10.95} = 511.1$ hours

   (1) Excess = 24.4 hours

C/P H.O. = 793.7 tonnes

Actual H.O. $= \dfrac{511.1}{24} \times 38 \times 1.03 = 833.5$ tonnes

   (2) Excess = 39.8 tonnes

C/P D.O. = 40.6 tonnes

Actual D.O. $= \dfrac{511.1}{24} \times 1.2 = 25.5$ tonnes

   (3) D.O. savings 15.1 tonnes

| | | |
|---|---|---|
| (a) 24.4 × $288 | = | $7,027 |
| Commission | = | ($261) |
| (b) 39.8 × $182 | = | $7,244 |
| (c) 15.1 × $250 | = | ($3,775) |
| Net underperformance | = | $10,235 |

This represented a saving to owners of $2,613 for a single voyage. It will be noted that no allowance was used on the diesel oil consumption which is normal when overperforming. It should also be noted that at the time in question the fuel costs were extremely high.

If only one speed and consumption are stated in the charterparty it would be most unusual for charterers to make an underperformance claim if they instructed the voyage be performed at a somewhat lower speed than that stated in the charterparty. Some charterparties, when giving additional speeds and consumptions, qualify the figures by stating that they are not guaranteed.

The effects of ocean currents are sometimes taken into account, depending on the voyages under consideration. For example, if repetitive transatlantic or Pacific voyages are under consideration, it would be reasonable to assume that they would cancel each other out.

However, if we take the trading pattern of a typical Panamax bulker, which could be Rotterdam–Newport News–Japan–Australia–Rotterdam, there is a definite disadvantage to shipowners. Westbound ocean passages in the Northern hemisphere are invariably adverse and the Australia–Europe portion generally likewise, leaving only the Japan–Australia sector as being generally favourable. This should be taken into account, especially if the vessel performs favourably on the Japan–Australia sector, but not on the other sectors.

Ocean currents can be estimated using ocean routeing charts, the weather routeing services or by relying on ships' staff to fill in a suitably designed log abstract, as mentioned in earlier chapters.

Ships' staff have to be encouraged to fill in these abstracts faithfully. In an actual case, the speed of a new vessel dropped by nearly two knots for a single day's entry without any explanation. This brought the performance into the penalty area and immediate enquiries revealed that a two knot current had been encountered without it being recorded in the log abstract then in use, which was not designed to record currents.

If we take a quite simple example of how one day's wind force entered incorrectly can effect the bottom line, we can go back to the example shown in Table 13.

Say that in the entry for 12 October the wind force had been entered as force 5 instead of force 4, the revised fairweather averages would be:

    12.40 knots     28.24 tonnes H.O.     2.11 tonnes D.O.

instead of:

    12.44 knots     28.23 tonnes H.O.     2.11 tonnes D.O.

Although the difference appears quite small, it would add about \$400 to the underperformance claim had the vessel been performing below warranted figures. This emphasises the need for extreme care when filling in abstracts, and it is all too often left to the second mate to attend to this most important task.

It is generally accepted that weather conditions calculated are on an average daily basis, even though weather conditions can change several times throughout the day. In the event of a dispute arising leading to an arbitration it is possible that deck log books could be produced and lesser periods than a day taken into account.

The latest NYPE charterparty gives protection to owners in the event of poor quality fuel being supplied by charterers as spelt out in clause 9(b):

"The Charterers shall supply bunkers of a quality suitable for burning in the Vessel's engines and auxiliaries and which conform to the specification(s) as set out in Appendix A.

The Owners reserve their right to make a claim against the Charterers for any damage to the main engines or the auxiliaries caused by the use of unsuitable fuels or fuels not complying with the agreed specification(s). Additionally, if bunker fuels supplied do not conform with the mutually agreed specification(s) or otherwise prove unsuitable for burning in the Vessel's engines or auxiliaries, the Owners shall not be held responsible for any reduction in the Vessel's speed performance and/or increased bunker consumption, nor for any time lost and any other consequences."

Readers' attention is drawn to the BIMCO fuel quality clause, mentioned in Chapter Three, which covers the question of poor quality bunkers.


## 2. GALLEY FUEL

Galley fuel and fuel used for crew purposes is not included in NYPE 1993 (charterparty) and charterers now pay for this fuel unless otherwise included in an additional clause. This fuel has been the subject of much discussion over the years culminating in the Court of Appeal judgment in 1986 over the "Sounion" case. For the benefit of owners who are still operating their vessels under a charterparty clause in which they pay for this fuel, the following will be of interest. The amount of fuel used for galley and crew purposes is rather difficult to calculate and the costs involved rather small.

The calculations have been further complicated by the now standard application of energy conservation measures employed in the generation of electrical power onboard modern vessels. These range from the use of blended or heavy fuel in conventional diesel alternators to steam turbo-alternators by which all electrical energy is supplied free when full steaming and partially when operating at reduced output (slow steaming).

The first step in applying a technical approach is to calculate the electrical load used for crew purposes which will, of course, vary from vessel to vessel depending on the capacity of the varied equipment installed.

A calculation carried out by the author taking into account loading, demand and diversity indicated that on a typical vessel the following electrical loads for crew purposes would be considered reasonable:

|                            | kW |
|----------------------------|----|
| Galley stove               | 5  |
| Condensing water           | 4  |
| Lighting, etc              | 6  |
| Refrigeration              | 4  |
| Air conditioning/heating   | 7  |
| Total                      | 26 |

We know that a modern diesel alternator has a specific fuel consumption of around 215 g/kW/hour when burning diesel oil and we can easily calculate that 1 kW is equal to $215 \times 24 = 5,160$ g/day or 0.00516 tonnes per day. So, if our typical vessel has an electrical load of 26 kW we can say that this is equal to 0.134 tonnes of diesel oil per day or $30.4 \times 0.134 = 4$ tonnes per month.

As previously mentioned, however, the generation of electrical power using diesel alternators burning diesel oil is now rarely used except for older vessels, which still have to be catered for in our calculations.

When using blended or heavy fuel the specific fuel consumption will increase due to the lower heat content of these inferior fuels. We can calculate that the daily fuel consumptions would be 0.139 and 0.142 tonnes per day respectively when using these fuels. In the case of a power take off we must use the specific fuel consumption of a modern Main Engine currently around 174 g/kW/hour or 0.109 tonnes heavy oil per day.

It should be mentioned that the actual heat in accommodation heating systems and also in freshwater evaporators is, in many instances, part of a heat recovery system and the electrical energy used is simply for ancillary circulation duties.

We now have to convert the electrical energy into money and a summary of the various alternatives is shown in Table 15.

In the case of the turbo-alternator slow steaming option it is assumed that the shortfall in electrical output is made up by a diesel alternator running on blended fuel. Not included in the table is the power turbine option, which in a suitably designed system could be treated in similar fashion to the turbo-alternator scheme. Fuel costs shown are applicable at the time of writing but

*Table 15. Galley fuel cost table*

| Power generation source | Fuel in use | Cost per tonne | Fuel per day | Monthly cost $ |
|---|---|---|---|---|
| Diesel alternator | D.O. | 150 | 0.134 | 611 |
| Diesel alternator | D.O./H.O. blend | 125 | 0.139 | 528 |
| Diesel alternator | H.O. | 100 | 0.142 | 431 |
| Power take off | H.O. | 100 | 0.109 | 331 |
| Turbo-alternator full steaming | — | — | — | — |
| Turbo-alternator slow steaming | D.O./H.O. blend | 125 | 0.100 | 380 |

such is the unpredictability of the bunker market that ruling costs could be somewhat different. Even so it is comparatively easy for the reader to insert the relevant H.O. or D.O. costs into the calculation.

## 3. HOLD CLEANING

It has been found that the fuel consumed when cleaning holds is rarely apportioned correctly. Normally, it is simply included in the diesel oil consumed by the generator. By rights it should be entered separately, and not included in any performance calculation when a vessel is time chartered. The amount involved is quite small, but it can be used to offset that claimed by charterers for galley fuel. An investigation by the author revealed that the hold cleaning kW consumption per ballast voyage amounted to 4,800. If we assume a 60-day round trip the hourly rate would be 3.33 kW, which with diesel oil at $150 per tonne amounts to $78 per month.

## 4. TANKERS

Unlike bulk carriers, who generally seem to favour the NYPE charterparty form, tankers have a whole selection to choose from. Each of the oil majors has its own forms, which are revised regularly, so we have a situation whereby Shelltime 3 or Texacotime 2 may be the form in use.

From the performance point of view, the main difference is that the word "about" is not used in the standard versions of the forms when referring to speed and consumption. Neither is there a reference to good weather conditions—it usually being spelled out as a certain Beaufort number. Shelltime 4 has a particularly severe weather clause which reads: "excluding . . . (II) any days, noon to noon, when winds exceed force 8 on the Beaufort Scale for more than 12 hours."

So the benefits normally expected when using the NYPE form, namely half knot tolerance on speed, 3% on fuel consumption, and weather conditions above force 4 excluded, cannot be taken for granted, and will not be allowed unless specifically stated.

Some of the standard tanker charterparty forms do, however, have a clause allowing owners to receive a bonus in the event of the vessel overperforming against the warranted speed and consumption.

As far as is known there is no agreed method of calculating an underperformance claim when a proportion of the voyage is spent in heavy weather; always assuming a separate weather clause has been added to the charterparty. On occasions it has been known for it to be spelled out on the lines described for the NYPE form which, readers may recall, is based on a principle that if a vessel underperforms in good weather it will similarly underperform in heavy weather. However, by not using this principle a difference does arise when making the calculations comparing NYPE with a standard tanker form.

If we go back to the previous example for the Panamax bulker the performance figures under the NYPE calculation were: 12.44 knots on 28.23/2.11 in good weather.

We will increase the charterparty speed to 13 knots to enable a quantitative result to be given, because the vessel was overperforming when applying the original NYPE calculation.

**NYPE revised calculation**

$$\text{Fairweather time} = \frac{5,000}{12.44} = 401.93 \text{ hours}$$

$$\text{C/P time} = \frac{5,000}{13} \times 384.61 \text{ hours}$$

(1) Time lost = 17.32 hours

$$\text{Fairweather H.O.} = \frac{401.93}{24} \times 28.23 = 472.77 \text{ tonnes}$$

$$\text{C/P H.O.} = \frac{5,000}{13 \times 24} \times 27.43 \times 1.03 = 452.77 \text{ tonnes}$$

(2) Excess H.O. = 20 tonnes

$$\text{Fairweather D.O.} = \frac{401.93}{24} \times 2.11 \times 1.03 = 36.40 \text{ tonnes}$$

$$\text{C/P D.O.} = \frac{5,000}{13 \times 24} \times 2.03 \times 1.03 = 33.50 \text{ tonnes}$$

(3) Excess D.O. = 2.9 tonnes

| | | |
|---|---|---|
| (a) Excess hire 17.32 × 215.45 | = $3,731.59 | |
| Commission | = ($139.93) | |
| (b) Excess H.O. 20 × $100 | = $2,000 | |
| (c) Excess D.O. 2.9 × $150 | = $435 | |
| Total | = $6,026.66 | underperformed |

**Typical tanker calculation**

$$\text{Fairweather time} = \frac{2,976}{12.44} = 239.30 \text{ hours (from log)}$$

$$\text{C/P time} = \frac{2,976}{13} = 228.92 \text{ hours}$$

(1) Time lost = 10.31 hours

Fairweather H.O. $= \dfrac{239.3}{24} \times 28.23 = 281.5$ tonnes (from log)

C/P H.O. $= \dfrac{239.3}{24} \times 27.43 = 273.5$ tonnes

(2) Excess H.O. = 8 tonnes

Fairweather D.O. $= \dfrac{239.3}{24} \times 2.11 = 23.04$ tonnes

C/P D.O. $= \dfrac{239.3}{24} \times 2.03 = 20.24$ tonnes

(3) Excess D.O. = 2.80 tonnes

| | | |
|---|---|---|
| (a) Excess hire 10.31 × 215.45 | = | $2,221.29 |
| Commission | = | ($83.30) |
| (b) Excess H.O. 8 × $100 | = | $800 |
| (c) Excess D.O. 2.8 × $150 | = | $420 |
| *Total* | = | $3,357.99 underperformed |

This illustrates that, by and large, a typical tanker charterparty underperformance claim when taking heavy weather into account is not as disadvantageous to owners as the NYPE heavy weather calculation. Some dry bulk charterers actually work out the result according to the tanker calculation and then multiply it by a Total Mileage Factor in the ratio:

$$\frac{\text{Total mileage}}{\text{Fairweather mileage}} = \frac{5,000}{2,976} = 1.68$$

This will then give a result according to the NYPE routes—not forgetting that the 3% allowance is not given in a typical tanker claim.

### 5. SUMMARY OF CHAPTER NINE

Underperformance claims should be thoroughly checked by owners using the points made in this chapter. The risk in accepting an all weather clause should be fully appreciated by all those involved. It is to be hoped that the question of galley fuel is now understood from a technical viewpoint. Tankers have their own charterparty forms, each having quite different clauses. Owners should realise what the significance of some of these clauses means with respect to underperformance and any subsequent claim.

# CHAPTER TEN

# COMPUTER APPLICATION

## 1. INTRODUCTION

In previous chapters we have read about performance monitoring and charterparty performance, both of which are ideal candidates for computer programs. There are many programs available on the market at varying levels of sophistication and, of course, cost. When deciding what program is best suited, it should be remembered that whatever is entered must, of course, be recorded on board. This will probably mean redesigning the logs and abstracts to make them computer friendly.

Another fundamental decision will be whether to provide a computer aboard the vessel or to have it based in the shipowner's office. A lot will depend on whether a computer is already provided aboard to perform other functions such as planned maintenance, inventory control or other subjects.

Most vessels already have a dedicated computer for carrying out loading calculations and one solution, especially with older vessels requiring this instrument to be renewed, is to replace it with a standard computer, thereby giving access to a host of programs, including of course loading calculations.

Probably all shipowners' offices have computers performing a variety of tasks related to payroll and accounts; the additional programs covered in this chapter would cause no problems.

## 2. COMPUTER REQUIRED

The author has favoured a personal computer for carrying out tasks related to ship performance, and this has been found adequate for dealing with over 70 ships on a hard disc. It covers such subjects as voyage printouts, which replace the abstract, charterparty calculations and main engine performance with many other programs possible depending on the extent of the raw data entered. It would be possible to use a larger mini computer, but to keep the cost at a reasonable level the choice of a modern personal computer is considered the best solution.

### 3. DATA INPUT

The computer can only analyse whatever data is entered, and it is important to spend some time deciding the exact amount of data necessary. This will depend on the shipowner's requirements; for example, does he have the trained staff necessary to carry out this duty?

Regarding what might be called a typical abstract, we can assume all the normal information is required; this will include a distance steamed, time, fuel consumption, kW loading and the like. In order to carry out a more detailed analysis of a vessel's performance, we should also consider other important parameters, most of which were touched on in Chapter Four.

When considering computer application only digital entries are suitable in the type of computer we are considering, so everything must be reduced to a digital entry and any analogue descriptions which may have been previously used must be converted to digital. This was the main purpose of converting weather conditions to digital as discussed in Chapter Four.

The format eventually decided on by the author is illustrated in Fig. 27.

Starting with the heading we have ship's name, sailing port and arrival port, with dates and voyage number.

Each day's entry comprises:

*Page one*
Date
Latitude
Longitude
Course steered
Wind force/direction (sector)
Swell force/direction (sector)
Current speed/direction (sector)
Distance—over ground
Distance—log
Pitch/roll
Deck wetness
Time
Speed (calculated by program)
RPM
Slip (calculated by program)


*Page two*

| *Heavy oil consumption* | Main Engine |
| | Cargo heating |
| | Tank cleaning |
| | Turbo-alternator |
| | Diesel alternator |
| | Total   (calculated) |

| *Diesel oil consumption* | Diesel alternator (propulsion) |
| | Diesel alternator (other) |
| | Main Engine |
| | Total   (calculated) |

*Electrical load kW*     Turbo-alternator
                         Diesel alternator
                         Total    (calculated)

It will be seen that for each day's entry there are a maximum of 27 entries if all possibilities are used. This is extremely unlikely, and the average in general use is around 21.

From this wealth of information we can cater for a comprehensive range of programs, which will be discussed later in the chapter. The only important parameter not allowed for in this program is brake horsepower, and for vessels fitted with a torsionmeter, a slight modification would be required to enable the torque reading to be entered.

A brief comment will be made on each of the entries, giving the reason why they have been included.

Ship Name
NOLA                                                    ROTTERDAM                                              0012L 10/05/95 28/05/95
Mask:                    Beaufort No.:  0               Current Speed:  0              Swell Force:  0          Pitch/Roll:  0

Page 1

| date | Lattitude Deg Min | Longitude Deg Min | C/S Deg | Wind S Bn | Swell S For | Curr. S Spd | Dist O.G. | Dist Log | Pitc Roll | Deck Wet | Time Hours | Speed Knots | RPM | Slip % |
|---|---|---|---|---|---|---|---|---|---|---|---|---|---|---|
| 10/05/95 | 27 29 N | 87 35 W | V | 2 5 | 2 2 | 0 0 | 138 | 138 | 2 | 1 | 12.3 | 11.22 | 55.7 | 5.38 |
| 11/05/95 | 24 30 N | 83 23 W | 128 | 1 4 | 1 2 | 4 15 | 290 | 263 | 2 | 1 | 24.0 | 12.08 | 58.0 | 2.14 |
| 12/05/95 | 26 51 N | 79 37 W | V | 8 3 | 6 2 | 8 15 | 308 | 260 | 2 | 1 | 24.0 | 12.83 | 57.2 | −5.39 |
| 13/05/95 | 31 0 N | 78 19 W | V | 1 5 | 3 2 | 8 10 | 259 | 251 | 4 | 1 | 23.0 | 11.26 | 57.4 | 7.84 |
| 14/05/95 | 34 59 N | 74 35 W | V | 5 3 | 5 2 | 8 20 | 309 | 263 | 4 | 1 | 24.0 | 12.88 | 57.6 | −5.00 |
| 15/05/95 | 37 52 N | 70 0 W | V | 8 4 | 8 5 | 8 18 | 289 | 247 | 4 | 2 | 24.0 | 12.04 | 58.7 | 3.64 |
| 16/05/95 | 38 56 N | 63 54 W | V | 8 6 | 8 5 | 8 25 | 298 | 227 | 4 | 2 | 24.0 | 12.42 | 57.9 | −0.74 |
| 17/05/95 | 39 34 N | 58 22 W | V | 5 5 | 7 5 | 0 0 | 266 | 236 | 4 | 1 | 23.0 | 11.57 | 57.4 | 5.35 |
| 18/05/95 | 40 14 N | 53 18 W | V | 5 8 | 5 8 | 0 0 | 238 | 237 | 5 | 4 | 24.0 | 9.92 | 57.5 | 18.99 |
| 19/05/95 | 40 42 N | 48 15 W | V | 5 8 | 5 8 | 0 0 | 244 | 233 | 5 | 4 | 24.0 | 10.17 | 57.7 | 17.23 |
| 20/05/95 | 42 26 N | 43 11 W | 65 | 5 6 | 5 6 | 0 0 | 252 | 242 | 5 | 2 | 23.0 | 10.96 | 57.4 | 10.33 |
| 21/05/95 | 44 22 N | 37 32 W | 65 | 3 4 | 5 5 | 8 13 | 273 | 251 | 4 | 1 | 24.0 | 11.38 | 57.3 | 6.75 |
| 22/05/95 | 45 48 N | 32 3 W | 70 | 2 4 | 2 2 | 8 5 | 248 | 237 | 4 | 1 | 23.0 | 10.78 | 57.4 | 11.76 |
| 23/05/95 | 47 14 N | 26 12 W | 70 | 4 5 | 2 3 | 8 10 | 257 | 234 | 4 | 1 | 24.0 | 10.71 | 57.4 | 12.37 |
| 24/05/95 | 48 15 N | 20 15 W | 76 | 4 5 | 4 5 | 8 10 | 249 | 227 | 4 | 1 | 23.0 | 10.83 | 57.4 | 11.40 |
| 25/05/95 | 49 9 N | 14 7 W | V | 7 6 | 7 7 | 0 0 | 249 | 247 | 6 | 2 | 24.0 | 10.38 | 57.7 | 15.53 |
| 26/05/95 | 49 35 N | 8 3 W | 84 | 5 6 | 5 8 | 0 0 | 240 | 235 | 6 | 3 | 23.0 | 10.43 | 57.6 | 14.90 |
| 27/05/95 | 50 2 N | 1 37 W | V | 5 4 | 5 4 | 0 0 | 252 | 189 | 4 | 1 | 24.0 | 10.50 | 57.5 | 14.22 |
| 28/05/95 | 51 57 N | 3 29 E | V | 5 4 | 5 4 | 0 0 | 206 | 200 | 3 | 1 | 18.3 | 11.26 | 57.4 | 7.88 |
| Totals/Averages | | | | | | | 4,865 | 4,417 | | | 432.6 | 11.25 | 57.5 | 8.14 |

Page 2

| Date | Heavy Fuel Oil (Tonnes) | | | | | Diesel Oil (Tonnes) | | | | | Electrical Load (kw) | | |
|---|---|---|---|---|---|---|---|---|---|---|---|---|---|
| | Engine | Cargo | Tank | T.A. | D.A. | Total | DA Pr | DA Ot | M.Eng | Total | T.A. | D.A. | Total |
| 10/05/95 | 7.55 | 0.00 | 0.00 | 0.50 | 0.00 | 8.05 | 1.20 | 0.00 | 0.00 | 1.20 | 0.0 | 400.0 | 400.0 |
| 11/05/95 | 15.10 | 0.00 | 0.00 | 1.20 | 1.60 | 17.90 | 1.00 | 0.00 | 0.00 | 1.00 | 0.0 | 410.0 | 410.0 |
| 12/05/95 | 14.35 | 0.00 | 0.00 | 0.85 | 1.40 | 16.60 | 0.90 | 0.00 | 0.00 | 0.90 | 0.0 | 400.0 | 400.0 |
| 13/05/95 | 14.30 | 0.00 | 0.00 | 1.00 | 1.20 | 16.50 | 1.00 | 0.00 | 0.00 | 1.00 | 0.0 | 400.0 | 400.0 |
| 14/05/95 | 15.00 | 0.00 | 0.00 | 1.00 | 1.60 | 17.60 | 1.10 | 0.00 | 0.00 | 1.10 | 0.0 | 400.0 | 400.0 |
| 15/05/95 | 16.60 | 0.00 | 0.00 | 1.00 | 1.40 | 19.00 | 1.00 | 0.00 | 0.00 | 1.00 | 0.0 | 410.0 | 410.0 |
| 16/05/95 | 16.40 | 0.00 | 0.00 | 1.00 | 1.50 | 18.90 | 1.00 | 0.00 | 0.00 | 1.00 | 0.0 | 410.0 | 410.0 |
| 17/05/95 | 14.20 | 0.00 | 0.00 | 0.90 | 1.45 | 16.55 | 0.85 | 0.00 | 0.00 | 0.85 | 0.0 | 410.0 | 410.0 |
| 18/05/95 | 16.60 | 0.00 | 0.00 | 0.90 | 1.55 | 19.05 | 0.95 | 0.00 | 0.00 | 0.95 | 0.0 | 400.0 | 400.0 |
| 19/05/95 | 17.35 | 0.00 | 0.00 | 1.00 | 1.40 | 19.75 | 0.90 | 0.00 | 0.00 | 0.90 | 0.0 | 400.0 | 400.0 |
| 20/05/95 | 14.50 | 0.00 | 0.00 | 0.90 | 1.30 | 16.70 | 1.00 | 0.00 | 0.00 | 1.00 | 0.0 | 390.0 | 390.0 |
| 21/05/95 | 14.30 | 0.00 | 0.00 | 1.00 | 1.40 | 16.70 | 0.90 | 0.00 | 0.00 | 0.90 | 0.0 | 390.0 | 390.0 |
| 22/05/95 | 13.70 | 0.00 | 0.00 | 0.90 | 1.50 | 16.10 | 0.90 | 0.00 | 0.00 | 0.90 | 0.0 | 390.0 | 390.0 |
| 23/05/95 | 16.80 | 0.00 | 0.00 | 0.95 | 1.58 | 19.33 | 1.06 | 0.00 | 0.00 | 1.06 | 0.0 | 380.0 | 380.0 |
| 25/05/95 | 14.05 | 0.00 | 0.00 | 1.20 | 1.40 | 16.65 | 0.85 | 0.00 | 0.00 | 0.85 | 0.0 | 370.0 | 370.0 |
| 25/05/95 | 16.70 | 0.00 | 0.00 | 1.30 | 1.40 | 19.40 | 0.90 | 0.00 | 0.00 | 0.90 | 0.0 | 360.0 | 360.0 |
| 26/05/95 | 15.70 | 0.00 | 0.00 | 1.10 | 1.30 | 18.10 | 0.90 | 0.00 | 0.00 | 0.90 | 0.0 | 360.0 | 360.0 |
| 27/05/95 | 15.20 | 0.00 | 0.00 | 1.20 | 1.35 | 17.75 | 0.90 | 0.00 | 0.00 | 0.90 | 0.0 | 360.0 | 360.0 |
| 28/05/95 | 12.75 | 0.00 | 0.00 | 2.50 | 1.05 | 16.30 | 0.65 | 0.00 | 0.00 | 0.65 | 0.0 | 360.0 | 360.0 |
| Totals | 281.15 | 0.00 | 0.00 | 20.40 | 25.38 | 326.93 | 17.96 | 0.00 | 0.00 | 17.96 | | | |
| Averages | 15.60 | 0.00 | 0.00 | 1.13 | 1.41 | 18.14 | 1.00 | 0.00 | 0.00 | 1.00 | 0.0 | 389.5 | 389.5 |

*Fig. 27  Passage summary—computer printout*

The date, of course, requires no explanation, and latitude and longitude have been included for possible expansion of the menu of programs, which could eventually include voyage strategy. It is possible to divide the world into sectors and, with the help of routeing charts, we can have a historical weather database available on a computer program. We must also consider electronic charts, which are gaining in popularity and, of course, a vessel's position is now displayed on demand with the universal use of satellite positioning devices with a good possibility of direct entry into the computer. For these reasons it was deemed necessary to include latitude and longitude. Also, we must not forget it gives a guide to the route taken for post-voyage analysis purposes. Course steered could also be placed in the category of latitude and longitude, namely for future possibilities related to voyage strategy.

Wind, swell and current need no additional comment except, perhaps, that they are in numerically ascending order of magnitude both in force and direction, which would also apply to the weather related effects of pitch/roll and deck wetness.

Distance over ground and by log are nowadays from instruments usually very accurate in the case of over ground and, dependent on the sophistication of the method employed, the recording of log distance.

RPM is usually very accurate and speed over ground and slip are calculated from the data entries relating to distance, time and RPM with the propeller constant already fed into the program.

Heavy fuel oil consumption has been divided into five separate consumers, namely Main Engine, cargo heating, tank (or hold) cleaning, turbo-alternator and diesel alternator. Whilst this extensive subdivision is mainly for tanker operation, it can be useful for identifying hold cleaning operations on bulkers in certain instances. If flashing a boiler is necessary to provide steam for the turbo-alternator the fuel consumed would, of course, be entered in the turbo-alternator column and, although this method of electricity generation is normally not efficient, a provision has been made for it. Neither is the turbo-alternator scheme used these days but many ships are still in service which are so provided.

Diesel oil consumption has been split into three consumers—namely diesel alternator propulsion, diesel alternator other and Main Engine. Diesel oil consumed entered in the other column would include tank and hold cleaning and also tank heating if this split was necessary for charterparty purposes. It is unlikely that the Main Engine would consume diesel oil, but a provision has been made in case emergency operation requires its use.

Finally, there is electrical load divided between diesel and turbo-alternators with the total kW load shown.

These, then, are the daily entries which form the basis of the various programs. There are other inputs relating to predicted performance, propeller constant, displacement curve and Main Engine parameters, but these will be discussed later.

## 4. PASSAGE SUMMARY

The first program is simply a printout of all the daily data for whatever voyage by whatever ship is selected as shown in Fig. 27. Included in the program is a weather mask which permits Beaufort number limits to be pre-selected and also current speed limits and swell intensity limits, so that a realistic performance in simulated good weather is available on demand.

The second program is a variant of the first, again on a daily basis, but concentrating on the speed aspect as shown in Fig. 28. It will be seen that speed over ground, log speed and speed over the ground with current effect are shown. This latter feature was developed to suit the requirements of a charterer who used this speed when calculating charterparty performance.

Current speed is indicated in tenths of a knot and the sectors are as described in Fig. 15. It will be noted that the log speed recorded is apparently inaccurate, and experience has shown that this is a feature throughout the fleet. It also brings into question the reliability of the figures entered for current speed.

The third program is shown in Fig. 29.

| NOLA | | | | ROTTERDAM | | | 0012L 10/0595 28/05/95 | |
|------|------|------|-----|---------|---------|----------|----------|------------|
| Mask: | | Beaufort No.: | 0 | Current Speed: | 0 | Swell Force: | 0 | Pitch/Roll: 0 |
| Date | Dist | Time | BN | Current Sector | Current Speed*10 | Over Grnd | Speed Knots Log | OG+Current |
| 10/05/95 | 138 | 12.3 | 5 | Variable | 0 | 11.220 | 11.220 | 11.220 |
| 11/05/95 | 290 | 24.0 | 4 | SECTOR 4 | 15 | 12.083 | 10.958 | 12.083 |
| 12/05/95 | 308 | 24.0 | 3 | SECTOR 8 | 15 | 12.833 | 10.833 | 14.333 |
| 13/05/95 | 259 | 23.0 | 5 | SECTOR 8 | 10 | 11.261 | 10.913 | 12.261 |
| 14/05/95 | 309 | 24.0 | 3 | SECTOR 8 | 20 | 12.875 | 10.958 | 14.875 |
| 15/05/95 | 289 | 24.0 | 4 | SECTOR 8 | 18 | 12.042 | 10.292 | 13.842 |
| 16/05/95 | 298 | 24.0 | 6 | SECTOR 8 | 25 | 12.417 | 9.458 | 14.917 |
| 17/05/95 | 266 | 23.0 | 5 | Variable | 0 | 11.565 | 10.261 | 11.565 |
| 18/05/95 | 238 | 24.0 | 8 | Variable | 0 | 9.917 | 9.875 | 9.917 |
| 19/05/95 | 244 | 24.0 | 8 | Variable | 0 | 10.167 | 9.708 | 10.167 |
| 20/05/95 | 252 | 23.0 | 6 | Variable | 0 | 10.957 | 10.522 | 10.957 |
| 21/05/95 | 273 | 24.0 | 4 | SECTOR 8 | 13 | 11.375 | 10.458 | 12.675 |
| 22/05/95 | 248 | 23.0 | 4 | SECTOR 8 | 5 | 10.783 | 10.304 | 11.283 |
| 23/05/95 | 257 | 24.0 | 5 | SECTOR 8 | 10 | 10.708 | 9.750 | 11.708 |
| 24/05/95 | 249 | 23.0 | 5 | SECTOR 8 | 10 | 10.826 | 9.870 | 11.826 |
| 25/05/95 | 249 | 24.0 | 6 | Variable | 0 | 10.375 | 10.292 | 10.375 |
| 26/05/95 | 240 | 23.0 | 6 | Variable | 0 | 10.435 | 10.217 | 10.435 |
| 27/05/95 | 252 | 24.0 | 4 | Variable | 0 | 10.500 | 7.875 | 10.500 |
| 28/05/95 | 206 | 18.3 | 4 | Variable | 0 | 11.257 | 10.929 | 11.257 |
| Average Speeds (knots) | | | | | | 11.246 | 10.210 | 11.939 |

*Fig. 28. Speed summary—computer printout*

In this program certain calculations are made based on information which has previously been entered and this is what might be called the expected performance. This is shown in Table 16.

If we consider the load percentage column this is, in fact, the absorbed load based on the assumption that the Main Engine fuel consumption and revolutions as per the above input are 100%.

| NOLA | | | | ROTTERDAM | | | | 0012L 10/05/95 28/05/95 | | |
| Mask: | Beaufort No.: | 0 | | Current Speed: | 0 | | Swell Force: | 0 | Pitch/Roll: | 0 |

| Date | Dist miles | Time hours | BN | Wind sect | Speed knots | RPM | Slip % | Load % | Speed diff | Fuel diff |
|------|-----------|-----------|----|-----------|-------------|-----|--------|--------|-----------|-----------|
| 10/05/95 | 138 | 12.3 | 5 | 2 | 11.22 | 55.7 | 5.38 | 112.77 | −0.57 | 2.04 |
| 11/05/95 | 290 | 24.0 | 4 | 1 | 12.08 | 58.0 | 2.14 | 102.37 | 0.25 | −2.09 |
| 12/05/95 | 308 | 24.0 | 3 | 8 | 12.83 | 57.2 | −5.39 | 101.43 | −1.09 | −8.46 |
| 13/05/95 | 259 | 23.0 | 5 | 1 | 11.26 | 57.4 | 7.84 | 104.37 | −0.55 | 2.12 |
| 14/05/95 | 309 | 24.0 | 3 | 5 | 12.88 | 57.6 | −5.00 | 103.83 | 1.06 | −8.11 |
| 15/05/95 | 289 | 24.0 | 4 | 8 | 12.04 | 58.7 | 3.64 | 108.57 | 0.03 | −0.25 |
| 16/05/95 | 298 | 24.0 | 6 | 8 | 12.42 | 57.9 | −0.74 | 111.76 | 0.43 | −3.43 |
| 17/05/95 | 266 | 23.0 | 5 | 5 | 11.57 | 57.4 | 5.35 | 103.64 | −0.23 | 1.18 |
| 18/05/95 | 238 | 24.0 | 8 | 5 | 9.92 | 57.5 | 18.99 | 115.51 | −2.10 | 7.46 |
| 19/05/95 | 244 | 24.0 | 8 | 5 | 10.17 | 57.7 | 17.23 | 119.47 | −1.94 | 7.53 |
| 20/05/95 | 252 | 23.0 | 6 | 5 | 10.96 | 57.4 | 10.33 | 105.83 | −0.88 | 3.16 |
| 21/05/95 | 273 | 24.0 | 4 | 3 | 11.38 | 57.3 | 6.75 | 100.55 | −0.36 | 1.19 |
| 22/05/95 | 248 | 23.0 | 4 | 2 | 10.78 | 57.4 | 11.76 | 99.99 | −0.95 | 2.80 |
| 23/05/95 | 257 | 24.0 | 5 | 4 | 10.71 | 57.4 | 12.37 | 117.51 | −1.33 | 5.50 |
| 24/05/95 | 249 | 23.0 | 5 | 4 | 10.83 | 57.4 | 11.40 | 102.55 | −0.95 | 3.04 |
| 25/05/95 | 249 | 24.0 | 6 | 7 | 10.38 | 57.7 | 15.53 | 115.00 | −1.65 | 6.31 |
| 26/05/95 | 240 | 23.0 | 6 | 5 | 10.43 | 57.6 | 14.90 | 113.40 | −1.55 | 5.83 |
| 27/05/95 | 252 | 24.0 | 4 | 5 | 10.50 | 57.5 | 14.22 | 105.76 | −1.34 | 4.47 |
| 28/05/95 | 206 | 18.3 | 4 | 5 | 11.26 | 57.4 | 7.88 | 116.96 | −0.77 | 3.93 |
| FC 150154 | 4,865 | 432.6 | | | 11.25 | 57.5 | 8.14 | 108.49 | −0.65 | 2.84 |

*Fig. 29. Performance summary—computer printout*

*Table 16. Expected performance—computer input*

| Output | RPM | M.E. H.O. | Boiler H.O. | Diesel gen. H.O. | Diesel gen. D.O. | Load speed | Ballast speed |
|--------|-----|-----------|-------------|------------------|------------------|-----------|---------------|
| 100% | 78 | 36 | — | — | — | 15.00 | 15.75 |
| 80% | 74 | 30 | — | 0.5 | 0.6 | 14.25 | 15.25 |
| 65% | 69 | 24 | — | 0.7 | 0.8 | 13.75 | 14.50 |
| 50% | 64 | 19 | 1 | 1.0 | 1.1 | 13.00 | 13.75 |
| 35% | 57 | 14 | 1 | 1.2 | 1.3 | 12.00 | 13.00 |
| 25% | 53 | 11 | 1 | 1.2 | 1.3 | 10.75 | 11.75 |

It will be noted that the Main Engine consumption entries are rounded off to suit charterparty consumptions, which are normally given in whole numbers. Rather than use more accurate fuel consumptions based on cube law revolutions and corrected test bed specific fuel consumption, it is felt that using charterparty figures avoids duplication.

The overload figure can then be used purely as a trend indicator, rather than an accurate reflection of the absorbed load. It is interesting to note that in this particular case a highly derated engine is fitted and the absorbed load indicates around 108% instead of the expected 100% for a non-derated engine. For non-derated engines it is considered dangerous to operate above 115% absorbed load for extended periods, especially if running at a high output. Deviations from the expected performance, with respect to speed and consumption, are shown in the two final columns, and do not require special comment. The weather screening option is available for all these programs.

## 5. DATABASE

Each voyage is summarised in Fig. 30.

Mask :– Beaufort No.   0:        Current Speed   0:        Swell Force   0:        Pitch/Roll   0

| Voyage No.<br>Index No. | Distance<br>Time hrs<br>Speed | M.E:– t/d<br>RPM<br>Load % | D.A :– Kw<br>HO/DO t/d<br>gm/bhp/hr | T.A :– Kw<br>HO t/d<br>Save t/d | Slip %<br>Speed Diff<br>Fuel Diff | Displ.<br>Trim<br>Fuel Coeff |
|---|---|---|---|---|---|---|
| NOLA | | ROTTERDAM | | | 10/05/95 | 28/05/95 |
| 0012L | 4865 | 15.60 | 389.47 | 0.00 | 8.14 | 66,821 |
| 22 | 432.60 | 57.48 | 1.41   1.00 | 1.13 | −0.65 | 0.00 |
| | 11.25 | 108.49 | 191.89 | −1.13 | 2.84 | 150,154 |

*Fig. 30. Database—computer printout*

The first three columns are self-explanatory, and do not need any comment. The fourth column relates to the performance of the diesel alternator giving average load, also daily consumption of heavy oil and/or diesel oil together with the specific fuel consumption. The next column shows the performance of the turbo-alternator in similar fashion as the diesel alternator but, additionally, shows the benefit of the turbo-alternator, expressed in tonnes per day fuel saved for the "free" kW produced. In this particular example, the turbo-alternator was not in use due to a defect in the economiser necessitating the boiler being flashed to support the steam load. An example of how this works will be shown later. In the sixth column deviations from the expected performance are shown as well as the slip. In the final column the vessel's displacement (not deadweight) is shown, as is the trim based on sailing and arrival draughts, also the fuel coefficient using the mean draught.

The database can be printed for single or multiple voyages with a selection option for loaded or ballast, or any other combination of voyages at will.

## 6. GRAPHIC ILLUSTRATION OF TREND ANALYSIS

A selection of graphic illustrations are available, all on an elapsed time basis. Whereas the previous programs have considered voyage performance in isolation, the next set of programs indicates long-term trends for selected voyages, either loaded, ballast or both, in chronological order.

These programs will process raw passage data for any specified voyages and correct for displacement, revolutions and weather. It is also possible to screen the data using the weather mask and current speed.

The corrected data will be displayed graphically with speed or fuel consumption plotted against elapsed time. Voyage number and start date of voyage will be indicated on the time axis and events such as dry dockings, bottom scrubs and propeller polishings shown. An illustration of the corrected raw data is shown in Fig. 31.

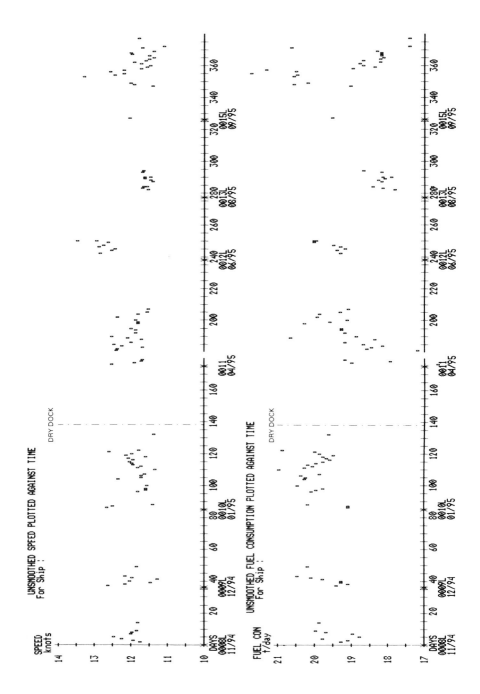

*Fig. 31. Unsmoothed trend graphs*

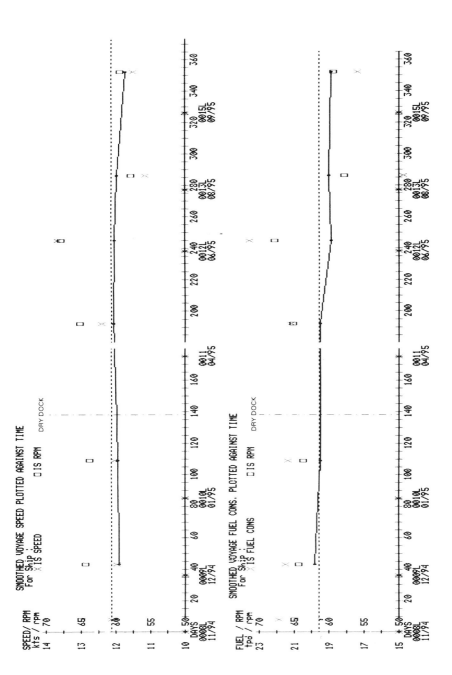

*Fig. 32.  Smoothed trend graphs*

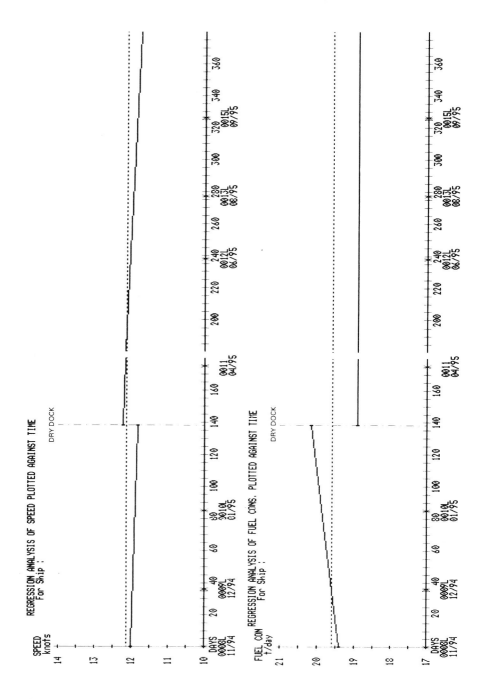

*Fig. 33. Regression analysis graphs*

From this corrected raw data a five-part moving average will then produce smoothed speed or fuel consumption in similar manner as shown in Fig. 32.

By introducing the dry dock date into the program, regression analysis graphs for speed and consumption can be produced which clearly show the beneficial effect of the dry dock on performance (see Fig. 33). This part of the program can also be used to illustrate what effect, if any, an underwater scrub or propeller polishing may have had on performance.

To complete this section of the program an analysis of absorbed engine loading with RPM reference points will be shown graphically as illustrated in Fig. 34.

This, more or less, covers the technical aspects of computerised performance monitoring, which has a distinct advantage over a manual system with respect to the speed of the calculations and the possibility of forecasting trends.

## 7. CHARTERPARTY CALCULATIONS

The raw data entered into the passage summary are normally adequate for dealing with most charterparty performance claims.

We have seen how weather screening possibilities can cover all known variations so far met with when dealing with underperformance claims. Such a comprehensive weather description used in the computerised passage data program is not normally required for charterparty calculations. It is, however, very important that the data must be identical. It is no use working out a claim submitted by charterers based on their own abstracts and then using the owners' abstracts to challenge the claim unless both sets of figures are identical on the important issues of distance, time, fuel and weather.

Charterers' abstract forms may, possibly, be laid out quite differently to the computerised passage summary described in this chapter; in all probability the charterers' form will not contain as much weather information, neither will it split fuel up into the number of consumers we have used in the computerised version.

Ship's staff must be encouraged to complete both owners' and charterers' abstracts using identical figures, and additional information, not catered for in the charterers' abstract, should be entered in the remarks column. This would generally relate to adverse currents, reductions in speed for fog or to prevent damage to the vessel in heavy weather. Fuel used for what might be called charterers' activities must also be separated from essential propulsion fuel. This would include cargo heating and tank or hold cleaning.

It is also important that charterers' steaming instructions are clearly indicated in the remarks column, both when starting the voyage and at each

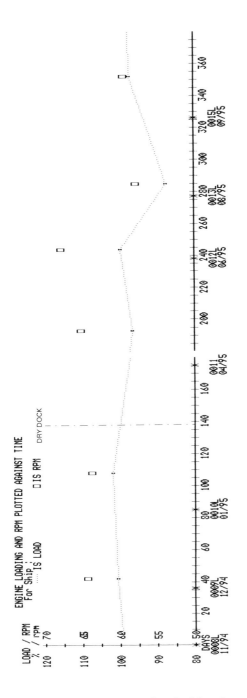

*Fig. 34. Main Engine absorbed load*

change in instructions received thereafter. This would include instructions to fit slow steaming fuel valve nozzles.

The computer program has a display in which all the various fuel consumers are clearly listed and can be included or omitted by the user. For example, Main Engine and diesel generator fuel would obviously be included in the performance calculations, whereas tank cleaning and tank heating would, in all probability, be omitted.

There is also an option for selecting NYPE calculations or typical tanker calculations as fully described in the previous chapter. Weather screening is included too in an option which allows Beaufort number, current speed, swell force and pitch/roll to be chosen at will.

In a typical charterparty only Beaufort number would normally be taken into the calculation, but unexplained inferior performances could be identified and perhaps negotiated with the charterer or at an arbitration. In the event of the charterer choosing to use a weather routeing service to challenge the recorded weather conditions, the weather section of the program would prove to be very useful should such a challenge be unfounded. It should be mentioned that weather routeing services very often route vessels away from heavy swells, as they consider their effect more devastating to a vessel's performance than a moderate wind force.

The program also allows a voyage to be split into five periods, each having different speed settings—should this have been asked for by the charterer.

When calculating the underperformance, or overperformance in certain cases, we must first enter the voyage reference number from the menu of voyages displayed on the screen. If there were no alterations in steaming orders, the start and finish dates of the chosen voyage will not require adjustment. If charterers have instructed the vessel to speed up or slow down, the date of the first change is entered and the program automatically rearranges the voyage into the requisite number of periods.

Next to be entered is the charterparty speed. This can be with or without the ½ knot tolerance depending on the terms of the charter. Charterparty heavy oil consumption and diesel oil consumption are likewise entered using whatever allowance is applicable. Fuel costs of both heavy oil and diesel oil are also entered.

Daily charter freight rate, deadweight and address commission are also entered. If the vessel is time chartered at a daily hire rate rather than a daily freight rate, it can be easily converted as shown:

$$\text{Daily Freight Rate} = \frac{\text{Daily Hire Rate} \times 30.4}{\text{Deadweight}}$$

If thought necessary, the address commission can be deducted from the daily hire rate and the address commission entered as zero. This would not, however, be suitable if an overperformance clause was included in the charterparty terms.

The weather mask limit is then entered, as is the charterparty form to be used, either NYPE or tanker. The various fuel consumptions to be taken into account are also selected, as previously mentioned. We can then display and print out the calculation. Should we decide that the end result is not beneficial and no allowances have been used, we can add these allowances before printing out the final version.

As an example, we will show a calculation for the voyage used in section 3 (see Fig. 27) of this chapter, which readers may recall was a New Orleans—Rotterdam laden passage on a Panamax bulker.

This is shown below in Fig. 35.

| CHARTER PERFORMANCE: VOYAGE—0012L | | | 10/05/95 to 28/05/95 | |
| SUMMARY | NOLA | | to ROTTERDAM | |
| Date From | Date To | Speed knots | Heavy Oil tonnes/day | Diesel Oil tonnes/day |
| --- | --- | --- | --- | --- |
| 1   10/05/95 | 28/05/95 | 12.00 | 16.260 | 1.320 |

| | |
| --- | --- |
| Heavy Fuel Oil Price ($/tonne) ......................................... | 100.0 |
| Diesel Oil Price ($/tonne) ................................................ | 150.0 |
| Tonnage (tonnes) ........................................................... | 63,650 |
| Charter Rate ($/tonne/month) ......................................... | 3.000 |
| Address (%) ................................................................... | 3.70 |
| Charterparty Type is ..................................................... | NYPE |
| Speed Type is ................................................................ | Speed over ground |

| NOLA | | ROTTERDAM | 0012L 10/05/95 to 28/05/95 | |
| Mask: | Beaufort No.: 0 | Current Speed: 0 | Swell Force: 0 | Pitch/Roll: 0 |
| --- | --- | --- | --- | --- |
| Leg 1 of 1 | | | Period: 10/05/95–28/05/95 | |
| | | | All Weather | After Mask |
| Total Distance (miles) ..................................... | | | 4,865.00 | 4,865.00 |
| Total Steaming Time (hours) ........................... | | | 432.60 | 432.60 |
| Average Speed (knots) ..................................... | | | 11.25 | 11.25 |
| Average RPM ................................................. | | | 57.48 | 57.48 |
| Average Fuel Consumption (tonnes/day) ......... | | | 18.14 | 18.14 |
| Average Diesel Cons. (tonnes/day) ................. | | | 1.00 | 1.00 |
| Excess Hire (US$) ............................................ | | | | −6,851.16 |
| Excess Heavy Oil Costs (US$) ......................... | | | | −5,226.03 |
| Excess Diesel Costs (US$) ............................... | | | | 650.91 |
| Charter Performance (US$) .............................. | | | | −11,426.28 |
| Cumulative Charter Performance ($) ............... | | | | −11,426.28 |

**Fig. 35. *Charterparty claim all weather: New Orleans–Rotterdam***

The charterparty performance figures were 12 knots laden on 16 l.t. heavy oil and 1.3 l.t. diesel oil which have been converted to metric tonnes to tie up with the abstract figures. It can be seen that an underperformance claim of $11,426.28 would be forthcoming from charterers if no allowances were taken into account. We can now re-calculate the underperformance using a ½ knot on speed and 3% on heavy oil and diesel.

The result is shown in Fig. 36.

The charterparty speed now becomes 11.5 knots and the heavy oil 16.74 tonnes, and the diesel oil 1.36 tonnes. The weather mask chosen was a limit of Beaufort 5 which means that the program will reject all Beaufort readings of five and above. The complete turn round in performance will be noted. It now shows an overperformance of $1,940.10 when using the fuel allowance and weather mask. Actually, this will not result in a claim by owners against charterers for overperformance, as it is not allowed to use the allowances and then claim for underperformance. The result would therefore be that the voyage was performed within the warranted performance with no claim on either side involved. In fact, cases have been known of charterers grouping

CHARTER PERFORMANCE: VOYAGE—0012L          10/05/95 to 28/05/95
SUMMARY                    NOLA                    to ROTTERDAM

| | Date From | Date To | Speed knots | Heavy Oil tonnes/day | Diesel Oil tonnes/day |
|---|---|---|---|---|---|
| 1 | 10/05/95 | 28/05/95 | 11.50 | 16.740 | 1.360 |

| | |
|---|---|
| Heavy Fuel Oil Price ($/tonne) ........................................... | 100.0 |
| Diesel Oil Price ($/tonne) .................................................. | 150.0 |
| Tonnage (tonnes) .............................................................. | 63,650 |
| Charter Rate ($/tonne/month) ........................................... | 3.000 |
| Address (%) ..................................................................... | 3.70 |

| | |
|---|---|
| Charterparty Type is ...................................................... | NYPE |
| Speed Type is ................................................................. | Speed over ground |

| NOLA | | ROTTERDAM | 0012L 10/05/95 to 28/05/95 | |
|---|---|---|---|---|
| Mask: | Beaufort No.: 5 | Current Speed: 0 | Swell Force: 0 | Pitch/Roll: 0 |

| Leg 1 of 1 | Period: 10/05/95–28/05/95 | |
|---|---|---|
| | All Weather | After Mask |
| Total Distance (miles) ......................................... | 4,865.00 | 2,175.00 |
| Total Steaming Time (hours) ............................. | 432.60 | 185.30 |
| Average Speed (knots) ....................................... | 11.25 | 11.74 |
| Average RPM ...................................................... | 57.48 | 57.64 |
| Average Fuel Consumption (tonnes/day) ......................... | 18.14 | 17.87 |
| Average Diesel Cons. (tonnes/day) ................................. | 1.00 | 0.95 |
| Excess Hire (US$) ................................................ | | 2,159.39 |
| Excess Heavy Oil Costs (US$) ............................................ | | −1,349.11 |
| Excess Diesel Costs (US$) ................................................. | | 1,129.82 |
| Charter Performance (US$) ............................................... | | 1,940.10 |
| Cumulative Charter Performance ($) ............................... | | 1,940.10 |

*Fig. 36. Charterparty claim fairweather: New Orleans–Rotterdam*

voyages together, choosing all those at, say, minimum power setting and all those at various other settings that they had elected to sail the vessel at.

In this case, the rather good result obtained when using the weather mask and fuel tolerances would improve voyages with poorer results. The computer program is arranged to deal with this groupage option, should it ever be exercised.

We can also show the computerised version of another example mentioned in Chapter Nine. This was a voyage some time ago from Newcastle NSW–Rotterdam with all weather conditions included by virtue of the fact that "under good weather conditions" had been deleted from the relevant clause in the NYPE charterparty.

Charterers did allow the ½ knot speed tolerance and also the 3% fuel tolerance so that the charterparty performance of 11 knots on 29 M.T.H.O. plus 2.5 l.t. D.O. became 10.5 knots on 29.87 M.T.H.O. plus 2.61 M.T.D.O. It will be

| CHARTER PERFORMANCE: VOYAGE—0012L | | | 26/09/95 to 21/11/95 | |
| SUMMARY | NEWCASTLE | | to ROTTERDAM | |
| --- | --- | --- | --- | --- |
| Date From | Date To | Speed knots | Heavy Oil tonnes/day | Diesel Oil tonnes/day |
| 1    29/09/95 | 21/11/95 | 10.50 | 29.870 | 2.610 |

| | |
| --- | --- |
| Heavy Fuel Oil Price ($/tonne) ......................................... | 152.9 |
| Diesel Oil Price ($/tonne) .................................................. | 238.6 |
| Tonnage (tonnes) .............................................................. | 29,913 |
| Charter Rate ($/tonne/month) ......................................... | 2.500 |
| Address (%) ...................................................................... | 3.80 |

| | |
| --- | --- |
| Charterparty Type is ...................................................... | NYPE |
| Speed Type is ................................................................. | Speed over ground |

| NEWCASTLE | | ROTTERDAM | 0012L 26/09/95 to 21/11/95 | |
| Mask: | Beaufort No.: 0 | Current Speed: 0 | Swell Force: 0 | Pitch/Roll: 0 |
| --- | --- | --- | --- | --- |
| Leg 1 of 1 | | | Period: 26/09/95–21/11/95 | |
| | | | All Weather | After Mask |
| Total Distance (miles) ...................................................... | | | 13,415.00 | 13,415.00 |
| Total Steaming Time (hours) ............................................ | | | 1,391.50 | 1,391.50 |
| Average Speed (knots) ..................................................... | | | 9.64 | 9.64 |
| Average RPM ................................................................... | | | 80.21 | 80.21 |
| Average Fuel Consumption (tonnes/day) ......................... | | | 29.41 | 29.41 |
| Average Diesel Cons. (tonnes/day) ................................. | | | 2.45 | 2.45 |
| Excess Hire (US$) ............................................................ | | | | −48,767.90 |
| Excess Heavy Oil Costs (US$) .......................................... | | | | −17,582.96 |
| Excess Diesel Costs (US$) ................................................ | | | | 801.45 |
| Charter Performance (US$) .............................................. | | | | −67,152.30 |
| Cumulative Charter Performance ($) ............................... | | | | −67,152.30 |

*Fig. 37.  Charterparty claim all weather: NSW–Rotterdam*

CHARTER PERFORMANCE: VOYAGE—0012L                26/09/95 to 21/11/95
    SUMMARY                    NEWCASTLE                to ROTTERDAM

| | Date From | Date To | Speed knots | Heavy Oil tonnes/day | Diesel Oil tonnes/day |
|---|---|---|---|---|---|
| 1 | 29/09/95 | 21/11/95 | 10.50 | 29.870 | 2.610 |

| | |
|---|---|
| Heavy Fuel Oil Price ($/tonne) ......................................... | 152.9 |
| Diesel Oil Price ($/tonne) ................................................. | 238.6 |
| Tonnage (tonnes) ............................................................... | 129,913 |
| Charter Rate ($/tonne/month) ......................................... | 2.500 |
| Address (%) ........................................................................ | 3.80 |

| | |
|---|---|
| Charterparty Type is ...................................................... | NYPE |
| Speed Type is .................................................................. | Speed over ground |

NEWCASTLE                    ROTTERDAM        0012L 26/09/95 to 21/11/95
Mask:            Beaufort No.: 5    Current Speed: 0    Swell Force: 0      Pitch/Roll: 0

| Leg 1 of 1 | Period: 26/09/95–21/11/95 | |
|---|---|---|
| | All Weather | After Mask |
| Total Distance (miles) .............................................. | 13,415.00 | 4,940.00 |
| Total Steaming Time (hours) ............................................ | 1,391.50 | 473.00 |
| Average Speed (knots) ...................................................... | 9.64 | 10.44 |
| Average RPM ....................................................................... | 80.21 | 80.26 |
| Average Fuel Consumption (tonnes/day) ........................ | 29.41 | 28.95 |
| Average Diesel Cons. (tonnes/day) ................................. | 2.45 | 2.47 |
| | | |
| Excess Hire (US$) .............................................................. | | −2,934.97 |
| Excess Heavy Oil Costs (US$) .......................................... | | 6,206.13 |
| Excess Diesel Costs (US$) ................................................ | | 1,596.71 |
| | | |
| Charter Performance (US$) ............................................. | | 4,867.87 |
| | | |
| Cumulative Charter Performance ($) ............................... | | 4,867.87 |

*Fig. 38.  Charterparty claim fairweather: NSW–Rotterdam*

noted that charterers used metric tonnes for H.O. and long tons for D.O., which
required converting to metric tonnes before entering into the program.

Ship Name:

Mask:–      Beaufort No. 5:      Current Speed 0:      Swell Force 0:      Pitch/Roll 0

| Voyage No. | Distance | M.E.:–t/d | D.A.:–Kw | T.A.:–Kw | Slip % | Displ. |
|---|---|---|---|---|---|---|
| Index No. | Time hrs | RPM | HO/DO t/d | HO t/d | Speed Diff | Trim |
| | Speed | Load % | gm/bhp/hr | Save t/d | Fuel Diff | Fuel Coeff |
| MUTSURE | | HAY POINT | | 28/08/95 | 11/09/95 | |
| 0026B | 2,289 | 21.72 | 333.75 | 132.75 | −3.27 | 38,632 |
| 1 | 186.50 | 88.83 | 0.00  2.05 | 0.00 | −0.14 | 2.06 |
| | 12.27 | 100.93 | 190.56 | 1.71 | 0.48 | 97,266 |

*Fig. 39.  Database printout*

Mask:–     Beaufort No. 0:     Current Speed 0:     Swell Force 0:     Pitch/Roll 0

| Voyage No. | Distance | M.E.:–t/d | D.A.:–Kw | T.A.:–Kw | Slip % | Displ. |
|---|---|---|---|---|---|---|
| Index No. | Time hrs | RPM | HO/DO t/d | HO t/d | Speed Diff | Trim |
| | Speed | Load % | gm/bhp/hr | Save t/d | Fuel Diff | Fuel Coeff |

| DUNKIRK | | NEWPORT NEWS | | | 14/11/95 | 28/11/95 |
|---|---|---|---|---|---|---|
| 0083B | 3,685 | 29.51 | 264.33 | 173.00 | 8.16 | 64,085 |
| 24 | 344.00 | 78.18 | 0.00   1.93 | 0.00 | −1.13 | 2.63 |
| | 10.71 | 100.97 | 227.25 | 2.23 | 5.95 | 66,704 |

Mask:–     Beaufort No. 5:     Current Speed 0:     Swell Force 0:     Pitch/Roll 0

| Voyage No. | Distance | M.E.:–t/d | D.A.:–Kw | T.A.:–Kw | Slip % | Displ. |
|---|---|---|---|---|---|---|
| Index No. | Time hrs | RPM | HO/DO t/d | HO t/d | Speed Diff | Trim |
| | Speed | Load % | gm/bhp/hr | Save t/d | Fuel Diff | Fuel Coeff |

| DUNKIRK | | NEWPORT NEWS | | | 14/11/95 | 28/11/95 |
|---|---|---|---|---|---|---|
| 0083B | 1,710 | 29.67 | 252.14 | 190.00 | 7.30 | 64,085 |
| 24 | 158.00 | 78.30 | 0.00   1.93 | 0.00 | −1.03 | 2.63 |
| | 10.82 | 101.16 | 237.81 | 2.45 | 5.55 | 68,433 |

Mask:–     Beaufort No. 0:     Current Speed 0:     Swell Force 8:     Pitch/Roll 0

| Voyage No. | Distance | M.E.:–t/d | D.A.:–Kw | T.A.:–Kw | Slip % | Displ. |
|---|---|---|---|---|---|---|
| Index No. | Time hrs | RPM | HO/DO t/d | HO t/d | Speed Diff | Trim |
| | Speed | Load % | gm/bhp/hr | Save t/d | Fuel Diff | Fuel Coeff |

| DUNKIRK | | NEWPORT NEWS | | | 14/11/95 | 28/11/95 |
|---|---|---|---|---|---|---|
| 0083B | 2,453 | 29.44 | 256.50 | 170.00 | 5.53 | 64,085 |
| 24 | 222.00 | 78.40 | 0.00   1.97 | 0.00 | −0.78 | 2.63 |
| | 11.05 | 99.84 | 238.43 | 2.19 | 4.19 | 73,389 |

**Fig. 40. Database weather screening**

The printout without any weather mask was $67,152.30 underperformed as shown in Fig. 37.

The printout with a Beaufort 5 weather mask was $4,867.87 overperformed as shown in Fig. 38, but of course this would not change the fact that owners were obliged to meet the claim of $67,152.30.

It will be noted that only 20 days out of 58 days were performed in good weather, which is typical of such a voyage.

The effect of the turbo-alternator is shown on the database printout for another voyage (see Fig. 39) and it will be seen that a saving of 1.71 M.T./Day arose.

We can also show the effect of swell force in another example and in this case three database printouts show that the best performance in terms of speed and Main Engine fuel consumption is when a swell force 8 limit is used as a weather mask (see Fig. 40).

It will be seen that the final example is the best. Any combination of Beaufort

Report No. ............................... 21
Voyage No. ......................... 0011L
Date ............................... 26/04/94
No. Cylinders ............................ 4

| | |
|---|---|
| Total IHP | 13,241 |
| Total BHP | 12,076 |
| Efficiency % | 91.20 |
| SFC gms/BHP/hr | 139.50 |

| Cylinder No. | 1 | 2 | 3 | 4 | | | Average |
|---|---|---|---|---|---|---|---|
| P Max (BAR) | 101.00 | 101.00 | 106.00 | 102.00 | | | 102.500 |
| P Comp (BAR) | 71.00 | 70.00 | 71.00 | 68.00 | | | 70.000 |
| P Ind (BAR) | 13.60 | 12.50 | 13.20 | 13.30 | | | 13.150 |
| HP Ind | 3,423.50 | 3,146.60 | 3,322.80 | 3,348.00 | | | 3,310.300 |
| Exh Temp | 355.00 | 360.00 | 360.00 | 365.00 | | | 360.000 |
| Jacket Temp | 85.00 | 85.00 | 85.00 | 85.00 | | | 85.000 |
| Piston Temp | 58.00 | 58.00 | 58.00 | 58.00 | | | 58.000 |
| Fuel Pump Ind | 81.00 | 81.00 | 81.00 | 82.00 | | | 81.250 |
| Cylinder Wear | 0.92 | 1.00 | 1.00 | 0.87 | | | 0.972 |

F1—General Data Entry
F2—More Cylinders    F3—Previous Entry    F4—Next Entry
F7—Results Box    TAB—Next Screen Section    F10—Save/Exit

***Fig. 41. Main Engine cylinder data—computer printout***

number, current speed, swell force and pitch/roll can be chosen to illustrate what effect the weather is having on performance.

## 8. MAIN ENGINE PERFORMANCE

We have seen how absorbed load has already been taken care of in the computer program and further aspects can now be considered. Main Engine performance, unlike overall ship performance, is not normally an on line continuous function receiving contributions in the form of regular watch readings and observations as the ship performance does. The main event is probably when power diagrams are taken and the results analysed; this is usually, perhaps, once per passage or if on long voyages, once per week depending on the shipowner's practice. Naturally other readings are regularly taken which would give early indication of trouble developing and these are usually under the control of an alarm and monitoring system permanently connected to essential pressures and temperatures. It is considered a good idea to take a set of indicator cards or power diagrams when weather conditions are good and preferably when the engine is running at high output.

From analysis of the indicator cards, or from the recently introduced engine analysers using cathode ray tubes, the following information is entered into the computer program which then calculates the IHP and BHP based on constants

| | |
|---|---|
| Voyage Number | 0011L | Report Number | 21 |
| Date ......................... 26/04/94 |

| | |
|---|---|
| Total IHP | 13,241 |
| Total BHP | 12,076 |
| Efficiency % | 91.20 |
| SFC gms/BHP/hr | 139.50 |

Speed (knots) ............... 16.13  RPM ............................ 80.10
Draft Fwd (m) .............. 11.52  Draft Aft (m) ................. 11.53
Slip (%) .......................... 5.40  Seawater Temp °C ......... 27.00
Eng. room Temp °C ....... 28.00

─────────────────────── Weather Data ───────────────────────

Wind Direction .................... 0  Wind Force .......................... 6  Swell direction ........................
Swell Force ........................... 0  Current Direction ............... 0  Current Speed/10 ....................
Pitch & Roll ......................... 0  Deck Wetness ...................... 0

─────────────────────── Fuel Data ───────────────────────

Fuel at Start LT ...................0  Fuel at End LT .................... 0  Fuel Cons LT/HR * ........1,871
Time (mins) ....................... 60  Fuel Temp °C ............... 129.00  Viscosity @ 50°C ......... 380.00
Density at 5°C ............. 0.9899  Sulphur % ........................ 3.00

─────────────────────── Engine Data ───────────────────────

Govenor Index ................ 6.80  Fuel Lever Index ........... 95.00  Spring Constant ............... 0.50
Cool P. Drop FWD ......... 0.00  Cool P. Drop AFT .......... 0.00  Scavenge Pressure ........... 1.30
Scavenge Temp °C ......... 37.00  Turbo RPM FWD ......... 6,000  Turbo RPM AFT ................. –
Turbo O/H FWD ...... 01/01/84  Turbo O/H AFT ............. ../../..

F1—Enter Cylinder Data      F3—Previous Entry
F4—Next Entry      F7—Results Bos      TAB—Next Screen Section      F10—Save/Exit

***Fig. 42. Main Engine general data—computer printout***

and curves held in the program. An example of this is shown in Fig. 41 which relates to a large bore four cylinder Main Engine.

Also entered into the program are other parameters relating to both the Main Engine and the vessel regarding their performance as shown in Fig. 42.

The analytical side of the program can then produce graphic illustrations of the following important ratios in similar fashion to those of speed and consumption mentioned earlier also on an elapsed time basis:

1. Compression/Scavenge Pressure
2. Maximum/Indicated Pressure
3. Fuel Pump Index/Indicated Pressure
4. RPM/Indicated Pressure
5. Scavenge/Indicated Pressure
6. Exhaust Temperature/BHP
7. Specific Fuel Consumption.

As we learnt in Chapter Four the ratio of compression and scavenge pressure is a good guide to the condition of the piston rings and amount of cylinder liner wear. We can graphically illustrate this in Fig. 43 which indicates a satisfactory performance.

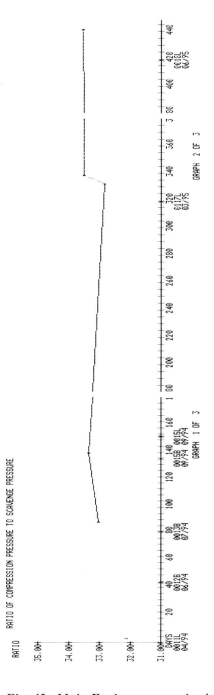

*Fig. 43. Main Engine compression/scavenge pressure ratio*

The other ratios can also be viewed if for some reason the performance of the engine gives cause for concern.

## 9. CARGO HEATING PERFORMANCE

Tankers carrying cargoes which require heating can consume quite large amounts of fuel oil; in extreme cases the daily fuel consumption used heating the cargo can approach that consumed by the main propulsion engine. It is considered that a useful program could be developed based on a databank of past voyages in which vessels with rather good results could be compared with the poor performers.

Even on sister ships carrying similar cargoes at similar times of the year, variances of 80% in the amount of fuel consumed have been recorded. A computer program based on many such voyages could provide a useful check for monitoring cargo heating performance.

## 10. VOYAGE STRATEGY

At the moment around 100 ship years of raw passage data is stored on hard disc, covering many hundreds of voyages.

Resulting from this, some sort of strategy program is envisaged which, amongst other things, would categorise voyages on a seasonal geographical basis. This would enable a prediction to be made of weather effect on ship type based on historical data. It is well known that attempts to make up time in adverse weather is not normally fuel cost-effective and the precise cost could be predicted by the envisaged program.

It is also well known that a voyage carried out under constant revolutions is more cost-effective than a voyage carried out with two or more speed changes. On many occasions we find vessels have to speed up or slow down to meet deadlines which should have been known earlier, and the program would cater for this. The miles steamed per tonne of fuel consumed could be used to illustrate this point to ship's staff who, on occasions, appear unaware of the penalties involved in changing speed intervoyage.

A recent development concerns the decision to use either the Suez Canal or Cape route on a voyage from Europe to the Middle East or Far East. This, of course, is related to fuel costs and the canal dues, and the decision-making process could easily be handled by the envisaged program.

Included in the program could be a bunker strategy section which would determine the amount of upliftings and bunker ports and the decision to shut out cargo to maximise bunker uplift as discussed in Chapter Three.

Using the trend analysis section of the existing program it would be possible to update the so-called expected performance figures, which, when used in conjunction with the strategy program, would provide an extremely reliable guide to the expected performance at any given time.

Also in the program would be a set of comprehensive distance tables giving alternatives when either Suez or the Cape route are being considered. Although weather routeing services are available they can be complemented by the use of these tables. A classic example is whether or not to use the UNIMAK pass route and the program would give the fuel costs, which could be related to increased revenue due to the shorter passage time. The expected performance of the vessel, by using the weather effect prediction, would form part of the calculation. It would also be possible to integrate the proposed strategy program with one of the electronic chart systems now becoming popular.

The program would be able to forecast the probable financial result of the voyage using updated performance figures modified for expected weather conditions. As mentioned earlier, other entries would include bunkering strategy. Finally, a program to indicate when it is considered to be the time to dry dock having regard to the fall off in performance, as indicated in the regression curves, and taking into account fuel costs and performance claims is a future possibility.

## 11. COMMUNICATIONS

At the moment, raw performance data produced on the ship in the form of log and abstract entries are posted at the voyage end and, generally, arrive at the author's shipowner office a week or so later.

It is then entered into the computer and analysed with respect to perform-ance, using both the technical and commercial programs. The actual time taken to enter the data takes, maybe, 20 minutes for an average voyage—so the task is not unduly onerous.

Several vessels have computers provided on board and submit floppy discs on a regular basis. The information on these floppy discs is then transferred to the hard disc of the office-based PC, and analysed in a similar manner. Ship's staff also have the possibility of analysing the data on board as they have been provided with all the analytical programs.

For all normal situations it would appear that, from a technical analytical point of view, these alternative procedures are satisfactory, with little to choose from except for the moderate cost for the provision of a personal computer.

It is rare for serious performance-related technical problems to develop without prior warning from the trend analysis program. This, of course, would not apply to sudden catastrophic breakdowns, which occur from time to time, and it is unlikely that they would be detected by any standard computer program anyway. However, in the event of sudden hull bottom fouling developing, it would be picked up rather quickly by either the computer or the manual system described earlier.

The commercial considerations depend on the type of charterparty in use and future business contemplated. For example, if the vessel's performance suddenly deteriorated due to the fouling problem mentioned earlier this must be communicated to the chartering department immediately, otherwise a commitment could be entered into which would have severe financial penalties—and we have already described the penal effects of underperformance.

A system has been developed that allows a coded telex message from the vessel to be entered directly into the office-based computer. This message contains the 20 or so daily performance figures and can be sent at whatever intervals are deemed necessary depending on the position of the vessel from a charter fixing point of view.

If a vessel is on a long-term charter then weekly messages would suffice. If a time charter with tight performance figures is being negotiated, then daily messages would appear more appropriate. The chartering manager would then be almost in the same position as the master in knowing the performance capability of the vessel at the time of fixing the charter.

For those vessels fitted with satellite communications similar arrangements could be provided with enhanced round-the-clock availability, albeit at a somewhat higher cost, but transmission costs are somewhat cheaper than telex.

It is an accepted fact that a satellite communication system is more satisfactory when used in conjunction with a personal computer. This leaves the door open for a host of software programs including electronic mail, crew lists, cargo stowage, planned maintenance and inventory control—all of which are presently available.


## 12. DIAGNOSTIC AND PREDICTIVE PROGRAMS

Planned maintenance programs have been in use for many years and need no special comment. In the natural order of things they have been updated and modified, and are generally incorporated into an inventory control and stock replenishment capability. Classification Society continuous survey of machinery computer records can now be accessed using a direct modem link into a microcomputer in the shipowner's office.

A development receiving attention is a diagnostic or predictive program which differs from the earlier planned maintenance schemes in that it is not elapsed-time based, but relies on a quite different approach.

The program is probably linked to condition monitoring systems and additionally requires some sort of input from an engine builder or research establishment to enable damage sensitivity criteria to be defined.

Previous problems and corrective action taken will be processed into a databank and trend analysis results from the Main Engine performance program will also be entered. This will be mentioned in the next chapter.

## 13. SUMMARY OF CHAPTER TEN

Shipboard or shore-based computers are being increasingly used to perform all manner of tasks relating to vessel operation and performance. Charterparty calculations and trend analysis techniques are ideal candidates for computer application.

In the foreseeable future most sophisticated owners will transmit data relating to vessel performance via satellite into the shipowner's office, giving instant access to current performance.

Classification Society records are now available via modem link and LLP Limited have a similar link called SEADATA, giving access to all manner of particulars of interest to shipowners and charterers alike, relating to around 80,000 vessels.

The computer programs used by the author's company are very low cost and no additional monitoring equipment is needed aboard. Many expensive, sophisticated systems are available, but it is doubtful if they are cost-effective.

The programs used were developed in conjunction with MCTS Cardiff who have considerable experience in maritime-related computer applications.

# CHAPTER ELEVEN

# REMAINING COMPETITIVE
# BY OPTIMISING PERFORMANCE

## 1. INTRODUCTION

The advent of the fuel crisis in 1973 was instrumental in producing very economical vessels mainly by a continual improvement in Main Engine efficiency, now probably approaching its practical limit. We must not forget that further improvements gained by ultra-sophisticated installations could be counterproductive, in that higher cost shipboard personnel may be deemed necessary. The latest strategy used by shipowners in remaining competitive is to reduce manning costs by various means, most of which are outside the scope of this book. The pressure to reduce the capital cost of a newbuilding is also at the forefront of most shipowners' minds to the detriment of what might be referred to as super economical designs that appeared a decade or so ago. There are, however, other aspects to be considered, and these are reviewed in this chapter.

## 2. DRY DOCKING

Dry dock and related costs figure high on the list of operational expenses and are probably the most important after fuel and manning, which can reverse pole position regularly dependent on fluctuations in crude oil prices.

Historically, most vessels dry docked on an annual basis and classification survey rules were more or less built up around this period. In those days dry docking costs were fairly cheap and there were no undue pressures on shipowners to extend this annual dry dock. Then, around 25 years ago, dry dock capacity could barely keep up with the demand, so costs started rising and intervals between dry dockings became longer.

Although dry dock capacity is now more than adequate and prices have softened considerably, most shipowners now dry dock at two to three year intervals. Some owners go to five years, which is the maximum allowed by the classification societies, and to achieve this period an intermediate "in water" survey is asked for.

These intermediate surveys must be held in clear water and are performed by divers using video cameras, and the transmitted pictures are witnessed by an attendant classification surveyor. However, restrictions on the toxicity of underwater paints has resulted in difficulties in achieving a five-year interval without suffering a serious loss in propulsive performance. Also, intermediate surveys conducted on tankers and bulk carriers to monitor corrosion have increased in content and severity and most owners appear to settle for a two- to three-year interval between dry dockings.

Another measure to reduce dry dock costs is the extended interval allowed between propeller shaft survey periods. When lignum vitae bushes were used to line stern tubes, propeller shaft surveys were held at two year intervals. As white metal bushes became increasingly used and securing arrangements between propeller and shaft improved, the interval progressively increased as the reliability of the superior methods were proven.

In the case of Lloyd's Register, for example, it is possible for owners to adopt an SCM (Screwshaft Condition Monitoring) assignment whereby screwshaft withdrawals may be waived altogether. This is dependent on the condition of the stern tube lubricating oil system being satisfactory during regular analysis results.

The toxicity restriction on underwater paints has dealt a severe blow to those owners who previously adopted a five-year interval between dry dockings. The paint manufacturers are of course working on the problem of producing a suitable paint acceptable to the authorities and at the same time discouraging the attachment of marine growth on the underwater hull, but a breakthrough does not yet appear to have taken place. It should be mentioned that toxicity restrictions are not yet applied worldwide but there is increasing pressure to do so and in the medium term TBT may be banned altogether.

Apart from adequate paint film thickness it is important that surface roughness is kept to an absolute minimum. Frictional resistance is directly related to the condition of the underwater hull, and when the vessel leaves dry dock it should be as smooth as possible. Meters are available for measuring hull roughness, and this should be done at each dry docking in order to check that no deterioration is taking place, and also provide a basis for measuring performance. It is not unknown for grit blasting operations to take place on an adjacent ship in a dry dock complex which deposits grit on a ship being painted with predicted catastrophic deterioration in the underwater surfaces.

Other items attended to at the dry docking include measurement of rudder and shaft clearances, renewal of anodes, examination/survey of sea valves and inlets and also ranging of anchors and cables. Hull steelwork damages and blemishes are also dealt with, usually with an underwriter's surveyor in attendance.

The next item highlights the difference between tanker and bulker operational scenarios. In the case of bulkers, it is normally expected that the ship's engineering staff can undertake most of the machinery survey items in service. Tanker operational patterns make this rather difficult, mainly because immobilisation of the main propulsion unit is not allowed at most tanker terminals. So the dry docking specification of a tanker will probably include many items not capable of being undertaken by ship's staff, whereas a bulker will have a much trimmed down specification.

Classification societies now allow approved chief engineers to carry out many machinery surveys on their behalf but no such relaxation is permitted with respect to hull structural surveys. Vessels' altered trading patterns and reduced inport periods have made surveys rather costly, and the societies have responded to the requests of shipowning organisations by allowing the relaxation mentioned above. It is unlikely that items of a purely safety nature would ever be entrusted to ship's staff.

The choice of dry dock is, of course, a very important aspect in the never-ending quest of reducing operating costs closely allied to improving the commercial performance. Currency rates also play an important part in the decision-making process, especially when related to the $US, the currency most frequently used for ship revenues.

Shipowners must spend a considerable amount of time drawing up a comprehensive dry dock specification, encouraging ship's staff to submit detailed drawings of any parts requiring renewal.

Scheduled rates for various standard jobs should also be obtained from the various shipyards asked to quote on the specification. These would include steelwork renewals per kg, and grit blasting per $M^2$. When the shipyard quotes are received, the cost of any vessel deviation must be added, and if a tanker is involved the cost of the slops removed taken into consideration. Removal of slops can be an expensive exercise in certain ports and it must be taken into consideration if, of course, it is necessary to remove the slops for work to be carried out.

An idea worthy of consideration is for the shipowner to draw up his own standard conditions, and have these accepted by the shipyard. Rejection or acceptance of this type of document is allied to the prevailing market conditions, which of late favour the shipowner. Included in this document would be the definition of the word "overhaul" when used in conjunction with a piece of machinery or equipment included in the specification. It should be clearly defined that overhaul means not only dismantling and assembling but also cleaning all the parts, calibrating those subject to wear and renewal of packings and jointings.

The condition of the vessel should be the same as when delivered to the shipyard, and additional costs for clearing up what might be called the contractor's mess and debris should be for their own account.

Costs for supplying dry dock services should be defined; in the case of electrical energy it is sometimes more cost-effective to run the ship's generators than to obtain the shipyard's supply. A modern diesel generator using heavy fuel oil can produce electricity at a cost of around $0.16 per unit and this should be compared with the shipyard's charge, which will include a cable connection fee.

Legal aspects concerning guarantee, contractor's liability and payment terms should also be included, especially when dealing with a shipyard for the first time. It is also a good idea to standardise the specification numbering, making it compatible with the accounts coding system, so that analysis of expenditure is made that much easier.

One unexpected result of the now accepted practice of extending dry dock intervals is the rather unknown condition of the underwater hull with respect to damaged steelwork. If major damage is found during the dry dock survey and no entry in the deck log is found that covers the incident then, after a three-year dry dock interval, it would be rather difficult to pinpoint the time. This could cause problems with the underwriters, and the vexed question of the number of voyage deductibles which would apply is raised. Ship's staff must record any incident in the official log-book, however trivial, so that damages with unknown causes are as far as possible eliminated.

By application of the measures mentioned in this section, coupled with close supervision by experienced personnel at the dry dock, it is possible to keep dry dock costs at a much reduced level. Part of this is due to the current depressed state of the ship repair industry, which, of course, cannot be guaranteed to continue. However, shipowners have made their own contribution in containing dry docking costs to today's reasonable level.

Dry docking operations are labour-intensive, and are not suitable for the volume production techniques employed by their cousins in the shipbuilding industry. It is, therefore, difficult for them to follow the cost-cutting exercises now standard in the shipbuilding industry with the possible exception of the major ship surgery operations.


## 3. VOYAGE REPAIRS/MAINTENANCE

Another operational expense is that incurred by voyage repairs and maintenance in the now lengthy periods between dry dockings. As vessels age, this becomes progressively difficult, and whereas ship's staff can normally overtake this function in the earlier years, they may not be able to do so in the latter part of a ship's economic life. Economic is the operative word as it may be found possible to physically carry out major renewals without too much disruption to the vessel's schedule, but the costs involved may prove uneconomical to the vessel's continued operation.

If we assume the average time between dry dockings equates to around 18,000 running hours on the main propulsion unit, we can run into difficulties on those parts which cannot bear this rather long interval without attention.

This is particularly directed to tanker operations in which, as previously mentioned, immoblisation of the main propulsion unit is not normally allowed by the port authorities. A planned schedule is, therefore, called for which would highlight these critical areas and arrange for a minumum period out of service for them to be carried out. It is unusual for bulk carriers to be faced with this problem as sufficient inport time is normally available, and immobilisation restrictions are rarely met with.

To encourage ship's staff to undertake as much maintenance as possible, they must be provided with the necessary tools and material to do the intended work. In the case of older vessels facing up to wholesale pipework renewals, sufficient lengths of the correct size pipe with adequate welding materials and a pipe bending machine must be made available in order that no delays are encountered.

If the scale of the operation is beyond the capabilities of the ship's staff then recourse to a so-called flying squad should be considered. Even taking into account repatriation costs, it has been found that using a flying squad is more cost-effective than using a shipyard—particularly so in what might be called high cost areas.

It is very important that several members of the ship's engine room complement are capable of carrying out all manner of welding jobs. It goes without saying that up-to-date welding equipment with adequate lengths of cable/gas piping to reach all parts of the vessel are provided.

A good selection of workshop machinery is essential if ship's staff are to help reduce dependence on expensive shore-based establishments. Training should be given in the overhaul of fuel pumps and injection valves and specialised lapping equipment obtained to facilitate this delicate type of work.

There are many other items of auxiliary equipment which must be kept in good order to maximise performance. Some of these tend to be overlooked, even though pressure and temperature sensors are generally fitted to indicate if they are functioning correctly.

Included in this category are the filters provided in the various main and sub-systems to protect delicate parts from the ingress of harmful particles. Failure to keep filters in good condition can lead to all sorts of operational problems, and the importance of maintaining their operational efficiency cannot be emphasised too strongly.

Other important pieces of equipment are the various heat exchangers which are used for such diverse purposes as heating the fuel for the Main Engine, boiler, generators—also for preheating the fuel prior to purification. They are also used for cooling scavenge air, jacket water and lubricating oil—also for condensing steam.

Any system malfunction resulting in high temperature conditions will probably cause precipitation of harmful impurities onto the heat exchanger surfaces, resulting in loss of efficiency. If the system temperature is not quickly restored to acceptable limits, serious damage can result.

In the case of main scavenge air coolers, an inbuilt chemical cleaning system is standard and should be used as recommended by the engine builders. The other heat exchangers should be cleaned when system operating conditions indicate fouling is starting to take place.

Turbo-chargers are another critical item in optimising performance and must be kept in good condition. They are subject to fouling, both on the gas and air sides. Arrangements are provided to water wash the gas side, and the air side can be similarly dealt with using a mild detergent. It is also possible to use a dry-cleaning technique on the gas side using rice or ground-nut shells instead of water. Dirty turbo-chargers have a knock-on effect on performance in that inefficient turbo-chargers provide insufficient combustion air to the engine, which results in imperfect combustion hence unburnt particles depositing themselves on the turbo-charger blades. If the situation is not restored quickly, a quite serious state of affairs can develop leading to all manner of problems in the combustion process.

Most of the subject matter that we have considered in this section relates to good housekeeping and this, of course, is a prerequisite of maximising performance.

There are other parts of the machinery to consider; for example, diesel generators, boilers and the electrical supply and distribution system.

Diesel generators require similar maintenance to that exercised on Main Engines and require no special comment except that in a well-designed engine room a diesel generator will always be available for overhaul at sea. This allows the ship's engineering staff sufficient time to undertake preventative maintenance tasks at sea, thus ensuring that the generators are in tiptop condition for cargo duties in port.

Boilers need to be kept clean both on the water and combustion sides, and are unlikely to survive between the two-yearly survey period without attention. Careful control should be kept on the boiler water and, in addition to the daily on board tests, the suppliers of the boiler water treatment should be asked for regular advice on the test results. Boiler corrosion can develop rapidly if the water is not kept in good condition and any signs of this not being the case should be followed up immediately.

One of the casualties in staff cutting exercises has been the ship's electrician and, except for vessels having complicated electrical systems, the electrician is nowadays rarely seen. It is a good idea to train the senior engineers in the rudiments of practical electrical knowledge so that they can deal with emergencies developing in the electrical systems.

Since a.c. replaced d.c. current 30 or so years ago, the preventative maintenance of electrical maintenance has decreased—especially in the case of generators and motors. Even so, routine electrical maintenance duties should be carried out by the engineers trained in this task.

## 4. CONDITION MONITORING

Of the machinery so far discussed in this chapter, we have not yet mentioned pumps, fans and other rotating equipment. One means of reducing the maintenance work-load on this type of equipment is to introduce condition monitoring in the form of vibration analysers and shock pulse meters.

Readings taken on a regular basis can be plotted on a time basis and indications of impending problems can be averted by taking the appropriate action. Classification Societies will accept this type of condition monitoring as an alternative to opening up the item for survey. Condition monitoring is only in its infancy when applied to the marine engineering industry, unlike many shore-based industries, which use it extensively.

Sophisticated condition monitoring systems can be used to measure wear on cylinder liners whilst the engine is running, they can also measure pressures and temperatures in the combustion process as a means of defining combustibility, to name but a few applications of their use. To be accepted they have to be cost-effective, and this aspect is presently being investigated by various professional institutions.

## 5. PLANNED MAINTENANCE

Planned maintenance systems became popular around 25 years ago and probably owed their popularity to the lack of continuity of serving engineer officers caused by unavaialbility of personnel. This made the previous method of committing the performance of each item of machinery to the then captive engineer's memory impossible. These systems can become paperwork generators inundating the shipowner's office with hundreds of forms he could well do without. When used in conjunction with a stock control and replacement ordering scheme these systems are very useful, providing the shipowner has the necessary checking procedure to intercept excessive overstocking.

It has been found beneficial to replace calendar-based intervals by running hour intervals, and cheap running hour meters have been connected to those pieces of equipment previously having unknown running periods.

Another beneficial move has been to allow those items of equipment due an overhaul or service under the planned maintenance system to be checked under working conditions, and if working satisfactorily the period can be extended. Items not normally capable of being unduly extended would include Main Engine pistons and turbo-chargers, and a fully developed condition monitoring system could help in these or similar cases.

Operational efficiency is dependent on the optimised performance of the vessel and its machinery, these two preprequisites could easily be stated in reverse order and still have the same meaning; the point being that whatever means are applied they must always be technically and commercially acceptable.

## 6. UNPLANNED MAINTENANCE

This particular aspect of the vessel's operational scenario is rather difficult to predict. Even in a well-run efficient vessel events can occur which will interfere with the schedule and also involve considerable cost. Most of these incidents will involve claims on the owner's hull and machinery policy and, such is the scope of the range of damages under this heading, it is difficult to single out any typical example.

One particular aspect which can progressively develop is the deterioration of steelwork due to the normal corrosion process, which, of course, is not covered by standard hull policy clauses. This can be visible in the case of the upper deck or out of sight as in the case of ballast tanks or cargo spaces.

The supply of a grit blaster and an adequate supply of grit can produce remarkable results with a well-motivated crew in a comparatively short time, given favourable weather conditions. This operation is ideally suited to the upper deck and hatch coaming area, but certain restrictions on their use in tanks and holds will, of course, apply.

Corrosion in ballast tanks, once started, can develop rather quickly and an adequate supply of sacrificial anodes can prevent costly steelwork repairs if applied at the onset of corrosion. It is very important that the paint schedule for a newbuilding is given careful consideration and, as mentioned earlier, ballast tank coatings are now part of classification regulations and so long as they are kept in good condition no serious problems should arise in service. It has been found that zinc silicate paint applied to the upper deck and other vulnerable areas will delay the onset of corrosion for many years.

Cargo gear, especially on tankers, is another item which can create havoc with the vessel's schedule. Cargo pumps, in many instances, rarely receive the priority treatment they deserve. Nowadays, diesel engineers account for a majority of certificated ranks and the steam certificated engineer is fast disappearing. The steam driven cargo pumps with horsepowers approaching that of some earlier Main Engines require careful attention and diesel engineers must be trained to give this otherwise expensive incidents will arise.

This could also apply to deck cranes, which nowadays are generally electro-hydraulic and require specialised maintenance techniques not normally acquired by seagoing engineers in the normal course of their career. Training courses at the manufacturer's works are strongly recommended if expensive breakdowns are to be avoided.

## 7. SPARES AND SUPPLIES

Expenditure under this heading accounts for a considerable proportion of direct operating expenses with spare part replacement probably taking the lion's share especially if the cost of air freighting these parts is included.

A critical examination of the actual stocks of spares held aboard some time ago did reveal that on average more parts than those disclosed in the inventory returns were held. It should be mentioned that the number of different items included in a complete inventory is quite large, the physical check time consuming and regular repeat examinations are therefore unlikely to be held.

This is an area in which strict controls can result in quite significant savings being made. One of the major faults is the more or less automatic ordering of replacements when parts are taken from the inventory into use.

When freight rates are high, and off hire periods can prove to be costly, it is rather important that spare part inventories are kept at a high level. When rates are low there is not the same importance in keeping to this philosophy, and some degree of risk can obviously be taken.

Most items of auxiliary machinery have a stand-by unit automatically brought into use when the on-line unit fails. This, in fact, is a Classification Society requirement for unmanned machinery space operation.

Given that the spare parts inventory will probably include the moving parts of the particular piece of equipment we have in mind, it follows that no less than three sets of parts subject to wear are carried for most auxiliary units. Obviously some sort of compromise can be made, taking into account that many shipowners are fighting for survival.

With respect to deck, engine and catering supplies—which include food— some sort of control should be exercised, whether it be by giving the master of the vessel a monetary spending limit or by screening the indents at head office.

When sterling is weak, it is has been found to be cost-effective to ship supplies to vessels on the European Continent from the UK and, in fact, this practice is extensively used.

A final point concerns airfreighting heavy machinery parts, which, of course, is a very expensive operation. Ship's staff should be made aware of this high cost factor and should be encouraged to plan overhauls, possibly requiring parts renewal, at ports having full spare part facilities; for example, Rotterdam and Yokohama. It is realised that this is not always possible, but efforts made in this direction can produce significant savings. It has been found that the provision of spare parts such as diesel generator crankshafts, turbocharger rotors and even propellers and tailshafts can avoid lengthy delays when they are found to be beyond repair. These rather expensive items can be held ashore if owners have two or more ships of identical design, so reducing the cost by having only one per series of ships instead of one per ship.

## 8. LUBRICATING OIL

Lubricating oil is a costly commodity and figures high on the list of operational expenses. A technical approach can be made to contain these expenses at what might be called acceptable levels of consumption.

Starting with cylinder oil, there is a distinct relationship between the amount of cylinder oil used and rate of wear on the cylinder liner walls. By supplying copious amounts of cylinder oil the rate of liner wear is much reduced, but a commercial viewpoint is necessary in order to consider all the facts.

Cylinder oil consumption is usually measured in grams per horsepower hour (g/b.h.p./hour) and liner wear rate is measured in millimetres per 1,000 running hours (mm/1,000 hours).

For an example, we could say that a cylinder oil feed rate of 0.7 g/b.h.p./hour gives a liner wear rate of 0.1 mm per 1,000 hours. On a 700 mm bore engine the maximum allowable wear is usually judged to be 5.5. mm so that the life of the cylinder liners would be:

$$\frac{5.5}{0.1} \times 1,000 = 55,000 \text{ hours}$$

say 9.2 years.

If we increased the feed rate to 1.0 g/b.h.p./hour we could, perhaps, reduce the liner wear rate to 0.08 mm/1,000 hours giving a liner life of:

$$\frac{5.5}{0.08} \times 1,000 = 68,750 \text{ hours}$$

or 11.4 years.

The cost of the increased oil can now be calculated. We will assume the engine in the example is 10,000 b.h.p. running 6,000 hours per year. With a feed rate of 0.7 g/b.h.p./hour the annual amount (kg) of cylinder oil consumed will be:

$$\frac{0.7 \times 10,000 \times 6,000}{1,000} = 42,000$$

and with cylinder oil at $0.90 per litre having a density of 0.96, the annual cost would be:

$$\frac{42,000}{0.96} \times \$0.90 = \$39,375$$

The annual cost of the increased feed rate would be:

$$\frac{1 \times 10,000 \times 6,000}{1,000 \times 0.96} \times \$0.90 = \$56,250$$

The question to be answered is can we justify paying $16,875 per year in additional cylinder oil to extend the life of the cylinder liners 2.3 years? The answer is probably "no", but it could depend on the shipowner's intentions about whether to sell the vessel and, if so, when.

What can be learned from this simple exercise is that an increase in the cylinder oil feed rate of 0.1 g/b.h.p./hour costs:

$$\frac{\$16,875}{3} = \$5,625 \text{ per year}$$

and must be balanced against any improvement in cylinder life, itself dependent on the owner's sales policy.

In the case of crankcase oil, the consumption is not a feed rate, as is the case for cylinder oil, but is really a loss rate caused by a variety of reasons. These include leakages from crankcase doors and piston rod glands, evaporation losses and losses in the purification system.

A well looked after machinery installation will have a crankcase oil consumption of around 0.3 g/b.h.p./hour. Because crankcase oil is cheaper than cylinder oil an increase of 0.1 g/b.h.p./hour in the example given earlier would have an annual cost of around $4,100 per year.

A brief word on the performance of these commodities may now be appropriate. Cylinder oil has a joint function in that it lubricates the cylinder liner piston ring interface and additionally neutralises the acidic products of combustion in this hostile area, thus preventing corrosion.

As Main Engine pressures and temperatures are increased to optimise thermal efficiency, the function of cylinder oil is approaching its limit in a hydrocarbon form. Research is proceeding to produce a pure synthetic or synthetic-based cylinder oil capable of meeting the rigorous requirements now demanded in order to contain cylinder liner wear at an acceptable level—which is proving difficult on these new highly rated long stroke engines.

The consumption of lubricating oil in diesel generator engines must also be considered, even though it is usually less than the lubrication consumption of the Main Engine cylinder and crankcase oil. Because of the comparatively low powers developed in diesel generators, it is not usual to relate the lubricating oil consumption to power as in the case of Main Engines, but simply to state it in litres per day. On a modern diesel generator engine we can expect a lubricating oil consumption in the range of 20 litres per day.

So how can we monitor the performance of lubricating oil? A simple table as indicated is considered sufficient for most purposes:

**Table 17. Lubricating oil performance**

| Vessel | Average output ME % | Liner wear | | Cylinder oil consumption | | Crankcase oil consumption | | Diesel generator consumption | |
|--------|---------------------|------|------|------|------|------|------|------|------|
|        |                     | 93/4 | 94/5 | 93/4 | 94/5 | 93/4 | 94/5 | 93/4 | 94/5 |
| A      | 65                  | 0.07 | 0.07 | 0.7  | 0.6  | 0.3  | 0.3  | 25   | 24   |
| B      | 71                  | 0.08 | 0.07 | 0.6  | 0.6  | 0.4  | 0.4  | 21   | 19   |

Vessels can be grouped into the various oil suppliers and average results compared with each other if more than one supplier is used. Target values for the liner wear and tabled consumptions can also be shown.

It is also possible to monitor the rate of cylinder liner wear indicating maximum liner wear readings on an elapsed time basis as shown in Fig. 44. This gives an accurate indication of cylinder liner wear, and the slope of the individual cylinder curves will indicate changes in the wear rate pattern. Feed rate changes, or even changes in the supplier of the oil, can be introduced and the result of these changes shown at subsequent cylinder calibrations.

Using this approach it was possible to demonstrate the rather remarkable increase in the rate of liner wear occasioned by the use of fuel with a high level of naphthenic acid and helped convince underwriters' surveyors of the creditability of our claim.

The condition of the system lubricating oils used in Main Engines and diesel generators is subject to vigorous attacks, usually connected with the combustion process. Lubricating oils must have an alkalinity reserve to combat the ingress of acidic particles, and regular checks must be made on the oil's condition. Simple test kits are provided by the oil companies for onboard testing and, in addition, regular more thorough tests are made in the oil companies' laboratories. These laboratory tests include sophisticated metallic particle counts which will indicate if any excessive wear is taking place on the metallic bearing surfaces and ideally will avoid serious breakdowns.

We have seen how by monitoring the consumption of the various lubricating oils we can effect savings, we can also monitor the performance of different suppliers' oils, but this is not normally immediately apparent and some time must elapse before any oil's superior performance is established. This would probably involve at least one piston overhaul during which cylinder calibrations are taken and a two-year period could be involved.

## 9. INSURANCE AND P & I

Premiums and calls paid by shipowners under the general heading of insurance are also a considerable part of direct operating expenses. They are directly related to what might be called the performance of the shipowner as reflected by the extent of his claims on underwriters and P & I clubs. Obviously the more efficiently an owner operates his vessels so the incidence of claims will be reduced, and this will be reflected in his premiums for the following year.

A significant amount of major hull damage claims concern groundings, and it is very important that up-to-date hydrographical charts are supplied to the vessels and that these are kept up-to-date by making corrections as regularly advised by the authorities.

In a recent arbitration it was ruled that shipowners have the ultimate responsibility in ensuring that this aspect is fully complied with, and negligent acts by ship's staff do not abrogate this responsibility. The significance of this ruling is far-reaching in that insurance cover for owner's negligent action must be covered—probably by the owner's P & I club.

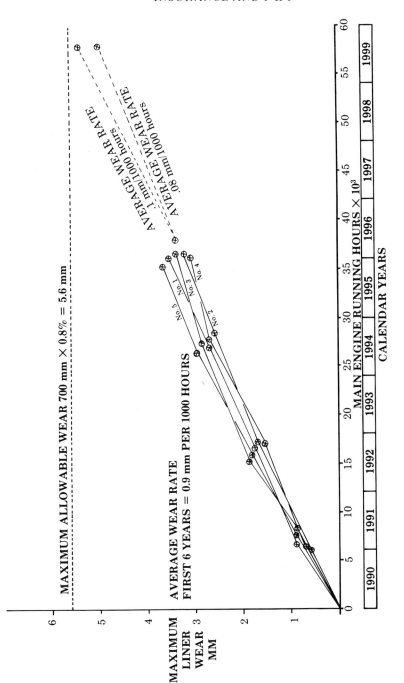

*Fig. 44. Cylinder liner wear graph*

If we assume that most hull damage claims can be attributed to a known incident, owners do not have any problem stating a cause. As previously mentioned, this does not include those damages discovered in dry dock, which may be delegated into a date and cause unknown category if log entries are not sufficiently detailed. Shipowners are then left with the problem of presenting underwriters with a cause when machinery damage claims are being examined by underwriter surveyors.

The main problem is to identify the cause with a relevant clause in the hull and machinery policy. These clauses do vary dependent on where the insurance cover is placed, whether it be London, New York or Gothenburg to name but a few of the more often used insurance centres.

It is in the shipowner's interest that the clauses applicable to his fleet are known to those members of his staff dealing with claims, and this should include the master and chief engineer.

Machinery damages are in some instances simply due to fair wear and tear and are, therefore, not covered by any standard hull and machinery policy clauses. It is, however, very important that each incident is fully investigated by competent personnel so that all avenues are exhausted before it is placed in this category.

Speedy settlement of legitimate claims is in the shipowner's interest as he has already paid the contractor for carrying out the work, and lengthy delays in dealing with the adjustment of the claim can be costly.

The question of seaworthiness is sometimes brought up, especially when cargo underwriters' interests are concerned, for example when a vessel is diverted to a port of refuge due to damage and general average is declared.

Normally the costs involved in general average, which can include substantial towage costs, are shared by the hull and machinery underwriters and cargo underwriters on a pro rata respective value basis.

If cargo underwriters can show that the vessel involved was at the commencement of the voyage in question unseaworthy then they will probably refuse to contribute to their portion of general average expenses. It is very important, therefore, that shipowners ensure that in all respects their vessels are seaworthy at the commencement of a voyage if they are not to be placed in this position.

Finally, if vessels are out of service or subject to excessive port delays this information should be communicated to the underwriters for a possible reduction in premium payment. Strictly speaking underwriters should be told every time a vessel makes a diversion or deviation, for example to pick up bunkers or land an injured seaman. Failure to do this could result in problems arising if the vessel was involved in a collision or grounding; the principle being that the vessel would not have had the accident had it prosecuted the voyage with utmost dispatch, to use the legal term.

## 10. MISCELLANEOUS CHARGES

The final category of operational expenses comes under the heading of miscellaneous. These will normally include radio traffic, agents' disbursements, various fees and, perhaps, a management fee in the use of managed vessels.

Radio traffic costs are usually monitored by one of several specialised firms who, for a nominal sum, will look after the commercial interests of the shipowner. In recent years telex and satellite communication systems have improved the performance of message transmission between the vessel and the owner/operator. On time-chartered vessels those messages sent which are related to charterers' activities should, of course, be paid by them.

Agents' disbursements require careful vetting by experienced personnel in order to properly apportion the various charges. Agents generally ask for, and usually receive, funds to cover owners' expected outlays during the vessel's visit. This also is an area requiring careful control as it is not unknown for some unscrupulous agents to ask for excessive funds, leaving owners the sometimes impossible task of retrieving the surplus.

Such is the nature and scope of the subject matter included in this section that it is very difficult to generalise. It does appear that, in some instances, the control of miscellaneous charges is not given the attention it deserves.

## 11. SUMMARY OF CHAPTER ELEVEN

We have learned how dry dock costs have effectively been reduced mainly by lengthening the interval between dry dockings, although this has suffered a set-back if the vessel dry docks in an area in which a TBT paint restriction applies. Various other measures open to shipowners to make them more competitive are described.

CHAPTER TWELVE

# PAST, PRESENT AND FUTURE

## 1. INTRODUCTION

Most of the various factors affecting performance of existing and proposed new-buildings have been reviewed. We should now stand back and look at the performance of past vessels and review this against current designs and possibilities for the future.

## 2. THE PAST

As we have generally confined our comments to what might nowadays be called conventional vessels, we will only go back in time to when the situation started to change and economies of scale played a big part in the development of new designs.

During the Second World War, and immediately after, the then standard vessel was a 10,000 TDW tween deck dry cargo bulker as typified by the large number of wartime Liberty, Fort and Empire vessels built during this period. Tankers tended to be slightly larger, probably on account of the fact that they did not use enclosed dock systems with their severe restrictions on vessels' dimensions.

The machinery on these wartime-built vessels was invariably steam reciprocating with oil fired boilers, the Liberty ships had an added attraction in being supplied with water tube boilers instead of the Scotch boilers used extensively during the period.

Performance was not a consideration when ordering a vessel in those days. They were all of a muchness, having a loaded speed of around 10 knots and a consumption of about 35 tons fuel oil. Coal burners were still to be occasionally found and their consumption rose to around 50 tons per day for a similar performance.

A small percentage of vessels were fitted with diesel engines and their consumption would be around 12 tons of diesel oil. Heavy fuel oil was not to become popular until the 1950s and diesel oil was used more or less exclusively until then.

Towards the end of the war the Victory design came into service; these vessels were turbine driven and had somewhat larger deadweights and higher speeds. The T2 tanker also came into service during this period and represented a major step forward in that they were provided with turbo-electric machinery with the main propulsion unit driving the propeller at sea, and the cargo pumps whilst in port.

Peacetime designs for bulk carriers followed the wartime standard vessels in that they were still tween deckers, but an increasing number of diesel engines were being specified.

British and Norwegian fleets then headed the league table of shipowning nations and Doxford, Harland & Wolff (B&W) Sulzer and Gotarverken engines gradually replaced steam engines.

In the case of tankers, steam turbines were also popular—especially with British and US fleets, both of whom were rather dominant in the oil industry. Norwegian owners tended to favour diesel propulsion and kept to this choice even when deadweight capacity started to rise in the mid-1950s.

Self-trimming bulk carriers also became popular around this time and the time-consuming practice of erecting shifting boards on tween deckers when carrying grain cargoes became a thing of the past.

As tankers and bulk carriers started their ever-increasing size leap-frogging tactics steam turbines occasionally were favoured if only because diesel engine designs could not keep pace with the increased outputs demanded by the higher deadweights. Even as late as 1973 steam turbine VLCCs were keeping up with diesel designs but the oil crisis in the autumn of that year was eventually to change all that.

This was the first of several oil crises which saw bunker prices rise from $20 a tonne to $80 then approaching $200, a peak reached in the early 1980s. These price hikes sounded the death knell for the steam turbine and even though oil prices have now softened, it would appear unlikely that steam turbines will reappear in any large numbers.

When oil prices are high, ship's speed is a very expensive commodity and horsepowers in general terms are then lower than they were during low oil price periods.

There was recently some interest shown in coal-burning steam turbine vessels and several were built in Korea and Japan. They owed their short-lived popularity to a period when oil prices peaked at nearly $200 a tonne and coal prices became competitive if the additional capital costs for these rather special ships were largely ignored.

The oil price hikes, as well as dealing a death blow to the steam turbine, also focused attention on the thermal efficiency of current diesel engine designs—then running at around 40%.

One of the problems with the then current diesel engines was their rather high revolutions. The first diesel VLCCs had propeller revolutions of 100–110 RPM whereas the steam turbine VLCC's propellers turned at around 70 RPM, which made them more efficient from a propulsive point of view.

Several slow-speed diesel vessels using gearboxes to reduce the propeller revolutions were designed but, as far as is known, none were built. It should be mentioned that medium-speed diesels are invariably geared down and have always had this advantage over their slow-speed rivals.

The derated slow-speed long stroke diesel then made its appearance and immediately the high revolution problem was solvable, albeit at additional cost. A derated diesel engined VLCC could be run at the same revolutions as an equivalent sized steam turbine. Derating proved to be rather costly for reasons previously explained and engine designers now tend to offer fully rated engines tailor made for ship types. Recent examples include engines for post Panamax container ships and low RPM engines for VLCCs.

Other technical developments during this period mainly revolved around energy conservation measures occasioned by the high fuel costs.

The size of tankers stabilised at around 540,000 TDW in the late 1970s even though designs for 1,000,000 TDW ULCCs were produced and several shipyards have the capabilities of building these mammoths.

Commercial reasons, rather than conservation measures, were largely the cause of the decline in the tanker market and it is only comparatively recently that replacement VLCCs have been contracted for. It would appear unlikely that ULCCs will ever again become popular, purely for commercial and *not* technical reasons.

Bulk carriers appear to have stabilised and the current maximum deadweight is around 350,000 TDW. These so-called VLBCs are generally designed for specific trades; for example, iron ore from South America to Japan.

Returning to diesel engine design, the thermal efficiency had—as previously mentioned—stabilised at around 40% ever since the introduction of two stroke turbo-charging in the early 1950s. Thermal efficiencies have steadily improved, mainly by increasing the degree of turbo-charging, which leads to higher cyclic pressures and temperatures and, of course, efficiency —and efficiencies can be as high as 53% if additional equipment such as power turbines are provided although this is not currently fashionable on economic grounds.

Automation of machinery spaces started gaining popularity in the early 1960s and eventually led to the unmanned engine room. In the beginning no serious attempt to substantially reduce manning as a result of introducing automation was made, probably because manning costs were not a problem. The recent prolonged trough the market is experiencing, however, has directed attention to manning costs. Some of the high crew-cost shipowning nations, notably Scandinavian ones, have made significant reductions in manning numbers, enabling nationals to be employed in the surviving berths. Even this drastic action does not always appear to be sufficient. Flagging out and offshore agreements now have the same sort of press coverage energy conservation had a decade or so ago.

## 3. THE PRESENT

This brings us up to the present, which, from a commercial point of view, is decidedly poor with many owners unable to match earnings with finance and operating costs.

Not so many newbuildings are being contracted for and most shipbuilding nations are reducing capacity in an attempt to weather the storm. The overlying trend in worldwide seaborne trade is not declining significantly, but too many vessels were built on purely speculative grounds and, until equilibrium is restored, the market is unlikely to substantially recover.

Present-day designs are not as efficient as those entering service several years ago, mainly because the emphasis has shifted from technical efficiency to reduced first cost. However, in the case of tankers and bulk carriers recent legislation has made it more expensive to operate older vessels.

Most surviving shipowners have made strenuous efforts to remain competitive by building efficient vessels and reducing operating costs on the lines mentioned in previous chapters.

European flag vessels have been reduced in numbers since the days when the UK and Norway headed the league and these former shipowning powers are now well down the list after Liberia, Panama and other emergent nations.

Shipbuilding costs in mid-1995 have softened compared with several years ago. A VLCC cost around $16m in 1968. This gradually rose to $40m in 1974. In the early 1980s it had risen to around $70m and in the third quarter, 1995, the price is around $85–$90 not forgetting the contribution that the provision of double hulls has made.

Many European officers and crew have been replaced, usually by lower cost Far Eastern employees. The haste with which this transfer was accomplished was quite remarkable and the situation of shortages in key ranks which was prevelant in Europe in the last decade could conceivably reappear.

A typical present-day vessel will have a main engine tailor made to suit its operating requirements but will in all probability not have any sophisticated energy conservation features. Registry will probably be Monrovia, Hong Kong or other currently fashionable port with the owner's name not immediately recognisable as coming from a familiar shipowning stable. Officers and crew will probably be a mixture of nationalities and supplied by an agency having its office in the Far East. The nationality of the master may give a clue to the identity and location of the beneficial owner, but this cannot always be relied on. Because of the fragmented nature of this type of operation it will be difficult to comply with the ISM code when it becomes mandatory in 1998 under SOLAS regulations.

The performance of the vessel may conceivably be lower than that of a comparable vessel built 10 years or so ago but in relative terms its capital cost will have been reduced by not specifying expensive energy saving measures. Advances in technology will mean that less maintenance is required and fewer staff needed to operate her. This coupled with comparatively low shipbuilding costs and perhaps favourable finance terms could make it attractive for speculators to move in and order newbuildings even though the initial return on investment looks bleak.

## 4. THE FUTURE

Viewed from the midst of the longest recollectable recession in the shipping industry, it is rather difficult to predict the future without becoming influenced by the current gloom. It can only be said that those shipowners who do survive will be leaner and fitter, to quote a well-known phrase.

There would appear to be very little scope for any significant improvement in the thermodynamic efficiency of Main Diesel Engines except for the re-introduction of the rather expensive derating approach favoured several years ago but nowadays only rarely used. Further slight improvements in efficiency may become possible due to the introduction of higher combustion pressures in fully rated engines. There is also a likelihood of introducing electronic activation of exhaust valves and fuel pumps if this proves to be economically and technologically attractive. A recent trend by the Main Engine manufacturers is to produce engines specifically aimed at ship types, for example large bore slow RPM engines with only five or six cylinders for the propulsion of VLCCs. The largest diesel engines now offered have outputs of over 90,000 BHP, these mammoths being aimed at the post Panamax container ships.

Propeller design has not drastically altered over the last decades and propellers will in all probability continue to be the main source of propulsion for conventional vessels in the short to medium term. An electromagnetic thrust system has been under development for many years and if proven to be successful could supersede screw propellers for propulsion of specialised vessels, but indications are that this could be some time off.

The recent introduction of HSS ships using either water jets or super cavitating propellers as their propulsive method was necessary on account of their high speed. Those HSS ships that employ various means to reduce the immersed hull area whilst at speed offer the greatest opportunity for improving hydrodynamic performance. By employing these means the penal effect of the cube law relationship can be reduced somewhat and resort to higher speeds commercially justified.

Even higher speeds have been proposed for the so-called "wing in ground" craft, which operate just above the surface of the sea at speeds approaching those usually identified with aircraft, whose aerodynamic principles they closely follow.

It would appear unlikely that really large vessels such as VLCCs and bulk carriers would adopt such novel propulsive methods in the short to medium term and they would generally be restricted to passenger vessels or perhaps small sized container ships.

The availability of crude oil reserves appears to be ever increasing and those gloomy forecasts of yesteryear no longer heard. Research into alternative fuels for marine propulsion is currently at a rather low ebb.

Those alternative fuels under investigation just a few years ago are now rarely mentioned and include coal, methanol and even plutonium. Unless some serious political unrest takes place the use of oil as the principal means of ship propulsion seems secure even in the long term.

However, should oil supplies become endangered or too costly it would be a fairly straightforward operation to switch to coal fired steam turbine or even steam reciprocating engine propulsion. Several coal fired steam propelled bulkers were built in the 1980s so the technology still exists even if the logistics involved in providing worldwide coal bunkering stations would severely tax the resourcefulness of the coal producers.

A much simpler solution would possibly be the direct conversion of the abundant reserves of coal into oil by methods already in use. Reserves of natural gas are considerably greater than crude oil at current consumption levels and gas is replacing oil in many shore-based plants to the obvious security of future oil supplies.

The world oil supply and demand situation has barely changed over the last five years or so and recent statistics from Intertanko are shown in Fig. 46.

Recent propulsion systems have incorporated the use of wind power, usually as a contribution rather than as the sole source of power. In certain applications they do make a positive contribution to the overall economy, but whether the capital cost coupled with the additional labour required for sail operation can be justified is the subject of much debate. It would appear unlikely that these would catch on from an international basis in that low cost Far Eastern operators would not be favourably impressed.


## 5. SUMMARY OF CHAPTER TWELVE

We have seen how diesel propulsion gradually took over from steam, leading to the virtual extinction of steam propulsion in the early 1980s.

The thermal efficiency of the diesel engine has steadily risen from 40% to the current 53%, providing rather expensive additional equipment is provided. A fully rated engine has the possibility of reaching around 55% by increasing cyclical pressures in the medium term. Research into alternative fuels is not presently the subject of serious thought mainly because oil supplies appear secure in the immediate future. Apart from the recent advent of the HSS ship there is very little research being undertaken into alternative means of propulsion for conventional ships, which form the major part of our study.

| | 1991 | 1992 | 1993 | 1994 Q1 | Q2 | Q3 | Q4 | 1994 | 1995 Q1 | Q2 | Q3 | Q4 | 1995 |
|---|---|---|---|---|---|---|---|---|---|---|---|---|---|
| Demand | 66.9 | 67.2 | 67.1 | 69.3 | 66.3 | 67.4 | 69.8 | 68.2 | 70.2 | 67.5 | 68.3 | 71.1 | 69.3 |
| Of which: OECD* | 38.2 | 38.8 | 39.1 | 40.6 | 38.7 | 39.7 | 40.7 | 39.9 | 41.0 | 39.3 | 39.9 | 41.3 | 40.4 |
| non-OECD** | 28.8 | 28.4 | 28.1 | 28.7 | 27.6 | 27.7 | 29.0 | 28.3 | 29.2 | 28.2 | 28.4 | 29.8 | 28.9 |
| Stock Change*** | 0.0 | 0.1 | 0.3 | -1.3 | 1.4 | 0.8 | -0.1 | 0.2 | -1.0 | 1.2 | 1.1 | 0.7 | 0.1 |
| Total Supply: | 66.9 | 67.3 | 67.4 | 68.0 | 67.7 | 68.2 | 69.7 | 68.4 | 69.2 | 68.7 | 69.4 | 70.4 | 69.5 |
| Non-OPEC Supply | 41.8 | 41.1 | 40.5 | 40.9 | 40.6 | 41.0 | 42.2 | 41.2 | 41.9 | 41.3 | 41.5 | 42.5 | 41.8 |
| OPEC Crude Prod. | 23.0 | 24.1 | 24.7 | 24.9 | 24.8 | 24.9 | 25.2 | 25.0 | 24.9 | 24.9 | 25.4 | 25.4 | 25.2 |
| OPEC NGL Prod. | 2.1 | 2.1 | 2.2 | 2.2 | 2.3 | 2.3 | 2.4 | 2.3 | 2.4 | 2.5 | 2.5 | 2.5 | 2.5 |

* Figures for German eastern states included in OECD Europe
** Includes estimated domestic demand figures for the FSU and China
*** Stock draw (−) or Stock build (+) and Miscellaneous to balance
The call on OPEC crude prod. for 1994 has been estimated on no change in oil stocks

[Source: IEA/INTERTANKO]

*Fig. 45. World oil supply and demand (million barrels daily)*

# CONCLUSION

The steady improvement in the performance of ships over the last decades has made the cost of sea transport much cheaper. Even so, most shipowners of the type of vessel reviewed in this book are finding it difficult to stay in business.

A 20-year-old diesel VLCC travels only 5.4 miles per tonne of fuel consumed, a modern VLCC will travel 7.7 miles per tonne. This 40% improvement in performance is typical for all the ship types reviewed in this book. From a technical point of view there is not the same possibility of improving the performance of a modern vessel as there was 10 years ago. Therefore, most owners have directed their attention to the reduction of direct operating costs and currently manning is under scrutiny. Efforts to reduce the capital cost of a new ship have generally been to the exclusion of providing performance enhancing equipment. The forthcoming introduction of the ISM code by the IMO could have a marked effect on those operators who will find it difficult to comply with the detailed procedures included in the code.

Flagging out, offshore agreements and outside management contracts are now the vogue and manning costs have been reduced substantially by employing various combinations of these. Some shipowners have retained their National Flag with personnel greatly reduced in number but highly trained and Panamax size vessels can be manned with a total complement of 18 using this approach. This would compare with around 28 when using a Far Eastern low cost management company but these numbers can vary so much that it would be dangerous to draw firm conclusions.

Another possibility for reducing operating costs gaining in popularity is to write down the ship's value to reflect a more accurate assessment of its current value, thus reducing depreciation costs. This specialised subject is, however, outwith the scope of this book. In a similar manner the insured value can also be reduced, thus effecting a saving in insurance premium payments. It is also possible to increase the deductible value of each casualty accident, which can result in savings in a well run fleet but could be counter productive in a not so well run fleet. By employing these various economies direct operating costs can be reduced from around $4,000 to approximately $2,500 per day, and even lower figures can be obtained at the expense of having a less efficient operation.

The large amount of surplus tonnage is the main reason that freight rates are depressed and no positive improvement can take place until this surplus is absorbed in some way or other. Owners of modern efficient ships with low operating costs will obviously stand a better chance of capitalising on this when the market recovers.

Up until the present time (fourth quarter, 1995) the freight market shows no signs of recovery. It has previously always staged a recovery for reasons not apparently obvious at the time. If and when the recovery comes, those owners who have taken steps to optimise performance without incurring too high an expense by providing equipment unlikely to recover its cost should have a reasonable future.

Finally, it should always be borne in mind that fuel costs are not under any form of control and the situation existing in the mid-1980s could easily reappear.

# GLOSSARY

**Aframax**
A size of tanker in the range of 80,000 DWT (deadweight) and above. It is a definition relating to chartering rather than operational or technical reasons.

**Air draught**
Is the distance from the waterline to the highest fixed point of a vessel's structure, usually but not necessarily the top of a mast. Air draught can be reduced by employing such means as hinged masts or by flooding cargo holds.

**Australian hold ladders**
These are angled ladders provided in the cargo holds of mainly bulk carriers and so designed to limit the vertical distance allowed. Rest platforms and handrails are also required as laid down in regulations issued by the Australian Waterworkers Union.

**Bar**
Is a unit of pressure used extensively in the marine industry. It is equal to a column of mercury in vacua of 750mm. For the convenient measurement of atmospheric pressure it is divided into 1,000 millibars. The Bar is not an SI (Système International) unit and eventually will be replaced with an approved SI unit, for example $Kgf/cm^2$, to take into account gravitational acceleration, hardly appropriate in the marine environment.

**Bending moment**
A mechanical assessment of the bending forces acting on the hull of a ship. In still water conditions the bending moments are easily calculated if the weights of cargo, ballast and bunkers are known and the ship then considered as a simply supported beam. At sea, bending moments are more difficult to determine due to the action of waves as they pass along the ship. Every ship must possess a loading manual and a loading instrument in order to determine the allowable still water bending moment. Allowable wave bending moments are prescribed in classification rules.

**Boil off gas**
Gas tankers generate a certain amount of gas when the liquid cargo receives heat through the insulation and this is known as boil off. In the case of LPG

(liquid petroleum gas) this boil off gas is re-liquefied onboard and returned to the cargo tank. The boil off gas from LNG (liquid natural gas) tankers is piped to the boilers and used as fuel to drive the steam turbines. It has not yet been used to provide fuel for diesel engines.

## Bow thruster

A bow thruster is a device arranged at the fore end of a ship and usually consists of a propeller housed in a transverse duct so arranged as to exert a sideways thrust at right angles to the lines of the ship. Thrust can be reversed by various means such as controllable pitch propellers or by a series of adjustable vanes. Bow thrusters are very useful during berthing operations and on some vessels stern thrusters are also provided.

## Bulbous bow

Most ships are now built with a bulbous bow. They fulfil a dual role, one being to increase buoyancy forward and therefore reduce pitching in bad weather. Their other function is to reduce the size of the bow wave and therefore reduce resistance from this source. The down side is that the wetted area is increased and with it the frictional resistance.

## Cape sized bulkers

Are simply those whose dimensions preclude them from using the Suez Canal and they therefore use the Cape of Good Hope route. They are usually around 150,000 DWT depending on Suez Canal restrictions in force.

## Carcinogenic

Are substances having properties exposure to which is thought to lead to cancer. Typical examples in the marine industry would be asbestos and certain chemicals carried as cargo.

## Cathodic protection

Electrolytic action occurs when dissimilar metals are immersed in an electrolyte, the metal with the highest electro-chemical number becomes a cathode and the lowest an anode. In a cathodic protection scheme the vessel's hull and propeller are cathodes and the seawater the electrolyte. Anodes usually in the form of zinc blocks attached to the underwater hull complete the electrolytic circuit with the result that they corrode away and in doing so protect the hull and propeller. Cathodic protection is also employed in ballast tanks using the same principle.

## CIMAC

Also known as the International Council on Combustion Engines. CIMAC is an international organisation concerned with all aspects of diesel engine design and operation. It is probably best known for its work on producing fuel oil specifications now accepted as the standard in the marine industry.

### Classification surveys

These fall into various categories such as annual, intermediate, docking, continuous and special surveys which are held to ensure that a vessel and its machinery are maintained according to classification rules and regulations. In recent years the survey of the hull structure on vulnerable ships has increased in severity due to repetitive problems found in service. The holds of bulk carriers and ballast tanks of all ships are cases in point and these must now be surveyed at 2½ year intervals instead of the five-year period previously allowed.

### Class shopping

An activity practised by some shipowners in order to reduce operating costs. If faced with the possibility of a huge repair bill for carrying out specified work by a classification surveyor the shipowner will contact another Classification Society in the hope that its specification for the work will be less onerous. This activity is strongly discouraged by members of the IACS (International Association of Classification Societies).

### Coulombi egg tanker

A design of tanker by Anders Bjorkman put forward as an alternative to the double hull tanker now required if trading to the US. The Coulombi egg design does not have a double bottom ballast tank but does have side ballast tanks extending to below the waterline. There is also a horizontal division in the cargo oil tanks. This design has not been approved by either the IMO (International Maritime Organisation) or the USGC (United States Coast Guard) as an acceptable alternative to the double hull design.

### Condition monitoring

A system used to monitor the condition of running machinery without the need to dismantle the parts for inspection. Vibration analysers and shock pulse meters are the main instruments used on rotating machines. In the case of propeller shafts regular analysis of the lubricating oil system is part of an acceptable condition monitoring system in lieu of withdrawing the shaft.

### Constant pressure turbocharging

Is now the standard method of turbocharging used on all slow speed, 2-stroke main diesel engines. In this method the exhaust gas from each cylinder exhaust valve is led into a common manifold running the length of the engine which acts as a constant pressure accumulator. Outlets from this manifold lead into the turbochargers, which are then fed with this steady gas flow leading to improved thermodynamic conditions.

### Container fittings

These are varied both in size and shape and perform the important function of keeping the containers safely secured even in the severest of weather conditions. Those containers stowed underdeck invariably rely wholly on the fixed cell guides as a restraint. Some modern container vessels are provided with on deck cell guides which are also capable of restraining the containers.

The majority of container ships, however, require loose fittings to secure the on deck containers. These include stacking cones, twistlocks, bridge fittings, lashing rods and chains, all of which form part of a system approved by the relevant Classification Society.

### Continuous Service Rating (CSR)

The power at which the main propulsion engine is capable of being operated at throughout its useful life. It is usually fixed at between 85 and 90% of the Maximum Continuous Rating (MCR), dependent on the practice of the shipowner.

### Contra rotating propellers

An arrangement whereby two propellers are mounted in tandem and in close proximity with each other. They are mechanically attached to shafting so arranged as to turn one propeller clockwise and the other in an anti-clockwise direction. They are claimed to give a vessel a high hydrodynamic efficiency.

### Controllable pitch propeller (CPP)

These are mainly used on passenger ferries and other such vessels engaged in frequent manoeuvring activities although they are occasionally used on deep sea cargo vessels. The blades of CPP propellers can be moved from the full ahead to the full astern position whilst the Main Engine is still turning at full revolutions, making for a speedy astern response.

### Deadweight (DWT)

Is the tonnage of cargo, fuel, fresh water and stores a ship can carry when at its respective freeboard marks, usually corresponding to the summer loadline draught when describing a ship for chartering purposes. The deadweight at other draughts can easily be determined by reference to the deadweight scale carried onboard.

### Deepwell pumps

These are generally used in the chemical carrier and product tanker trades. They are typically arranged with one deepwell pump in each cargo tank. This is a particularly good arrangement in avoiding cross-contamination of cargoes via suction lines, not required when using these pumps. Deepwell pumps are located at the lowermost part of the cargo tank and are usually driven by deck mounted hydraulic motors. The practice of stripping cargo tanks is particularly effective when using deepwell pumps.

### Derating

A method used to increase the thermal efficiency of a Main Diesel Engine albeit at considerable cost to the shipowner. It involves operating an engine at reduced output whilst still maintaining the maximum combustion pressure (P Max) for which it was designed. The unit cost of a derated engine expressed in $ per horsepower is therefore higher when compared with a fully rated engine as the delivered cost of the engine is the same in both instances.

## Displacement

The actual weight of a vessel and all it contains at a given draught. It is the sum of the deadweight plus the lightship weight and, in similar vein to the deadweight, can be determined from the deadweight scale.

## Distillate fuels

These are fuels which have been through the refinery distillation process and generally have densities of between 0.85 and 0.90 Kg/litre dependent on the level of distillation employed. So-called straight-run distillate typically had a density of 0.85 but is rarely called for in the marine industry. Nowadays, distillate fuels have densities approaching 0.90 usually controlled by admixture with a heavier grade at the refinery.

## Doppler logs

Are an extremely accurate method of measuring ship's speed. They work on the principle of the Doppler effect which can be likened to the apparent change in pitch of a fast moving train's whistle. The whistle has not actually changed its pitch but the sound waves approaching the observer are altered by the speed of the train.

## Double hulls

Double hull ships in the form of certain chemical carriers have been the norm for many years as reflected by the dangers posed by the cargoes they can carry. The double hull forms an effective barrier completely around the bottom and sides of the cargo spaces to prevent the escape of cargo in the event of a collision or grounding. This philosophy is now being extended to other ship types and oil tankers are the most recent example with other ships also being targeted by the IMO (International Maritime Organisation).

## Draw cards

These are superimposed on an indicator diagram (which see) in order to study the critical part of the combustion process in a diesel engine when fuel injection takes place. The curve so traced clearly shows the maximum compression pressure (P Comp) reached, as well as any pressure fluctuations occasioned by faulty fuel injection equipment for which the draw card was first introduced.

## Drop valves

These are fitted at the lower ends of the topside ballast tanks in a conventional bulk carrier, especially those having larger deadweights. They are simply open ended sluice valves operated from the upper deck or from a console if a remote operation system is provided. They are independent of the main ballast system and can quickly "drop" the ballast water in the tanks overboard. They are particularly useful at terminals with high capacity loading rates.

## Dual fuel engines

Dual fuel diesel engines are designed to operate either on heavy viscosity fuel or boil off gas from LNG (liquid natural gas) tankers or both. The fuel system is rather complicated as it has to deal with high temperature fuel oil and high pressure gas simultaneously. It is usual in dual fuel installations to supply pilot fuel oil along with the gas when running in the gas mode. Fuel oil can be used alone when gas is not available, for example when an LNG is on a ballast leg. The safety measures necessary to run on LNG are rather onerous and at this moment in time only steam boilers have duel fuel capabilities.

### Economisers

In its original application an economiser was used to preheat the feed water on steam boilers by means of the flue gas, so improving boiler efficiency. Nowadays an economiser is provided in the exhaust gas uptakes of most diesel Main Engines in order to produce free steam for various auxiliary purposes by extracting useful heat from the exhaust gas.

### Economy of scale

This philosophy could also be dubbed the larger the better and is based on the principle that unit costs are invariably lowered when the largest possible sized ship is used having regard to the physical limiting dimensions posed by its area of operation.

### Electro-hydraulic systems

A system used for distributing energy usually by means of a centralised power source having localised energy consumers via a hydraulic piping network. A typical example is that used for the deck machinery of many modern vessels in which all the winches and the windlass are so connected.

### Electronic charts

Are a recent improvement over the previously used paper charts used in ship navigation for many years. They are now usually arranged as ECDIS (Electronic Chart Display Information Systems) integrated with the radar images, thus producing a much improved map display of a ship's moving position relative to the area involved.

### Flag of convenience (FOC)

Ships flying so-called flags of convenience are those associated with open registers as opposed to closed or traditional registers. FOC countries are headed by Liberia and Panama who have relaxed attitudes to the employment of their nationals, leaving the way open to the engagement of low cost crews. Many FOC countries are signatories to the various IMO (International Maritime Organisation) Conventions but the loss rate of their vessels is generally somewhat higher than those of the traditional flag states.

### Flying squads

These consist of specialised groups of workers who undertake suitable repairs whilst a vessel is maintaining its sailing schedule. Repairs to the main propulsion machinery are excluded for obvious reasons but such items as heating coil repairs, tank coating refurbishment and boiler retubing have all been satisfactorily dealt with at sea usually at a competitive cost and, more importantly, without loss of hire.

### Freeboard
Is the distance from the waterline to the freeboard deck measured amidships. The freeboard deck is the uppermost complete deck exposed to the sea and weather which has permanent means of closing all openings affecting the watertight integrity of the ship. The assignment of freeboard marks (Plimsoll) is regulated by the International Convention on Load Lines and usually delegated to the relevant Classification Society.

### General cargo ship
Is a ship without any dedicated equipment or special design features permitting the carriage of nominated cargoes. A typical general cargo ship will have five holds/hatches, a tweendeck and a cargo system comprising derricks or cranes. The Liberty ship was an example of the archetypal general cargo ship.

### Global Marine Distress and Safety System (GMDSS)
This communication system is gradually being phased in by the IMO (International Maritime Organisation) and all ships must comply with the GMDSS Convention by 1999. Already in force is the provision of NAVTEX, a telegraphic printing facility transmitting safety and weather reports. EPIRBs (Emergency Position Indicating Radio Beacons) have also already been introduced by the IMO. The remaining equipment involving satellite communications between ship and shore stations will progressively be introduced to meet the 1999 deadline.

### Handy sized vessels
A strictly chartering term with no particular relevance to technical aspects or to any limiting dimensions. It generally refers to bulk carriers in the 20,000 to 40,000 plus DWT size. At the upper end of this range they are often referred to as "Handymax".

### Heat exchangers
Are used aboard ships in a variety of applications but in general terms they either heat or cool a liquid or gas in order to fulfil its designed function. For example, Main Engine jacket water, scavenge air and lubricating oil are cooled to dissipate heat generated by cyclic conditions within the engine. Conversely fuel oil is heated to reduce its viscosity to that required by the engine.

### Hoistable car decks
These are generally used on short sea ferries of Ro Ro design to maximise car carrying capacity by introducing additional deck space at busy periods. When not in use they can be conveniently stowed underneath the deckhead so as not to interfere with loading/unloading operations. Before the advent of the PCC

(Pure Car Carrier) many new cars were carried aboard conventional vessels by the provision of hoistable car decks.

## Horsepower

Is the unit used to measure the output usually of the Main Engine. It has two separate designations, namely metric of 75 kg metres per second and British of 550 ft lbs per second. Horsepower is historically linked with the measured output of a rather large horse many years ago. It is not a recognised SI (Système International) unit and will eventually be replaced by Kilowatts, already in use by many engine manufacturers.

## Hydrodynamics

Expressed in simple terms, hydrodynamics is a branch of physics concerned with the study of water in motion as opposed to hydrostatics, water at rest. In the shipping industry hydrodynamics is mainly concerned with the resistance and drag of a vessel whilst moving through water, a subject thoroughly investigated by Froude in the 19th century.

## Hydrostatic balance

A method of loading an oil tanker so that the total pressure exerted by the depth of oil in a cargo tank is balanced by the pressure of seawater acting on the hull by the draught of the tanker. Seawater has an average density of around 1.025 whereas crude is typically 0.85 depending on source. The principle involved is if cargo is loaded to a depth equal to that of the draught having regard to the difference in density, no cargo will flow out in the event of a bottom damage.

## Ice class

Ships that are designed to operate in ice conditions must have an equivalent Classification Society notation if they are to remain covered by insurance for any ice damage. The notation will equate the degree of ice protection required with the severity of ice expected. The hull and other parts of the ship affected by ice have to be strengthened, the main protection being the provision of an ice belt at the vulnerable waterline level. Many other requirements are included in an ice class notation, for example increased strength of propeller, shafting and rudder and means of ensuring cooling water supply whilst in ice.

## IMO Conventions

There are nearly 30 IMO (International Maritime Organisation) Conventions currently in force but not all of these affect safety, technical or environmental issues. The main conventions affecting these issues are the SOLAS (Safety of Life at Sea) Convention, which first entered force in 1974 but has had many subsequent amendments, and the MARPOL (Marine Pollution) Convention, which first entered force in 1973 and has also had many subsequent amendments. Other IMO Conventions and their entry into force dates include: Load Line (1968); Tonnage Measurement (1982); Collision Prevention (1977); Marine Satellites (1979); and Training Standards (1984).

### Impulse turbocharging
A method used prior to the introduction of constant pressure turbocharging (which see). In impulse turbocharging the exhaust gas outlets from each cylinder are led directly into the turbocharger serving a particular group of cylinders. Impulse turbocharging was rather inefficient but had the advantage of a quick response from the turbochargers at initial start and it did not usually require an auxiliary blower for this purpose.

### Impressed current cathodic protection
A method of protecting a vessels underwater hull against corrosion from seawater used as an alternative to sacrificial anodes. It involves passing an electric current through anodes attached to the underwater hull whose output is automatically controlled according to the difference in potential required. It has been found to be superior to sacrificial anodes when operating in ice conditions.

### Indicator diagrams
These are taken from a PV (Pressure/Volume) indicator directly connected to the cylinders of a diesel engine and driven by a mechanical device. The diagram so produced is fully representative of the work done in the cylinders and leads to the calculation of mean indicated pressure (P Mean) which in turn leads to the calculation of indicated horsepower. Maximum pressure (P Max) and compression pressure (P Comp) are also readily obtained from the indicator diagrams. (*See also* Draw cards.) More recently CRT (Cathode Ray Tubes) have been used instead of the PV indicator.

### Inert gas
On steam turbine driven tankers it is usual to use treated flue gas from the main boilers as an inert gas blanket to protect the cargo oil tanks against fire and explosion. Diesel propelled tankers cannot use the exhaust gas from their engines as inert gas because of its high oxygen content and they use a separate gasifier for this purpose. The ballast tanks of some recently built double hull tankers have been connected to the inert gas system to combat the danger from oil or gas leakage from the adjacent cargo tanks, although this is not a requirement.

### Inwater surveys
These surveys came about several decades ago mainly as an alternative to the nominal 2½ year dry dock surveys asked for by most Classification Societies. By adopting the inwater survey approach owners could go to a five-year interval between dry docking providing they had this intermediate inwater survey which was witnessed by a classification surveyor but actually carried out by a diver using video camera scans.

### International Standards Organisation (ISO)
This organisation is responsible for literally hundreds of standards in use throughout the whole spectrum of industrial activity. In the case of maritime

operations they have recently been involved in setting standards of account-
ability in management systems, for example the ISO 9000 series leading to
acceptance of the ISM (International Safety Management) code.

### Lightship weight
Is the weight of the basic ship, which includes the weight of steel, machinery,
furnishings and fittings. It is usually calculated by the shipyard and checked
against results from an inclining experiment taken shortly before delivery of a
new ship to its owners.

### Liquid natural gas (LNG)
A gas found in many locations throughout the world and used as a fuel after
being passed through a refining process. It can be transported through pipelines
or by sea in LNG gas carriers in liquid form at extremely low (cryogenic)
temperatures. The boil off gas produced by heat passing through the insulation
is used as fuel in the steam propulsion boilers.

### Log abstracts
Deck and engine room log books are official documents which record the actual
events taking place in both these critical areas. These large documents are
condensed into what are usually called log abstracts making it easier for owners
and charterers to determine the average daily speed and fuel consumption over
a voyage. Log abstracts are the documents most frequently used when
determining performance claims relating to charterparty warranties.

### Long stroke engines
The relationship between the length of stroke and cylinder diameter of a typical
slow speed 2-stroke engine was usually in the ratio of two to one. To improve
both the thermal efficiency of an engine and the hydrodynamic efficiency of the
ship the stroke/bore ratio has progressively increased and is now approaching
four to one, making for an extremely long-stroke engine sometimes referred to
as a super long-stroke engine.

### Loop scavenge
A formerly used scavenge arrangement for slow speed 2-stroke engines which
obviated the need for exhaust valves in the cylinder covers. Both the scavenge
ports and exhaust ports were located at the lower end of the cylinder liners,
which resulted in a loop form of scavenge air movement when the piston
uncovered the liner ports. The system was not compatible with the extremely
low specific fuel consumptions now demanded.

### MARPOL
The IMO (International Maritime Organisation) Marine Pollution (MAR-
POL) convention which first entered force in 1973. It currently has five annexes
covering pollution from oil, chemicals, packages, sewage and garbage, although
the annex relating to sewage has not yet entered into force. An Annex covering
gaseous emissions is expected to be introduced shortly.

**Maximum Continuous Rating (MCR)**
This is the rating of a diesel engine at which it can continuously operate and for which the strength of the various parts were designed. It is usual to allow a degree of tolerance with respect to wear, ageing and fouling and for this reason most owners operate their engines at around 90% MCR. (*See also* CSR.)

**Mechanical efficiency**
Is the ratio between the indicated horsepower of a diesel engine and its brake horsepower. The mechanical efficiency of a modern diesel engine is around 93% and it is measured by calculating the indicated horsepower from the PV diagram and comparing the result with the power measured at a dynamometer at the shop trials or from a torsionmeter in service.

**Medium speed engines**
These are usually 4-stroke (cycle) trunk piston engines operating at around 500 RPM. Unlike the larger 2-stroke crosshead engines, medium speed engines have no arrangement for separating the combustion space from the crankcase and rely on the piston/scraper ring pack to perform this important duty. Medium speed engines are very popular both in the large and small size passenger ship market where the emphasis is on reduced headroom, making the medium speed engine eminently suitable in these applications.

**Mid-deck tanker**
A design offered as an alternative to the double hull tanker insisted on by the USCG (United States Coast Guard) for tankers visiting US waters. The mid-deck tanker has a separation between the upper and lower halves of the centre cargo tanks and the design is acceptable under MARPOL, Annex I regulations as an equivalent design to the double hull but is not acceptable to the USCG.

**New York Produce Exchange (NYPE)**
One of the most frequently used charterparty documents in the dry bulk sector. It was first introduced in 1913 when coal was the normal fuel in use and has seen many modifications over the years culminating in the NYPE 1993 charterparty now in general use.

**OPA 90 (Oil Pollution Act 1990)**
A draconian measure introduced by the US Government following the "Exxon Valdez" incident in 1989. The main technical requirements included in OPA 90 are the unilateral adoption of double hulls on all tankers visiting US ports and the possession of a VRP (Vessel Response Plan) for all vessels.

**On/off hire surveys**
Prior to a vessel being time chartered and immediately before it is redelivered to owners on completion, it is normal practice to conduct on and off hire surveys. These are held to ensure that the physical condition of the ship (wear and tear excepted) is the same at the end of the charter as it was at the

beginning. In addition, the fuel quantities onboard at the time of these surveys are measured.

## Panamax

Refers to the maximum size of vessel capable of passing through the Panama Canal. It is usually associated with a beam restriction of closely 32.2 metres. Other restrictions such as those relating to maximum draught and length are only rarely referred to when a Panamax vessel is being discussed.

## Planimeter

A mechanical device used in marine applications to determine the area of a PV (Pressure/Volume) diagram taken from a diesel engine. The Planimeter sensor is carefully moved around the trace of the diagram, usually taking an average of three or so readings, from which the mean indicated pressure (P Mean) and, thereby, the horsepower, is derived.

## Planned maintenance

A method used to deal with the maintenance of machinery in an orderly or planned manner so that recognisable vulnerable items are regularly inspected having regard to historical experience. Using this approach the mean time between overhaul (MTBO) can be optimised as more data is analysed.

## Post Panamax

Is a term used particularly with regard to the recent breed of large container ships with TEU (Twenty foot Equivalent Units) capacities above 4,000. These vessels have beams in excess of the 32.2 metres limit imposed by the Panama Canal, hence the term post Panamax.

## Pressure maximum (P Max)

The maximum cyclical pressure reached in the combustion space of a diesel engine and used to determine the required mechanical strength of various components within the engine. P Max is also closely related to the thermal efficiency of an engine and in general terms the higher the P Max, the more efficient the engine.

## Propeller law

Also known as the cube law in that the propulsive power of a ship is proportional to the third power of the speed. A modern diesel engine has a broadly constant specific fuel consumption over its operating range and we can say that the fuel consumption of a ship is proportional to the third power of the speed. The third power is only an approximation and has been found to be much higher in many cases.

## Purifiers

Purifiers are the standard method used to remove water and unwelcome particles from fuel oil prior to its being supplied to the Main Engine and auxiliary diesel engines, but they are never used to purify fuel for steam boilers, which can tolerate such contaminants. Purifiers work on the centrifugal force principle, which generates extremely high gravitational forces leading to rapid removal of matter with densities above that of the fuel being treated.

**Redundancy**
Is related to the reserve capacity or availability of usually propulsive machinery especially that of passenger ships. The redundancy of a typical bulker or tanker is non-existent as the failure of the single Main Engine results in immobilisation of the ship. Multi-engine arrangements as provided on most passenger ships and cruise liners have high redundancy levels dependent on the complexity of the chosen plant.

**Re-liquefaction**
A method used to re-liquefy gas formed by heat leaking through the insulation and into the cargo carried at cryogenic temperatures. It is usually provided on LPG (liquid petroleum gas) tankers and consists basically of a refrigeration plant capable of dealing with the low temperatures involved, typically $-45°C$.

**Residual fuel oil**
An alternative term for heavy viscosity fuel oil, so called because it is all that remains of a crude oil after all other lighter fuels have been removed by the distillation process at the refinery.

**Safety of Life at Sea (SOLAS)**
The so-called SOLAS Convention which was introduced by the IMO (International Maritime Organisation) in 1974. SOLAS regulations are constantly being updated by various amendments to ensure safety measures are introduced when circumstances dictate that existing regulations are in need of improvement. Sub-division of Ro Ro ferries is one area currently concentrating the minds of those formulating SOLAS regulations.

**Satellite communications (Satcom)**
Most vessels now employ as standard a satellite communication system regulated by the IMO (International Maritime Organisation) through the INMARSAT (International Marine Satellite) Convention which entered force in 1979. There are various INMARSAT terminals in use depending on the needs of the shipowner. The IMO's involvement with communications is mainly concerned with improved safety and distress systems leading eventually to the full adoption of GMDSS (Global Marine Distress and Safety System) in 1999.

**Satellite navigation systems (Satnav)**
Satellite navigation systems are also standard equipment on most vessels and are extremely accurate now that all GPS (Global Positioning Satellites) are in position. The present move is towards integration of all navigational positioning equipment such as Satnav, radar and electronic charts.

### Scantlings

A term used to describe the size and strength of component members of a ship's structure. If, for example, increased scantlings are referred to it means that the frames or other such sections require increased dimensions, hence strength.

### Sea margin

An allowance prescribed to adjudge the power requirements of a Main Propulsion Engine compared to the power it required at sea trials to reach a certain speed, usually the expected service speed. Sea trials are conducted in conditions somewhat more favourable than those expected in subsequent service and the sea margin is used to calculate what additional power is necessary to take this into account. It is normally pitched at around 15 to 20% above the sea trial power, dependent on the owner's experience in his area of operation.

### Segregated ballast tanks (SBT)

A pollution combating arrangement whereby completely separate ballast tanks and cargo oil tanks are provided on oil tankers. Since 1982 all oil tankers must have segregated ballast tanks and it is expected that all tankers built prior to 1982 will be phased out by the year 2003. Protectively located SBT tankers are acceptable under present IMO (International Maritime Organisation) MARPOL regulations but are not acceptable under OPA 90 regulations issued by the US Government.

### Self-tensioning winches

These are essentially a labour-saving device which obviates the need to maintain a presence of seamen on the deck of a vessel moored in a port or at a berth having large tidal movements in water level. These tidal differences require constant attention by those attending the mooring lines and the provision of self-tensioning winches allows for differences in water level to be taken care of by automatically paying out or heaving in mooring lines to maintain a preset tension.

### Selective catalytic reduction (SCR)

A system primarily designed to reduce the nitrous oxide (NOx) content of a diesel engine's exhaust gas to meet anticipated future legislation under MARPOL regulations. In an SCR system urea is used as the reducing agent and the whole system is rather expensive and difficult to operate.

### Shear force

Is a mechanical force acting on a ship's structure occasioned by the distribution of weight either of the structure proper or from the weight of cargo, ballast or bunkers etc. The allowable shear force is given in the loading annual and also the loading instrument for various operating conditions expected in service.

### Shifting boards

Used to be a common feature when general cargo ships were employed in the grain trade. They were usually made from timber and erected on the longitudinal centreline, their purpose being to prevent the cargo shifting when the vessel was rolling in heavy seas. When not in use shifting boards were usually stowed in the tween decks. They are not required to be fitted on a modern self-trimming bulk carrier.

### Slow speed diesel engines

Are diesel engines operating on the 2-stroke (cycle) principle, they are provided with crossheads and guides for transferring reciprocating piston movement via connecting rods into shaft revolutions. They are normally associated with somewhat large cylinder bores but in recent years have been built with bores as low as 260mm. It is probably safer to refer to such engines as crosshead engines to avoid confusion with trunk piston engines having similar cylinder bore sizes.

### Special sea areas

These are designated by the IMO (International Maritime Organisation) as sea areas in which for ecological reasons it is deemed that pollution by any means must be avoided. Included in this category are the Mediterranean, Baltic and Red Sea areas.

### Special surveys

These are the main surveys included in classification regulations which take place at five-year intervals. At this time all vulnerable spaces and compartments are examined by a classification surveyor in order to assess their condition. As vessels age the scope and intensity of these examinations increase, reflecting the effect that fatigue and corrosion have on a vessel's structure.

### Spontaneous heating

Many cargoes carried in bulk carriers are susceptible to spontaneous heating. All these are listed in the IMDG (International Maritime Dangerous Goods) code first adopted by the IMO (International Maritime Organisation) in 1965 and periodically revised. Coal, direct reduced iron (DRI) and metal cuttings are amongst those listed as being subject to spontaneous heating and special fire precautions must be taken if they are to be considered as cargo, for example total flood $CO_2$ or a nitrogen blanketing system.

### Stability

Is the ability of a ship to avoid capsize either when its structure is intact, then known as intact stability, or if the structure is damaged, then known as damage stability. In general terms stability is related to the distance between the metacentric height and the centre of gravity (known as the GM) which must always be positive in order to effect a righting moment when a ship is rolling in bad weather. Damage stability survival is established using a variety of possible scenarios relating to damage in vulnerable compartments.

**Standards of Training Certification and Watchkeeping (STCW)**
This IMO (International Maritime Organisation) Convention entered into force in 1984 and lays down standards relating to each of its component subjects. Because of the high level of criticism made against its apparent ineffectiveness, the IMO has recently made radical amendments to a new STCW code, which is expected to enter into force in 1997. The new STCW code will tighten up procedures and IMO member administrations will have to establish training and certification arrangements in order to effect implementation, which the original convention did not effectively address.

**Stroke/bore ratio**
The stroke/bore ratio is generally used to relate this parameter of a diesel engine with its thermodynamic potential. A stroke/bore ratio of around two was originally the norm for 2-stroke slow speed diesels and perhaps 1.2 for medium speed 4-stroke engines. Whilst the stroke/bore ratio for 4-stroke engines has barely changed, that of the 2-stroke engine is now approaching four in, for example, engines destined for VLCCs with low RPM propellers.

**Sub-division**
Is the practice of dividing the ship's compartments underneath the freeboard (which see) deck in order to contain the total amount of seawater entering the ship in the event of a grounding or collision. The sub-division of the vehicle decks on Ro Ro ferries is presently under discussion at the IMO (International Maritime Organisation). Sub-division is the responsibility of SOLAS and is not part of classification rules for ship construction.

**Super cavitating propellers**
Cavitation is a phenomenon in which water vapour is entrained usually on the suction side of propeller blades and manifests itself by noise and erosion of the blade material. It is usually associated with poor propeller design, poor water flow into the propeller or if blade speeds are very high. In this latter case it is possible to move the area of cavitation away from the blade surfaces by the use of super cavitating propellers, usually associated with high speed craft.

**Test tanks**
Ships' scale model tests conducted at a test tank can give an extremely good indication of a full size vessel's performance with considerable savings in time and expense. Powering and seakeeping qualities can all be determined by extrapolating test tank results into full-scale predictions.

**Thermal efficiency**
Is the amount of useful heat extracted from the fuel in the form of energy compared with the heat value contained in the fuel. A modern diesel engine will have a thermal efficiency of over 50%.

**Thermal overload**
Thermal overload occurs when the heat load cannot be satisfactorily removed by the cooling system if a mechanical overload has been introduced. Poor

combustion due to insufficient supply of air or poor quality fuel oil can also cause thermal overload. A heavily fouled underwater hull or even a damaged propeller are the main causes of mechanical overload. The symptoms usually manifest themselves in fractured cylinder liners or piston crowns.

**Thermodynamics**
The first law of thermodynamics states that heat and work are mutually convertible and in the case of marine diesel engines we usually express the thermodynamic performance as the thermal efficiency in which the output of the engine is converted into heat units and compared with the heat units in the fuel.

**Ultra large bulk carriers (ULBC)**
These vessels are in the range of 250,000 to 350,000 DWT and are usually built with a specific trade in mind. They have obvious port restrictions on account of their dimensions and have not proved to be commercially popular.

**Ultra large crude carriers (ULCC)**
ULCCs had a comparatively short period of popularity in the mid 1970s culminating with the "Seawise Giant" of 568,000 DWT built in 1979. Like the ULBC they have not proved to be commercially popular.

**Uniflow scavenge**
The now standard method used by slow speed 2-stroke diesel engines whereby scavenge air is introduced at the lower end of the cylinder liners and scavenges the products of combustion through exhaust valves located in the cylinder cover.

**Unimak Pass**
A high latitude North Pacific route taken north of the Aleutian Islands into the Bering Sea via the Unimak Pass. Although somewhat longer than a great circle route it has the advantage of having improved average weather conditions.

**Unmanned engine rooms**
Have been in general use since the late 1960s and, subject to the relevant classification rules being implemented, a vessel can operate without any personnel being in the engine room at sea. It is usual to operate unmanned during overnight periods when the supervisory equipment advises the bridge watchkeeper and the appointed duty engineer of any malfunction of the equipment. During daytime periods it is usual for personnel to be present in the engine room normally attending to routine maintenance, leaving supervisory and control functions to the equipment so provided.

**Viscosity**
Viscosity is the property of a liquid to resist flow and in marine applications is usually used to describe the grade of fuel oil supplied, for example high viscosity fuel. The higher the viscosity of a fuel oil, the higher its resistance to flow and in order to reduce this resistance it is necessary to raise its

temperature. The unit of viscosity currently in use is the centistoke and viscosity is usually measured in a viscometer in which flow through an orifice or other such means is measured over a timed period.

## Viscotherm

A device for automatically controlling the viscosity of a fuel oil delivered to a diesel engine prior to it being injected into the cylinders. It is important that the viscosity at injection is to the engine designer's prescribed limits in order both to ensure efficient combustion and to avoid unwelcome stresses in the mechanical side of the fuel injection equipment, and the viscotherm attends to this.

## Water spray systems

A comparatively recent fire extinguishing system aimed primarily at machinery spaces and now making inroads into previously used $CO_2$ and Halon (not now allowed) systems. The fixed water spray system comprises nozzles located at vulnerable locations known for their fire hazard and connected to high pressure pumps remotely operated in an emergency. The system is divided into several circuits so that only the area under threat is water drenched at the outbreak of fire. The nozzles introduce an extremely fine mist which, as well as being an extremely good extinguishing medium, causes minimal damage to sensitive parts in the vicinity.

## Water sprinklers

These are now compulsory in all passenger ships and consist of a network of pipes throughout vulnerable areas thought likely to be a fire source. Each cabin and public space where passengers gather is provided with a sprinkler head sensitive to temperature which is activated by a temperature rise causing water to drench the incipient flame and prevent propagation. It is remarkably efficient in preventing the spread of fire.

# INDEX

Absorbed load, 65, 139, 140, 145, 146, 153
Accommodation heating, 19
Adaptive steering modules, 15
Additives, fuel, 50–52
Admiralty Constant, 3, 4
Affreightment contract, 85
Aframax tankers, 77, 187
Agents' disbursements, 175
Air draught, 76, 187
Air lubrication, underwater, 16
Air-cooled turbochargers, 7
Airfreight, 81, 168, 169
Alcohol and drug
   abuse, 109–110
   testing, 116
Alumina charter, 72
Aluminium plus silicon limit, 46
Ambient temperature, 62, 64
Ammonia as refrigerant, 119
"Amoco Cadiz", 114
Anemometers, 56
Anti-fouling paint, 15, 17, 119–120
Asphaltenes, 44
Asymmetrical stern, 13
Audit
   energy, 17
   quantity (of fuel), 52
Automatic coal handling, 24
Automation, 179
Automobile fuel, 39
Automobile lubricants, 46
Aviation fuel, 39

B & W engines, 8, 28, 178
B & W Panamax, 2, 20
B-60 freeboard, 17, 71
Ballast, minimum, 14–15
Baltic Exchange, 71
Baltic ferry, 32, 34
Bareboat charter, 85, 90
Barging charges, 52
Beaufort Scale, 60, 123, 125, 132, 139, 147,
   149, 152
Bilge wells, 91

BIMCO clause, 49, 130
Black box recorders, 105
Blended fuel, 6, 7–9, 37, 44
Boilers/incinerators, 19
"Bolt-on" improvers, 5–14
Bow thruster, 92, 188
Box rate, 81
Brake Mean Effective Pressure (BMEP), 25,
   28
Bulk carriers, 71–77, 83, 86, 90, 91, 99, 104,
   105, 106, 111, 114, 179
   CAPE-sized, 17–18, 71, 188
   charterparty performance, 123–130
   dry docking, 162, 163
   maintenance, 165
   post-war, 178
   propulsion, 24, 26, 33–35, 181
   sail-assisted, 184
   and sea trials, 4
   underwater hull, 2
Bunker Delivery Note, 48–49
Bunker purchasing, 52–53
Bunker receipt notes, 64

Calcium, in fuel, 46
Calorific value, 25, 45–46
CAPE-sized bulker, 17–18, 71, 188
Capital cost
   alternative power sources, 182
   of coal burners, 178
   deadweight increase, 18
   Doppler log, 55
   of engine, 26
   of newbuildings, 161
   performance improvers, 14
   SBT conversion, 115
   of vessels, 26, 78, 79, 107, 180, 185
Carbon
   CCAI, 50, 51
   in fuel, 37, 40
Carbon residue, 46, 47
Cargo
   carrying capacity, 2, 28, 30
   cleaning operations, 75, 90–91

Cargo—*cont.*
  deadweight, 53, 71, 87, 89
  discharge operations, 86
  gear, 85, 168
  heating, 86, 156
  heating coils, 27
  loading rates, 76
  separation, 78, 79
Catalyst fines, 46
Catalytic cracker, 38
Catamaran, 31
Cathode ray tube, 55, 57, 63, 153
Cathodic protection, 16, 94, 188, 195
CCAI (Calculated Carbon Aromacity Index), 50, 51
Centistokes viscosity, 41
Channel Tunnel, 82
Charter of affreightment, 89–90
Charterparty
  calculations, 145–153, 159
  clauses, 127
  fuel costs, 53
  long-term, 26
  NYPE, 86, 87
  performance, 86, 123–134, 139, 140
  warranties, 56
  weather conditions, 60
Charters, long-term, 71, 85–87, 158
Chemical carriers, 77, 78–79, 92, 117
Chemical pollution, 117
Chemicals, in fuel, 46, 50–51
Chief engineer surveys, 104–105, 163
Classification records, 96, 159
Classification Societies, 18, 85, 102–108, 110, 169
  bulk carriers, 73
  condition monitoring, 167
  dry docking intervals, 161
  fuel, 46
  surveys, 158, 163, 189
  tanker design, 77
CO$_2$
  fire extinguishing, 101
  in holds, 73, 76, 91
  as refrigerant, 119
Coal
  cargo, 73
  conversion to oil, 182
  ships that burn, 24, 177, 178, 182
Code of Safe Working Practices, 111
Combination carriers, 74–75, 104
Combustibility, 41, 46, 50, 167
Combustion chamber, 29
Combustion pressures, 5, 18, 25, 181
Communications, 157–158
Compatibility, of fuel, 44–45, 47
Computer application, 26, 135–159
Condition monitoring, 166–167, 189

Constant pressure turbochargers, 9, 25, 64, 189
Container ships, 56, 79–81, 82
  Fastship project, 32, 81
  propulsion, 24, 28, 30–31, 182
Container storing, 92
Container trade, 74
Contaminants, fuel, 8, 46, 47–48
Contra rotating propellers, 12, 190
Contracted and Loaded Tip (CLT), 12–13
Controllable pitch propellers, 2, 13, 31, 190
Conventional screw propeller, 32
Copolymer paint, 15
Coverless container ships, 79–81
Crew lists, 158
Crude oil, 37–38, 40, 161, 182
Crude oil tankers, 114
Crude oil washing (COW), 78, 91, 100, 115, 121
Cruise market, 27, 30, 81–82
Cube law, 31, 58, 181
Currents, ocean, 56, 60
Cylinder liner wear, 29, 63, 64, 154, 167, 170, 171–172, 173
Cylinder oil feed rate, 67, 170–171

Data, 135, 136–138, 157, 159
Database, 141, 152, 153
Deadweight, 53, 190
  increase, 17–18, 27, 29
Deck cranes, 73, 74, 168
Deep tanks, 19
Density, of fuel, 39, 40, 41, 44, 47, 50, 59
Derating, 1–2, 5, 179, 181
  definition, 190
  diesel engines, 25–26
  Main engine, 35, 67, 88, 89
"Derbyshire", loss of, 73
Dew point corrosion, 52
Diagnostic programs, 158
Diesel engines, 25–27, 79, 177
  *See also* Medium speed; Slow speed
  and container ships, 30
  conversion to, 24
  design, 179, 181
  fuel, 5, 34, 41
  increase in use, 178
  introduction of, 23
  maintenance, 28
  multi-engined configuration, 31
  replace steam, 28, 30, 32, 178, 182
  and tankers, 29
  upgrading, 9
Diesel generators, 7–9, 18, 163, 166
Diesel oil, 6, 37, 39, 41, 45–46, 138, 141
  costs, 17
  density, 44
  in manoeuvring, 18
  viscosity, 7

Direct reduced iron (DRI), 91
Discharge port, 28, 53, 89
Distillate fuel, 6, 37, 38, 41, 44, 45, 50
    classification, 42
    contaminants, 8
    costs, 7, 9, 33
    definition, 191
    SFC, 23, 25
Doppler log, 55, 191
Double bottom tanks, 19, 59, 71, 91, 107
Double hulls, 27, 75, 76, 83, 180
    definition, 191
    design, 27
    tankers, 73, 77, 78, 91, 104, 116, 121
Doxford engines, 178
Drop valves, 76, 191
Drug and alcohol
    abuse, 109–110
    testing, 116
Dry docking, 4, 15, 16, 18–19, 120, 141, 145,
    157, 161–164, 175
Duty free sales, 82–83
Dynamic blender, 8

Economies of scale, 81, 82, 177, 192
Economisers, 6–7, 46, 64, 86, 192
Economy fuel pump, 5
Economy rating. *See* Derating
Electric magnetic logs, 55
Electrical load, 17, 131, 138
Electro-hydraulic systems, 86, 168, 192
Electro-magnetic propulsion, 35, 181
Electronic charts, 109, 138, 157, 192
Electronic mail, 158
Empire vessels, 177
Energy audit, 17
Energy conservation, 14–19, 83, 131, 179, 180
Engine room fires, 101
"Estonia" accident, 100–101, 110
Exhaust gas
    emissions, 119
    recovery, 6–7, 64
    temperatures, 52, 64
    turbochargers, 7, 25, 27
"Exxon Valdez", 114, 116, 120, 121

Fastship container ship project, 32, 81
Feltham Tank, 16
Filters, 165
Fixed pitch propellers, 9, 13, 32
Flags of convenience, 96, 100, 108, 121, 192
Floppy discs, 157
Flow straightening nozzle, 9–10
Flowmeters, 56, 58, 59
Flying squad, 165, 192–193
Fort boats, 177
Fractionating columns, 39
Freight rates, 53, 94, 107, 169, 185–186
    bulk carriers, 74, 77
    daily, 147

Freight rates—*cont.*
    and fuel efficiency, 26
    tankers, 79
Freon gas, 119
Frictional losses, 18
Frictional resistance, 15, 18, 32, 56, 57, 162
Fuel. *See also* Viscosity *and* individual fuels
    additives, 50–52
    calorific value, 45–46
    cells, 34
    classification, 42–43
    coefficient, 2–4, 67, 96
    compatibility, 44–45, 47
    consumption, 55–56, 58–59, 62, 67–68, 69,
        86, 87, 88, 138, 141, 145, 147, 148–149,
        150, 152, 177. *See also* Charterparty
        (performance); Specific fuel
        consumption
    cost hikes, 5, 15, 23, 24, 25, 26, 79, 83, 178,
        179
    costs, 14, 45–46, 52–53
    documentation, 48–49
    injection, 5, 63, 64
    quality, 6, 18, 29, 37, 38, 39, 40, 46–47, 51,
        53
    quantity audit, 52
    storage tanks, 19, 50, 58–59
Fully open bulker, 74, 75

Galley fuel, 130–132, 134
Gantry cranes, 92
Garbage, 82, 118
Gas oil, 39, 41
Gas turbines, 31, 32, 35, 81
Gaseous emissions, 114, 119
Gearbox transmission losses, 2
GMDSS, 102, 193
Gotarverken engines, 178
Grain trade, 71, 72, 73, 75, 76, 90, 91, 125, 178

Halon gas, 101, 119
Hard disc, 135, 156, 157
Harmful substances, 40, 117–118
Hazardous cargoes, 91
HCM (Hull Condition Monitoring), 105
Heat exchangers, 165, 193
Heating coils, 27, 91, 92
Heavy cargoes, 72, 73, 104
Heavy fuel oil, 3, 6, 37, 40, 45, 46, 65, 86, 163,
    177
    combustibility, 50
    contaminants, 8
    costs, 7, 23, 24, 52
    density, 44
    in manoeuvring, 18
"Herald of Free Enterprise" disaster, 100–101
High skew propeller, 12
Hold cleaning, 90–91, 132, 138

Horsepower
  and Admiralty Constant, 3
  definition, 194
  main propulsion system, 1, 2
  monitoring, 55, 57, 65
  post Panamax ship, 30
  requirements, 86, 87, 89
  and speed, 5
HSS ships, 31–32, 33, 34, 181, 182
Hulls. *See also* Double hulls
  damages, 162, 164, 172–174
  design, 2–5, 21
  fouling, 4, 16, 57, 87, 157–158
  frictional resistance, 56
  HSS ships, 31, 32
  roughness, 15, 18–19, 162
  semi-planing, 31, 81
  strengthening, 72
  structure, 104, 105, 163
Hydrodynamics
  calculations, 3
  container ships, 30
  definition, 194
  derating, 89
  engines, 26, 27
  horsepower measurement, 57
  HSS ships, 33, 181
  hulls, 21
  slip, 58
  tanker design, 77
Hydrogen, in fuel, 37, 40

IACS, 102–103, 104, 110
Ice strengthening, 76
ICS (International Chamber of Shipping),
  48–49, 108
IMO (International Maritime Organisation),
  96, 99–102, 103, 104, 105, 108, 110, 185,
  196
  Conventions, 194
  loss rate: bulk carriers, 73
  pollution issues, 113, 114, 116, 117, 118
  and Ro Ro ferries, 82
  and tankers, 77
Impulse turbochargers, 9, 25, 195
Incinerators, 19, 119
Indicator PV, 63, 195
Insurance, 102, 172–174, 185
Integrated duct, 10–11
INTERCARGO, 108
Intermediate surveys, 103–104, 161–162
INTERTANKO, 108, 182
Inventory control, 135, 158, 169
Iron, in fuel, 46
Iron ore trade, 72, 73, 104, 179
ISM code (International Ship Management),
  96, 98, 101–102, 108, 109, 110, 111, 180,
  185, 196

ISO standards, 62, 63, 195–196
  ISO 8217, 40, 46, 48, 50
  ISO 9000, 108

Jacket water temperatures, 64
Japanese coal burners, 24, 178
Japanese trading houses, 85

Kerosene, 37, 39
"Knock down" staging, 92
Korean coal burners, 24, 178

Labour saving devices, 92–94, 97
Lead, in fuel, 46
Liberty ships, 177
Licensors, engine, 23, 29, 30
Lignum vitae bushes, 162
Lloyd's Intelligence (Colchester, UK), 97
*Lloyd's List*, 53
Lloyd's Register, 44, 104, 162
LNG gas carriers, 23–24, 196
Loaded displacement condition, 4
Loading port, 28, 53, 74, 76, 89, 115
Log abstract (passage summary), 61
Logs, 96
  Doppler, 55, 191
  Venturi, 55
Long stroke engines, 2, 64, 88, 171, 179, 196
Long-term charters, 71, 85–87, 158
Loop scavenged engines, 51, 196
Loss rate: bulk carriers, 73, 75, 99, 104, 106
Lubricating oil, 9, 37, 67, 94, 162, 165, 169–172

Main Engine, 85, 94, 155, 156
  absorbed load, 146
  of bulk carriers, 32, 34
  choice of, 26
  derating, 35, 67, 190
  efficiency, 161
  exhaust gas recovery, 6, 7
  fuel, 37, 45, 49, 165
    consumption, 138, 139, 140, 152
    contaminants, 46, 47–48
  lubricating oil, 171, 172
  maintenance, 166, 167
  monitoring, 55, 56, 65
  performance, 14, 153–156, 158
  power take-offs, 6
  recent design, 181
  requirements, 87, 88, 89
  slow steaming, 17
  of tankers, 27, 28, 77
  temperatures, 18, 63, 64
  upgrading/improving, 9, 14
Main propulsion system, 1–2, 23–35, 55, 178
  fuel, 58
  maintenance, 164
Management companies, 95–96, 108–109, 185

Manning, 52, 108
  costs, 81, 95–96, 97–98, 161
  reductions, 62, 92, 110, 179, 185
Manual performance system, 65, 66, 67
MARPOL, 77–78, 104, 196
  Annexes, 82, 91, 92, 114, 117, 118, 119
  environment, 47, 100, 113, 116, 119, 120–121
  fuel quality, 40, 53
  minimum draught, 14
"Matsu", 35
MCTS Cardiff, 159
Mean face pitch, 57, 58
Medium speed engines
  definition, 197
  diesel, 1, 2, 29, 30, 32, 179
Metallic particle counts, 172
Methanol, 182
Miles per tonne, 5
Mixing fuels, 59
Modem, 158, 159
Monitoring systems, 65–67
Montreal Protocol, 119
Mooring equipment, 86, 92
MSC (Marine Safety Committee), 99, 100, 101
Multi-engined configuration, 30, 31
Multi-purpose vessel, 74

Naphthenic acid, 46, 172
Newbuildings, 85, 89, 96, 97, 180, 181
  capital costs, 161
  paint schedule, 168
NLS (Noxious Liquid Substances), 117
Nomograph, 50, 51
NOx emission, 52
Nuclear propulsion, 23, 35
NYPE (New York Produce Exchange), 123–
  124, 125, 130, 132–134, 147, 148
  charterparty, 86, 87
  definition, 197
  time charters, 62

OBO carriers, 74, 75
Ocean
  currents, 56, 60
  routeing, 56–57
Off hire, 50, 53, 56, 59, 76, 90, 94, 107, 169,
  197–198
Offshore agreements, 95, 98, 179, 185
Oil
  pollution, 47, 100, 113–116
  world supply/demand, 24, 183
Oil tankers, 27–29, 77, 78, 79, 86, 100, 103, 113
On deck cell guides, 80, 81
On hire, 53, 59, 197–198
"One fuel ships", 8
OPA 90, 73, 75, 77, 114, 197
Optimal trim, 14–15
"Overhaul", 163

P & I clubs, 172
Paint, 72, 91, 94, 104, 175
  anti-fouling, 15, 17, 119–120
  choice of, 18
  schedule, 168
  self-polishing underwater, 15–16, 87
  underwater, 4, 162
Paint film thickness, 15, 162
Panamax vessels, 20, 21, 53, 65, 185
  bulkers, 14, 34, 71, 73–74, 86, 87–89, 97, 125,
    133, 148
  container ships, 29, 30, 79
  definition, 198
  speed/fuel consumption, 68
  tankers, 77
  underwater hull design, 2
Paraffin, 115
Parcel tankers, 77, 78, 79
Passage summary, 61, 125–126, 137, 139–140,
  145
Passenger ships, 27, 81–83, 99, 101, 102
  propulsion, 24, 30–32, 182
  underwater hull design, 2
Petcoke, 39, 91
Petrol, 37, 39, 115
"Phoenix World City" project, 82
Pipework, 76, 78, 79, 165
Pitching, 61, 138
Planimeter, 55, 198
Planned maintenance, 94, 135, 158, 164–165,
  167, 198
Plutonium, 182
Pollution. See Chemical pollution; Oil
  pollution
Port of refuge, 46, 174
Port of registry, 96
Port State Control, 100
Post Panamax vessels, 30, 179, 181, 198
Power take-offs, 6, 7, 8
Power turbines, 7, 27–28, 179
Pressures
  monitoring, 56, 62–64
  P Comp, 63
  P Max, 25, 26, 63, 65, 190, 198
  P Mean, 63
  P Scav, 63
Product carriers, 78, 86, 91, 92
Propellers
  CLT, 12–13
  contra rotating, 12, 190
  controllable pitch, 2, 13, 31, 190
  conventional screw, 32
  damage, 65
  design, 181
  diameter, 27, 28, 30, 32
  efficiency, 1
  fixed pitch, 9, 13, 32
  flow straightening nozzle, 9–10
  high skew, 12

Propellers—*cont.*
  horsepower, 57
  improving flow into, 21
  integrated duct, 10–11
  law, 3, 198
  polishing, 16, 145
  reaction fins, 11
  roughness, 4
  shaft surveys, 162
  vane wheel, 11–12
Pumps, two-speed, 19–20
Purifiers, 19, 59, 94, 198–199

QEII passenger ship, 24
Quality
  of distillate fuel, 41
  of fuel, 6, 18, 29, 37, 38, 39, 40, 51, 53
Quality testing, fuel, 46–47
Quantity audit of fuel, 52

Radars, 17, 109
Radial cranes, 92
Radio traffic, 175
Radiocommunications, 102
Re-liquification, 24, 199
Reaction fins, 11
Redwood No. 1 (fuel viscosity), 41
Refinery process, 38–40, 41, 46
Registry, 95–96, 108, 180
Regression analysis, 144, 145
Residual fuel, 37, 38, 39, 40, 41
  classification, 43
  combustibility, 50
  definition, 199
  use in diesel generators, 7–9
"River Boyne" (bulk carrier), 24
Ro Ro ferries, 82, 83, 100–101, 102, 104, 111, 117
Rolling, 61, 138

Safety performance, 99–111
Sail-assisted vessels, 35, 182
Satellite communications, 158, 159, 175, 199
Satnav, 55, 56, 109, 199
SBT (Segregated Ballast Tanks), 27, 77, 78, 104, 114, 115, 121, 200
"Scandinavian Star" accident, 101, 110
SCM (Screwshaft Condition Monitoring), 162
SCR (selective catalytic reduction), 119, 120, 200
Scrubbing, underwater, 16–17
SDA (Structural Design Assessment), 105–107
Sea Margin, 4, 87, 88, 200
SEA (Ship Event Analysis), 107
Sea trials, 4, 23, 56, 58, 65, 67
SEADATA, 159
Seaworthiness, 174
Secondhand tonnage, 96–97

Self-polishing underwater paint, 15–16, 87
Self-tensioning winches, 92, 200
Self-trimming bulk carriers, 71, 75, 178
Self-unloading equipment, 73–74
Service speed
  of bulk carriers, 32
  fuel oil costs, 27
  HSS ship, 31
Sewage, 118
Shaft generators, 6, 13, 31
Shelltime 3, 4, 132
Shifting boards, 71, 75, 178, 200–201
Shipbuilding
  contract, 97, 98
  costs, 87, 89, 180, 181
  market, 6
"ShipRight" procedure, 107
Ship's speed
  doubling of, 31–32
  fuel consumption, 67–68, 69, 87, 88, 139
  fuel costs, 178
  main propulsion system, 1, 2
  performance monitoring, 55, 56–57
  power take-offs, 6
Shipyards
  choice, 85–86, 89
  dry docking, 163, 164
Shop tests, 51, 52
Shop trials: Main Engine testing, 65
Short sea trade, 31
Shot blasting, 15–16
Slip, 57–58, 67, 138
Slow speed engines, 1, 2, 29, 30, 179, 201
Slow steaming, 2, 5, 17, 52, 87, 131
Sludge, 19, 45, 50, 51, 56, 59, 100, 114, 115
Sodium, 40, 46
SOLAS (Safety of Life at Sea), 99, 100, 101, 102, 113, 180, 199
"Sounion", 130
SOx, 40
Spare parts, 94, 168–169
Specific fuel consumption (SFC), 1, 3–4, 131, 140, 141
  diesel engines, 5, 25, 26, 27
  engine performance, 23
  improvement in, 65
Specific gravity, of fuel. *See* Density
Speculative charters, 85, 87–89
SPMH ship, 31
Spot market, 26, 71, 78, 85
Spot test, 45
Spot voyages, 53, 87–89
Static blender, 8
STCW Convention, 108, 202
Steam alternator, 19
Steam turbines
  demise of, 23–24, 27
  early container ships, 29
  exhaust gas recovery, 7

Steam turbines—*cont.*
  maintenance, 28
  passenger ships, 31
  relative efficiency, 9, 25, 30
  replaced by diesel, 30, 31, 178
  slow steaming performance, 5
  twin screw, 79
Stern thruster, 92
Stock control, 158, 167
Storage tanks, fuel, 19, 50, 58–59
Stroke/bore ratio, 1, 9, 27, 30, 202
Suez Canal, 156, 157
Suezmax tankers, 77
Sullom Voe oil terminal, 119–120
Sulphur, 40, 91
Sulzer engines, 178
SWATH ship, 31
Swell, 60, 138, 139, 147, 152

T2 Tankers, 178
Tachometer, 57
Tank cleaning operations, 86, 91, 92
Tank soundings, 56, 59
Tank tests, 2, 15
Tankers, 77–79, 82, 83, 104, 119
  *See also* Oil tankers
  charterparty performance, 132–134
  charters, 62
  design, 73
  dry docking, 162–163
  maintenance, 164
  propulsion, 178
  size, 179
  in wartime, 177
TBT paint, 15, 87, 120, 162, 175
Telex, 158, 175
Temperatures
  combustion, 25
  exhaust gas, 52, 64
  of fuel, 41, 59
  of Main Engine, 18
  monitoring, 56, 62–64
Test kits, 47, 172
Texacotime 2, 132
Thermal efficiency, 23, 64
  definition, 202
  diesel engines, 9, 178, 179, 182
  improvements in, 7
  Main Engine, 18, 171
Thermodynamic efficiency, 23, 28, 29
  definition, 203
  derating, 1, 89
  diesel engines, 25, 26, 27, 30, 181
  economy fuel pump, 5
  higher RPM engine, 30
  overloading, 29
  pressures/temperatures, 63
  and slow speed engine, 2
  of steam turbines, 24

Timber: as cargo, 74
Time charters, 97
  BIMCO clause, 49
  long-term, 71, 85–87
  NYPE, 62
  speculative, 85
Time-chartered vessels, 59
Topside tanks, 71, 76, 91
"Torrey Canyon", 114
Torsionmeters, 55, 57, 137
Trend analysis, 141, 142–143, 145, 156, 157,
  159
Turbo-alternators, 64, 67, 131, 138, 141, 152
Turbochargers, 46, 166, 167, 179
  air-cooled, 7
  exhaust gas, 7, 25, 27
  impulse/constant pressure, 9, 25, 64, 189,
    195
Tween deckers, 71, 177, 178
Two-speed pumps, 19–20

ULCC vessels, 77, 179, 203
Underwater paints, 4, 15–16, 87, 162
UNIMAK pass, 157, 203
Unit cost of energy, 45, 52
Unmanned engine-rooms, 94, 179, 203
Unplanned maintenance, 168
Unseaworthy, 174

Vanadium, 40, 46
Vane wheel, 11–12
Vapour return lines, 119
Variable injection timing (VIT), 63, 65
Venturi logs, 55
Vibration analysers, 105, 167
Viscosity, of fuel, 7, 23, 41–44, 45, 47, 50, 64,
  203–204
Viscotherms, 64, 204
VLBC vessels, 71, 179
VLCC vessels, 115
  cost, 180
  diesel engines, 178, 179, 185
  fuel consumption, 4, 27–28
  Main engines, 28
  propulsion, 12, 36, 181, 185
  slow steaming, 5
  steam turbine, 178
  tankers, 77–78
Voyage repairs/maintenance, 164–166
Voyage strategy, 156–157

Wake improvement duct, 9–10
Waste disposal, 82
Watchkeeping, 108, 109, 110, 202
Water, in fuel, 40, 44, 47, 52, 56, 59
Water jet propulsion, 31, 32, 33, 34, 81, 181
Wax, in fuel, 46
Weather
  and ballast condition, 14

Weather—*cont.*
  conditions, 71, 123
  disasters, 101
  and energy conservation, 18
  fairweather conditions, 86, 87, 125–126, 149,
      152
  and hull strain, 105
  mask, 148, 149, 150, 151, 152, 153
  monitoring, 56, 57, 60–62, 67
  routeing, 147, 157
  screening, 140, 145, 147, 156

Weather—*cont.*
  and Sea Margin, 4
  warnings, 102
Welding equipment, 165
Wind, 138
  force, 60, 147, 182
  speed, 56
"Wing in ground" craft, 181
World oil supply/demand, 24, 183

Zinc silicate, 94, 168